Balancing Dilemmas in Assessment and Learning in Contemporary Education

Routledge Research in Education

Balancing Dilemmas in Assessment and Learning in Contemporary Education

Edited by
Anton Havnes and
Liz McDowell

Routledge
Taylor & Francis Group
New York   London

Routledge
Taylor & Francis Group
270 Madison Avenue
New York, NY 10016

Routledge
Taylor & Francis Group
2 Park Square
Milton Park, Abingdon
Oxon OX14 4RN

Printed in the United States of America on acid-free paper
10 9 8 7 6 5 4 3 2 1

International Standard Book Number-13: 978-0-415-95584-3 (Hardcover)

Library of Congress Cataloging-in-Publication Data

EARLI/Northumbria Assessment Conference (2004)
    Balancing dilemmas in assessment and learning in contemporary education / edited by Anton Havnes and Liz McDowell.
       p. cm. -- (Routledge research in education ; 10)
    Includes bibliographical references and index.
    ISBN 978-0-415-95584-3 (hardback : alk. paper)
    1. Educational tests and measurements--Social aspects--Congresses. I. Havnes, Anton, 1951- II. McDowell, Liz. III. Title.

LB3050.5.E27 2004
371.26--dc22
                                             2006037148

Visit the Taylor & Francis Web site at
http://www.taylorandfrancis.com

and the Routledge Web site at
http://www.routledge.com

Contents

Table and Figures

Tables

Figures

Part I

Introduction

1 Introduction

Assessment dilemmas in contemporary learning cultures

Anton Havnes and Liz McDowell

SETTING THE SCENE

Assessment of learning in schools, colleges, universities, and in professional and workplace settings, is increasingly being questioned. We are in a period of rapid change and innovation in relation to assessment polices and practice. Critical debate amongst assessment experts and educational researchers has questioned the relevance of dominant policies and practices of assessment. In recent years this has focused on the inadequacies of traditional exams and the failure of mainstream assessment policies and practices dominated by tests, exams, and other forms of summative assessment. The critique has been based on the assumption that these forms of assessment do not support high quality learning associated with 'deep' learning, critical thinking, sustainable knowledge, and lifelong learning. In other words, the widely shared everyday view of assessment in the form of exams and tests as a safeguard for the quality of education is brought into question. As Knight and Yorke (2003, p. 15) put it, 'the everyday trust we put in grades, marks and classes is not shared among experts in assessment'. They refer to Linn's (2000) thought-provoking statement:

> As someone who has spent his entire career doing research, writing and thinking about educational testing and assessment issues, I would like to conclude by summarizing a compelling case showing that the major uses of tests for student and school accountability over the past 50 years have improved education and student learning in dramatic ways. Unfortunately, that is not my conclusion. (p. 14)

The criticism of so-called 'traditional' tests and exams cuts across different types of educational institutions, levels of the educational system (primary and secondary schooling, higher education), and academic disciplines and professional programs. Worldwide, researchers, teachers, and institutions across these boundaries are currently searching for new and more learning-oriented assessment structures. Birenbaum (2003, p. 22) describes the emergence of a new assessment culture. There is a move from a 'conservative *testing culture*' dominated by the use of a single total score with the ranking of students as its aim, to a 'contextual-qualitative paradigm' that emphasizes descriptive profiles aimed at providing multi-dimensional feedback to foster learning.

What we are experiencing is much more than a change in assessment and testing methods. Supporting Birenbaum's claims of a shift in culture are studies taking a broader historical and social perspective on assessment. Gipps (1997, p. 356) highlights that the most pervasive role of assessment over the years has been selection. In Europe, examinations were introduced from the late 18th century, first to control access to professions and government and next to universities. At the University of Copenhagen, law students were required to take an exam from 1788 (Thomsen, 1975). In Britain, the medical profession instituted qualifying exams in 1815, solicitors followed in 1835, and accountants in 1880. The purpose of these exams was to limit access to membership of the professions. In the mid-19th century, British universities instituted entrance exams. The certification given by exam-based assessment became a primary means of upward mobility, thus ensuring a widespread vested interest in the system:

> In Europe, as the industrial capitalist economy flourished, there was an increasing need for trained middle-class workers. Access to the professions had been determined, before the 19th century, by family history and patronage rather than by academic achievement or ability. Soon after the turn of the century, this picture began to change. The economy required more individuals in the professions and in managerial positions. Society, therefore, needed to encourage a wider range of individuals to take on these roles.... The expanding middle classes realised that education was a means of acquiring social status, and they could see that it was in their children's interests to encourage them to aim for the professions. This was the first time that upward mobility became a practical proposition on a wide scale. (Gipps, 1999, p. 357)

The motive underlying the development of the examination system was selection of the fittest person, allowing individuals to compete for positions in government and professions, instead of social background and patronage providing privilege. In the early 20th century, assessment moved beyond selection for the professions and was institutionalized within the school system: 'with IQ testing playing a central role in both identifying those considered able enough for an academic secondary education and selecting out of the system those deemed ineducable' (Gipps, 1999, p. 358). The selection purpose of assessment has predominated and the ranking of students has become part of teachers' and students' everyday life. In addition to providing access to education or employment, assessment also provides access to a rank or a position within the student population. Critiques of traditional assessment have drawn attention to the unintended effects of assessment for selection and ranking, particularly emphasising the often counterproductive effects of assessment on learning.

Shepard (2000) identifies the dominant educational paradigm in the 20th century as being based on:

> the central ideas of social efficiency and scientific management in the curriculum circle ... closely linked, respectively, to hereditarian theories of individual differences and to associationist and behaviourist learning theories. These psychological theories were, in turn, served by scientific measurement of ability and achievement. (p. 4)

This led to a consistent and largely stable system. As a result of the so-called cognitive revolution, the understanding of learning and instruction changed. A constructivist paradigm, strongly influenced by Piaget and others, had a major impact on the conceptions of learning and instruction. The growing interest in Vygotskyan theory in the 1980s (in the West) led to an understanding that both development and learning are primarily social processes. Participation in social problem solving activity was a precursor to individual development. As a result of these complementary developments in psychology and education, conceptions of learning and instruction were changing. But, Shepard argues, the assessment practices continued in the same way as under the previous paradigm. The earlier congruence between approaches to learning, teaching, and assessment was replaced by an inconsistency, or imbalance, in the educational system. The current situation is characterized by an attempt, both theoretically and practically, to re-establish a new balanced system where the alignment of teaching, learning, and assessment is based on research about teaching and learning.

Shepard (2000, p. 12) concludes her analysis of the historical development of assessment practices by stating that 'Clearly, the abilities needed to implement a reformed vision of curriculum and classroom assessment are daunting'. The challenges are, she argues, 'to create new contexts and new cultural expectations that will fundamentally alter the very relations we are trying to study' (p. 13). This is not simply a question of the assessment practices of individual teachers. Shepard argues that the *social meaning of assessment* is changing, firstly, from an act performed at the end of a learning trajectory to an act in the course of learning, and secondly, from an act by teachers *on* students to an act performed also *by* students.

Assessment is being redefined. From being a way of controlling student learning it is becoming a way of communicating to students what counts as valid knowledge. Current views are expressed in statements such as 'students learn what is assessed' and 'you get what you assess'. The so-called backwash effect (Biggs, 1996) alerts us to the unintended and unexpected side-effects of assessment, alongside those which can be readily anticipated. There is a drive to use assessment as a positive tool for learning. Dunn et al. (2004, p. 3) state that 'researchers have placed student assessment at the peak of the learning pyramid as regards its importance in determining students' approaches to learning'. Emphasis is placed on 'gradually integrating instruction and assessment and involving students as active partners in the assessment process' (Gielen, Dochy, & Dierick, 2003, p. 51). Students' participation in assessment is a crucial aspect of new assessment cultures. When students assess their own work and the work of their peers, assessment is no longer limited to the vertical relationship between teachers and students. Assessment becomes part of the horizontal relationship between students. This strengthens the practice of assessment as communication about and negotiation of what counts as valid knowledge within a domain. Additionally, a shift in priorities between formative and summative assessment (Scriven, 1967) is key to new thinking about assessment. The consequences cut across the whole spectrum of formal education. Since the beginning of the 1990s interest in the significance of formative assessment has been particularly strong. Sadler's article from 1989 on formative assessment and more recently Black and Wiliam's (1998) review article 'Assessment and Classroom Learning' fuelled the discussion and the change process. A substantial body of research indicates that integrating formative assessment in classroom practice improves students' learning.

MODES OF ASSESSMENT IN THE NEW CULTURE

The research-driven agenda, initially determined by assessment experts, is now having considerable effects on the practice of assessment:

> Since there is a significant consensus about the main features of effective learning, and the influence of assessment on student learning, on instruction and on curriculum is widely acknowledged, educators, policy makers and others are turning to new modes of assessment as part of a broader educational reform. The movement away from [traditional test and exams] to new modes of assessment has included a wide variety of instruments. (Segers, Dochy, & Cascallar, 2003, p. 5)

The new modes of assessment take diverse forms, such as performance assessment, portfolios, learning logs, self-assessment, peer assessment, group-work assessment, and oral/poster presentations. Although the methods and the contexts in which they are used are diverse, they can be traced back to conceptual shifts in thinking about assessment, emphasising:

- Students as active learners and, consequently, their responsibility for their own learning and participation in the assessment process;
- Change of the teacher role with a shift of focus from teaching to learning;

- The significance of making learning goals and assessment criteria transparent for learners
- An enhanced emphasis on criterion-referenced assessment of achievement and a shift away from norm-referenced ranking of performance;
- The backwash effect, or consequential validity (Gielen et al., 2003), of assessment on learning, leading a shift of focus from summative to formative assessment;
- The whole learning environment, and consequently, the importance of structuring a didactic system where teaching, learning, and assessment are aligned in accordance with new insight regarding the inter-relatedness between assessment, teaching, and learning;
- The dilemma of balancing diverse purposes of assessment (summative, formative, accountability).

The social meaning of assessment is changing as it becomes an integral part of teaching and learning, rather than a separate event after teaching and learning have taken place. The social meaning of assessment as judgement and selection continues, but now in interplay with assessment practices that bear a different social meaning, that of assessment as a tool for learning for all students. Often, for example, as coursework assessment increases in an attempt to integrate teaching, learning and assessment, summative assessment squeezes out the hoped for benefits of formative assessment and becomes an even more pervasive controlling factor in students' learning. New dilemmas become apparent, in this case between assessment *for* learning (formative assessment) and assessment *of* learning (summative assessment). We need to move beyond contrasting conventional and alternative assessment and arguing for a cultural shift towards examining the social meanings, theory, and practice of assessment in a new context.

BALANCING DILEMMAS IN ASSESSMENT PRACTICE

Until very recently, criticism of 'traditional' assessment has dominated amongst researchers and leading edge practitioners. The arguments for new modes of assessment as *alternatives* to inadequate *traditional* methods have been in focus. As new modes of assessment have been applied, as their rationales have been developed and their consequences have emerged, this has changed. From being potential solutions to the inadequacies of 'traditional' assessment, new modes of assessment are being addressed more critically. For example, Segers et al. (2003) examine new modes of assessment using a wide range of criteria. For the most part these are the same criteria used to evaluate 'traditional' assessment: validity, reliability, authenticity, cost-benefit, practical concerns, and so on. However, there has been considerable debate about new evaluation criteria that may need to be developed for the evaluation of new modes of assessment, practised within a new assessment culture.

We propose that a useful starting point is the new dilemmas which appear as the spectrum of assessment forms in use widens. How do teachers apply pre-defined criteria when they assess portfolios which encapsulate learners' personal, individual approaches? How do teachers deal with the fact that the same portfolio is subject to both formative and summative assessment, often by the same teachers? When performance assessment is developed, what aspects of the assessment are most crucial to warrant authenticity? What are the requirements that should be attended to if we are to realize the potential of formative assessment as a tool for learning? Teachers may put a lot of effort into giving feedback to students, but this acts as formative assessment only when the feedback is actually used by the students to meet learning needs (Black et al., 2003). What do we know about how students use the feedback? Do they value it as support for further learning? Self-assessment by learners is practised in a wide variety of ways but does it serve the purpose of empowering students as active and self-directing learners or is it a sophisticated means of controlling and directing learners? How is group-based assessment viewed? Whilst some might attribute value to it as fostering collaborative learning, their practices may be limited by perspectives on assessment that foreground the 'dangers' of collusion and the potential inaccuracies in judging individual capabilities. These are some of the questions that are raised in the chapters to come.

Our agenda is to highlight the ongoing processes of improving assessment practices by highlighting dilemmas inherent in assessment and the balancing of them. The idea of 'balancing dilemmas' may seem to be a contradiction in terms; however, we use it quite deliberately. Balancing dilemmas has connotations with Piaget's use of the notion of equilibrium, described as the balance between assimilation and accommodation, and also to Hegel's thesis–antithesis–synthesis model. Freely interpreted, we could say that Piaget explains development as a result of human striving towards equilibrium as a solution to the imbalance between our inherent capacities and the requirements (or facts) of the surroundings. But the state of equilibrium can only be temporary. As we interact with the world and we have new experiences, imbalance reoccurs between us and our experiences of the world. We are again are in a state of striving for equilibrium. In Hegel's terms any assertion or position takes the form of a thesis, which directly establishes an antithesis. A synthesis of the two again creates a new antithesis with a need for a new synthesis. In this way we move along in a dialectical relationship to the world around us and our position within it. In other words, when we take the balancing of dilemmas as the starting point, we presuppose that this is also a process of continuous creation and solving of imbalances. Likewise, when new assessment practices take form as solutions to dilemmas inherent in earlier, traditional or dominant practices, new dilemmas emerge from the new practices. Working on these new dilemmas, and the search for solving the dilemmas inherent in the ongoing practice, is part of a process of optimising new modes of assessment.

LEVELS OF SOCIAL MEANING AND ASSESSMENT PRACTICES

Dilemmas in assessment practices, and the need for balancing, can be addressed at different levels of analysis. The broadest is the societal level which is addressed in the first section of this book. Since assessment is an important interface between education and the wider society, the social meanings and purposes of assessment are of crucial importance. Secondly, assessment may be viewed as an institutional practice within education, training, and workplace settings. Finally, assessment may be considered in terms of the practices of individual teachers and learners.

Assessment is a phenomenon operating at the boundaries of the educational institution and representing an interface with the wider society, such as workplaces or political–social life more generally. However, the social meanings of assessment at this level have been given insufficient attention and may not be clearly linked to practices in education. Assessment is given material form as students leave the educational institution with a certificate or a diploma that states their status or competence. This document may provide certification for professional practice, accompany a job application, or support an application to further levels of study. Professional groups, politicians, and the society in general have expectations and claims regarding skills and knowledge that educators should develop in their students. Assessment is a minefield of competing interests amongst social groups in society.

The new assessment culture has emerged alongside other ideas about the place of education, training, and learning in society. Learning as a means of developing an educated and innovative workforce is central to economic and political strategies based on ideas of human capital and the need for knowledge workers (Ducatel, Webster, & Hermann, 2000). Learning has become part of work life; lifelong learning is an aspect of both work and life more generally. The meaning of assessment as a boundary construct between education and society is changing. Certification and selection are still important, but more is expected. Knight and Yorke (2003) approach assessment from the perspective of employability; that is, both gaining a job and being successful in employment. They highlight the importance of lifelong learning. In relation to assessment they emphasize:

- Standards of effective formative assessment.
- Limits of assessment in warranting of learners' achievements and capabilities.

- Standards for maximising the effects and reliability of summative assessment.

Boud (2000, p. 151) sees assessment as 'an indispensable accompaniment to lifelong learning'. He emphasizes that assessment must meet 'the specific and immediate goals of a course as well as establishing a basis for students to undertake their own assessment activities in the future'. He emphasizes sustainable assessment, that is, assessment that fosters future learning. A crucial aspect of this is to use assessment in educational settings to develop students as lifelong (self) assessors prepared 'to take a full place in a learning society' (Boud, 2000, p. 166). However, he suggests that current practice has not yet integrated such an approach to assessment into educational programs and calls upon well-established criticisms of traditional assessment, for example that it: 'too easily locates responsibility of making judgments in the hands of others and undermines learners' ability to be effective through simultaneously disguising the criteria and standards of performance' (p. 155).

There are many connections between new (and traditional) forms of assessment and the conceptualization and realization of a learning society. Shepard (2001, p. 11) emphasizes the importance of assessing students' understanding rather than recall of factual knowledge, proposing: 'a close relationship between truly *understanding* a concept and being able to *transfer* knowledge and use it in new situations'. Similarly, Knight and Yorke (2003, p. 8) attribute transfer from educational settings to the wider context, to the development of personal dispositions. Their 'USEM' model also describes employability as being promoted by understanding (U) but also by other interrelated components, namely: skills (S); efficacy beliefs, students' self-theories, and personal qualities (E); and metacognition, encompassing self-awareness regarding the student's learning, and the capacity to reflect on, in, and for action (M).

At the institutional level, assessment is attributed meaning in the context of social groupings and organizations. These differ in their interpretations of the broader social context and their positioning within it. Educational institutions are frequently held accountable on the basis of assessment practices and results. How assessment is done, when it takes place, and who is assessing are matters often decided or approved by institutional level decision-making bodies. Assessment is thus grounded in institutional guidelines, traditions, and priorities. Based on previous and current practices, institutional meaning is negotiated. This is made manifest in social and material forms such as formalized rules and guidelines and the institutional or disciplinary customs or traditions, within which the practices and ideas about assessment operate in the institution. In this way, relatively consistent practices are established and maintained, usually as a result of a compromise or balance between diverse interests and viewpoints. However, assessment is both context and content dependent. Different subjects, disciplines, and professional programs have their own specific perspectives and assessment practices. Kvale (1996) suggests that, in universities, the social meaning of summative assessment can be viewed as establishing consensus on what is regarded as valid academic knowledge amongst academics in the disciplinary community. Within the contemporary assessment culture we would want to ask questions about, for example, the transparency and the opportunities for sharing and construction of assessment criteria and standards. Do the institutional structures afford negotiations of criteria and communication between teachers and students about what counts as valid knowledge within the domains?

The most commonly held view on assessment is that it is a practice performed by teachers, students, and professionals and this remains an important area for analysis and development. Assessment is a crucial part of teachers' work. It is something that is of paramount importance for their students and has to be carried out with vigilance. As teachers assess their students' work and progress, they can also see how well they have succeeded in their teaching. What to assess and how, is in fact an aspect of planning an educational trajectory. At this level, assessment acquires its social meaning partly at the level of individual agents and their interaction, and dilemmas emerge within and between individuals. Implementation of new modes of assessment involves individual action and, often, negotiations between immediate colleagues. How do teachers and students perceive and approach assessment? What conceptions do different teachers have about assessment and how it is aligned within the overall process of teaching, learning, and assessment? Changing teachers' approaches to assessment is an essential aspect of the transformation of assessment practices. For students, assessment is something that is important as a guide to what should be learned and it also has significant consequences for their futures. As Shepard (2000) and others have argued, research on learning has documented that learning is a constructive process involving the learners as active agents and participants. Students are active in constructing the meaning of assessment and their own responses to it (Sambell & McDowell, 1998).

In summary, the current situation is typically characterized by multiple social meanings of assessment. Assessment is no longer considered only as an end-point judgement, serving the purposes of certification and selection. As assessment has become an integral part of teaching and learning, it also concerns what teachers teach and what students learn, as well as how teachers teach and how students learn. It has become a site for pedagogical debate. More broadly, assessment in educational institutions is viewed as having impacts on and being part of lifelong learning. There is more to discuss and resolve, more considerations need to be taken into account. There are more dilemmas to balance.

THE STRUCTURE OF THE BOOK

Our approach is based on a broad conceptualization: assessment as social practice. The chapters are structured according to different levels, or social contexts, that is, the societal level, the institutional level, and the individual or agency level. The challenges of assessment, and the inherent dilemmas, emerge with specific characteristics at these different levels. However, the levels are linked. Even though they provide a useful analytical device, it is not possible, either logically or practically, to make rigid and impermeable boundaries between them. The assessment practice of the individual assessor is carried out within an institutional context. The institution has its societal mandate that is performed through the acts of individuals. Neither is there a one-way influence from society, via institutions to individual practice, or vice versa. Assessors have a degree of freedom and use their professional expertise as they assess. Students have a capacity to act and to influence or adapt to the assessment context. Institutions have their degree of autonomy. There are tensions to be balanced both within each level and between the levels.

Innovation to improve assessment practices faces challenges at these different levels. At the societal level, we may consider the mandates given to education by a series of external forces, and the ways in which educational institutions influence societal thinking and develop their missions and aspirations within a wider societal perspective. At the institutional level, formal policies and guidelines come to the fore. At the agency level with a focus on individuals, we may consider individual conceptions of assessment and the many factors which affect teachers' practice and competence. The sections of the book address the three levels of analysis. The order of the sections is deliberate. We regard the societal function of assessment as the main driving force and institutional policies as intermediary. Assessment practices at the level of individual actions are addressed in the final section.

In this book we focus on dilemmas inherent in the practice of assessment in the contemporary context where new forms of assessment are being introduced and cultures and understandings of assessment are shifting. Chapters address the practice of assessment, reporting empirical research on modes of assessment, and specific features within a variety of educational contexts. Conceptual and theoretical aspects of assessment are also addressed. As a whole, we illustrate the conceptual and practical dilemmas of assessment and raise issues that are relevant and applicable across a variety of modes of assessment and across contexts where assessment takes place. The chapters are a selection of papers presented at the EARLI /Northumbria Assessment Conference 2004, a biannual conference where research and innovations in assessment are presented and discussed with the explicit intention of linking assessment research and assessment practice. As a result we have a set of papers which relate the principles and theories of 'new assessment' to the practicalities of the classroom, the lecture hall, and the workplace, offering insights into ways of balancing and re-balancing the dilemmas of assessment of and for student learning.

REFERENCES

Biggs, J. (1996). Assessing learning quality: Reconciling institutional, staff and educational demands. *Assessment and Evaluation in Higher Education, 21*(1), 5–15.

Birenbaum, M. (2003). New insight into learning and teaching and their implications for assessment. In M. Segers, F. Dochy, & E. Cascallar (Eds.), *Optimising new modes of assessment: In search of qualities and standards,* 13–36. Dordrecht: Kluwer Academic Press.

Black P., Harrison, C., Lee, C., Marshall, B., & Wiliam, D. (2003). *Assessment for learning: Putting it into practice.* Maidenhead: Open University Press.

Black, P. & Wiliam, D. (1998). Assessment and classroom learning. *Assessment in Education, 5*(1), 7–71.

Boud, D. (2000). Sustainable assessment: Rethinking assessment for the learning society. *Studies in Continuing Education, 22*(2), 151–167.

Ducatel, K., Webster, J., & Hermann, W. (2000). *The information society in Europe: Work and life in an age of globalisation.* Lanham, MD: Rowman & Littlefield.

Dunn, L., Morgan, C., O'Reilly, M., and Parry, S. (2004). *The student assessment handbook: New directions in traditional and online assessment.* London: Routledge Falmer.

Gielen, S., Dochy, F., and Dierick, S. (2003). Evaluating the consequential validity of new modes of assessment: The influence of assessment on learning, including pre-, post-, and true assessment effects. In M. Segers, F. Dochy, & E Cascallar (Eds.), *Optimising new modes of assessment: In search of qualities and standards,* 37–54. Dordrecht: Kluwer Academic Press.

Gipps, C. (1999). Socio-cultural aspects of assessment. *Review of Research in Education, 24,* 355–392.

Knight, P. & M. Yorke (2003). *Assessment, learning and employability.* Buckingham: Open University Press.

Kvale, S (1996). Evaluation as knowledge construction. In R. Hayhoe & J. Pan (Eds.), *East west dialogue in knowledge and higher education,* 117–140, London: Sharpe.

Linn, R. (2000). Assessment and accountability. *Educational Researcher, 29*(2), 4–16.

Sadler, R. (1989). Formative assessment and the design of instructional systems. *Instructional Science, 18,* 119–144.

Sambell, K. & McDowell, L. (1998). The construction of the hidden curriculum: Messages and meaning in the assessment of student learning. *Assessment and Evaluation in Higher Education, 23*(4), 391–402.

Scriven, M. (1967). The methodology of evaluation. In R. W. Tyler, R.M. Gagné, & M. Scriven (Eds.), *Perspectives of curriculum evaluation,* 39–83. Chicago: Rand McNally.

Segers, M., Dochy, F., & Cascallar, E. (Eds.), *Optimising new modes of assessment: In search of qualities and standards.*Dordrecht: Kluwer Academic Press.

Shephard, L.A. (2000). The role of assessment in a learning culture. *Educational Researcher, 29*(7), 4–14.

14   *Anton Havnes and Liz McDowell*

Thomsen, O.B. (1975). *Embedsstudiernes universitet: en undersøgelse af København havns universitets fundats af 1788 som grundlag for vores nuværende studiestruktur.* København: Akademisk Forlag København.

2 The challenges of assessment in a new learning culture

Olga Dysthe

INTRODUCTION AND OVERVIEW

A *new learning culture*, in my definition, is a culture based on the insights of constructivist, socio-cognitive, and socio-cultural perspectives of learning that grapples with the changes in society and the new demands on education in the 21st century. The basic premise for this chapter is that a new learning culture is emerging and that it needs alternative assessment forms in order to develop. I have chosen to organize the chapter around five challenges:

The first challenge is the 'backwash effect' of assessment, meaning that assessment has a strong influence on how teachers teach and how students learn. This alone makes assessment a crucial topic. Assessment practices are difficult to change, but if they remain unchanged, important aspects of a new or emergent learning culture are in danger.

The second challenge comes from developments in society and the ensuing expectations of what knowledge and competence students have acquired while studying. My claim is that alternative assessment forms are needed to meet these expectations.

The third challenge is the importance of alignment or congruence of theories of learning and assessment. Today we experience a gap between theories underpinning a new learning culture and the tacit theories underlying traditional assessment practices.

The fourth challenge is how teachers and students, who are socialized into traditional assessment practices, deal with the new modes of assessment.

The fifth and last challenge I want to focus on is how to meet the strong international trend of measurement and accountability. I will argue that unless alternative assessment practices are theoretically grounded and quality secured, and unless educational researchers and teachers join forces, the strength of the international testing regime may sweep alternative assessment away before it has grown strong roots and bring the emerging learning culture with it.

Because I have been working in the interface between writing research and education for many years, I have chosen an example from writing research to frame this chapter.

THE CHALLENGE OF THE BACKWASH EFFECT
OF ASSESSMENT: A HISTORICAL EXAMPLE

The strong influence of assessment on teaching and learning is much talked about but rarely documented. I will therefore start by telling a true story about the transformation of a learning and assessment culture. It is based on firsthand experience, but it is also documented in a unique research study reported by Murphy (2003).

In 1985 and 1986, on leave from my job as a teacher in a Norwegian secondary school, I spent a year in southern California, where I visited classrooms all over the San Diego School district. I had a small grant to study the use of computers in schools, but I ended up studying the way they taught and assessed writing. I had discovered the writing process movement and happened, by sheer luck, to be caught up in the midst of an incredible period of educational change. In the mid-1980s, the state of California challenged the pervasive testing culture in the United States, and became a progressive innovator in assessment development and in the professional development of teachers. The California Assessment Program (CAP) initiated the most ambitious writing test in the nation, where students would actually write in a variety of genres and forms. The CAP was the product of a broader movement toward performance assessment that had begun earlier. Politicians had been convinced by educational researchers and teachers that multiple-choice was too narrow a way of assessing students' knowledge and abilities and it had to be supplemented or replaced.

The well-known California Writing Project supported the change and provided staff development, also in assessment. The reformers worked from a pragmatic position, formulated by an American colleague: 'We cannot remove the testing system, and teachers will always teach to the test,—therefore our job is to create tests worth teaching to'.

I happened to arrive in the middle of all this and experienced what in effect was a transformation of a learning and assessment culture in this largest American state. When I came back in 1990 as a doctoral student at the University of California, Berkeley, writing research was burgeoning, portfolio assessment was being introduced in writing classrooms, and there was a shift in the predominantly cognitive theory base of writing towards a socio-cognitive and socio-cultural basis in writing theory and pedagogy. I will return to the second part of this story, which does not have a happy ending, but let us consider what lessons can be drawn from the first part of the California story:

- First of all it is encouraging because it tells us that learning and assessment cultures can change.
- Second, it confirms that assessment is 'the tail that wags the dog'. There is no doubt that the change in assessment became the engine of the change process, and a strong engine was needed to move this large state, where the measurement culture was just as entrenched as in the rest of the United States.
- Third, it documented that educational researchers deeply committed to classroom practices in coalition with teachers represent a strong force. The change was teacher driven, but needed the theoretical anchoring in learning theory provided by eminent scholars.
- Fourth, new assessment forms involve a major conceptual shift, and both teachers and students need support in order to change their practices. We must be alert to the danger of trivialized and subjective assessment practices under the guise of new assessment.

The driving force behind the innovation of the teaching and assessment culture in California was the conviction that students needed a much broader writing competence to meet the demands of their future lives. This meant a change from just teaching and testing writing as a decontextualized skill to more authentic forms of writing. Schools and universities have a duty to prepare their students for the demands of the future. If 'what you assess is what you get', what *do* we assess, and *how*, and does this correspond to what students will need in the 21st century?

THE CHALLENGE FROM DEVELOPMENTS IN SOCIETY

What knowledge, skills, and experiences do students in the 21st century need? It is common knowledge now that students need to develop a broad range of competences to function in the information society and to become life long learners in a fast changing society. Our job is to educate students for *their* future and not for *our* past. This is indeed challenging. Our students still need solid basic knowledge, but they also need to develop a broad range of competences beside disciplinary content knowledge. The society of tomorrow will require people who are flexible and able to continue to acquire new knowledge and learn new skills. All this is common knowledge now.

The information age is characterized by a steadily growing, dynamic and changing mass of information. Students need digital literacy, but also a variety of competences in order to function well in the information society. Birenbaum (1996) has analyzed and categorized these competences and skills in the following way:

a) cognitive competences such as problem solving, critical thinking, formulating questions, searching for relevant information, making informed judgments, efficient use of information, conducting observations, investigations, inventing and creating new things, analyzing data, presenting data communicatively, oral and written expression; b) meta-cognitive competences such as self-reflection, or self-evaluation; c) social competences such as leading discussions, persuading, cooperating, working in groups, etc. and d) affective dispositions such as for instance perseverance, internal motivation, self-efficacy, independence, flexibility, or coping with frustrating situations. (p. 4)

It can be discussed to what extent these competences are actually new or more important than before. The main point, however, is not the newness, but the fact that a learning culture for the 21st century must help students develop these competences as an integral part of acquiring content knowledge. In higher education there is an increasing awareness that traditional lecture based teaching and exams are insufficient to meet such goals, and at the same time the previous strong division between learning in school and learning at work is becoming less clear.

In Europe, OECD has conducted a large scale investigation ('Tuning Education Strategies in Europe') among university graduates, employers, and academics in 16 countries to establish a list of the most needed competences in higher education (also called 'capabilities', 'generic attributes', 'key skills', or 'key learning outcomes'). The result is as follows for all the three groups (the numbers indicate the ranking of the different items):

1. Capacity for analysis and synthesis
1. Capacity to learn
1. Problem solving
2. Capacity for applying knowledge in practice
3. Capacity to adapt to new situations
3. Concern for quality
4. Information management skills
4. Ability to work autonomously
5. Teamwork
7. Capacity for organisation and planning

Interestingly, 'teamwork' is much higher on the list of employers and university graduates, than among academics!

It should be obvious to most people that 'back to basics' and traditional testing is not the way to foster such competences—a new learning culture is needed. Introducing new technology is not in itself a solution, because unfortunately educational programs that utilize information technology, too often digitalize old-fashioned knowledge instruction (Engelsen, 2003).

Shavelson and Huang (2003), specialists in psychometrics and testing, protest against the narrowing of competences to those that can be tested. They discuss assessment in relation to the broad range of cognitive, personal, social, and civic goals which the higher education institutions themselves promoted. A national poll in the United States ranked higher education's goal in the following order (Immerwahl, 2000):

- Sense of maturity and [ability to] manage on [one's] own (71%)
- Ability to get along with people different from self (68%)
- Problem solving and thinking abilities (63%)
- High-technology skills (61%)
- Specific expertise and knowledge in chosen career (60%)
- Top-notch writing and speaking ability (57%)
- Responsibility of citizenship (44%)

Shavelson and Huang (2003) make two important points:

- First, that in debates about learning, assessment, and accountability the goals of higher education are almost always confined to cognitive output measures.
- Second, that those who advocate large scale tests don't realize the narrow scope of what it is actually possible to test.

Their advice is therefore to assess a broader range of what we value, not just the cognitive outcomes of education.

THE CHALLENGE OF ALIGNING ASSESSMENT WITH THEORIES OF KNOWLEDGE AND LEARNING

Several researchers have discussed the theories of knowledge and learning that underpin different forms of assessment and come to the conclusion that the testing culture is aligned to outdated theories of learning, and that new modes of assessment are needed today to fit and support new theories of teaching and learning.

Changing paradigms

Shepard (2000, 2001) has shown how the dominant paradigm in the last century was a combination of behaviorist learning theories, hereditarian theories of intelligence, curriculum theories and scientific measurement and how this supported traditional testing (see chapter 1).

The point Shepard (2000) is making is that constructivist and sociocultural perspectives on learning have created *new* theoretical foundations for teaching. Still dominant theories of the past continue to affect current practices and perspectives and the measurement perspective still dominates over our ways of thinking:

> Belief systems of teachers, parents and policymakers are not exact reproductions of formal theories. They are developed through personal experience and form popular cultural beliefs. Nonetheless formal theories often influence implicit theories that are held and acted upon by these various groups. Because it is difficult to articulate or confront formal theories once they have become a part of popular culture, their influence may be potent but invisible long after they are abandoned by theorists (p. 1068).

To Shepard, theories of learning are primary and assessment should follow. For instance, when learning according to *constructivist theories* is an active process of sense making, instead of passive reception of knowledge, assessment tasks cannot just test reproduction, but must give space for production of knowledge. One of the reasons why portfolios have become so popular is that they provide space for such assignments.

New modes of assessment aligned to cognitive and situated views of what it means to know

In the landmark article 'Cognition and Learning' in 1996, James Greeno, Allan Collins, and Lauren Resnick outlined some basic differences between the three main views of knowing and learning: behaviourist, cognitive, and situated or socio-cultural, and they have formulated succinctly some important differences in views of assessment:

> The traditional behaviorist perspective supports a quantitative view of knowing and learning, in which assessment involves independent samples of knowledge or skills to estimate how much of the domain a student has acquired. The cognitive view of assessment emphasizes questions about whether students understand general principles in a domain and whether they use methods and strategies that are useful in solving problems in the domain. The situative view of assessment emphasizes questions about the quality of students' participation in activities of inquiry and sense-making, and considers assessment practise as integral components of the general systems of activity in which they occur. (p. 37)

Tests of ability or knowledge composed of atomistic items make sense from *a behaviourist perspective* when the question we need to answer is some version of 'How much?'—How much does a student know in some domain such as mathematics, history, or biology? But when from a *cogni-*

tive perspective knowing is seen as understanding general principles in a certain domain and the ability to reason and to solve problems, alternative assessment forms are needed where students, through projects or other extended performance, can demonstrate their ability to understand, reason, solve problems, and communicate.

'*Performance assessment* provides a bridge between the cognitive and the situative perspectives on learning, because the extended performances needed to assess conceptual understanding and reasoning often also involve engagement with other people and with tools and artefacts that create natural, or 'authentic', situations of activity' (Greeno et al., 1996, p. 39). This is one reason why there are many points of agreement between proponents of the cognitive and the situative perspectives on learning when it comes to assessment. Another reason is their common need to fight the still so pervasive measurement paradigm of assessment.

In the situative or socio-cultural perspective, knowing in a domain is closely associated with the ability to participate in communities of practice, for instance disciplinary communities like biology, history, or literature or professional communities like teaching, engineering, or nursing, with their particular activities and discourses. It follows logically that assessment should be contextual and closely bound up with the normal activities in the community of practice, whether this is a classroom or a workplace, hence 'classroom assessment' and 'authentic tasks' (Lave & Wenger, 1991; Wenger, 1998; Wenger, McDermott, & Snyder, 2002). And since a characteristic of a community is that its members are dependent on one another, collaborative and collective tasks are combined with individual tasks.

It also follows from a situative or socio-cultural perspective that students are not just *objects* of assessment, they are *participants* in all aspects of assessment, from the formulation of criteria and quality standards to creating meaningful assignments and assessing their own and other students' work. This is an integral part of the socialization process, of learning what it means to know in a particular domain and what it involves of qualifications and responsibilities to be, for instance, a biologist, a teacher, or a nurse. This is formative assessment in its true sense, and it includes the formation of identities.

Theories of learning do not only deal with epistemology, but include ontology; i.e. what it means for somebody to be. 'Learning involves not only becoming a member of a community, not only constructing knowledge at various levels of expertise as a participant,... Learning entails both personal and social transformation' (Packer & Goicoechea, 2000, p. 228). There is greater awareness today of how historical and cultural factors constitute or form identities, images of possible selves, and how important this is in learning. Assessment plays a crucial role in identity formation. When students are assessed, whether by a teacher or by peers, the very language that is used is important for how they gradually come to view themselves as learners. The individual evaluates himself or herself in the light of how others judge them: 'Students' perceptions of their abilities are particularly sensitive to social comparison of information' (Gipps, 1999, p. 383). When fostering identities is seen as an important aspect of learning, it is necessary to design assessment forms that give space for students to express themselves and their emerging identities. One of the reasons why portfolios have become so popular in basic schools is probably because their use offers pupils such a space.

Here is also a connection to *theories of intelligence*. While hereditary theories focused primarily on students' inborn abilities, the focus changed to how cognitive abilities could be developed through socially mediated learning opportunities (Shepard, 2000, p. 1074). Earlier narrow views of intelligence have been replaced by notions of *multiple intelligences* (Gardner, 1984). When the need to foster and value a wide range of creativity as well as social and emotional development is foregrounded, not just scholastic aptitude, this demands new modes of assessment.

NEW MODES OF ASSESSMENT—CHALLENGES TO TEACHERS AND STUDENTS

Portfolio assessment will serve as an example of new forms of assessment here.

> Portfolio assessment is a purposeful, multidimensional process of collecting evidence that illustrates a student's accomplishments, efforts, and progress (utilising a variety of authentic evidence) over time. (Gillespie et al., 1996 p. 487)

In higher education, portfolios have their origin in one of two very different traditions. One is 'the competency movement', which is basically instrumental in its approach, and the other is humanism and constructivism.

The focus of the first one is on documenting competence in relation to detailed learning goals. One notable example of this is the *European Language Portfolio* based on the Common European Framework of Reference. It represents a top-down assessment initiative with considerable consequences for the learning culture in the classroom. The portfolio contains detailed descriptions of levels of competence for listening, reading, speaking, and writing in the foreign language. It is planned as an instrument to empower the students to take responsibility for self-assessment. The danger is that externally defined goals and criteria may be just imported.

When portfolios have their origin in humanism and constructivism, their aim is to enhance disciplinary and personal development through reflection, collaboration and peer response, and to develop new levels of understanding. Ideally students are invited into the process of formulating and negotiating criteria and there is wide scope for the students to document their learning. These two approaches to portfolios have created some confusion both in the literature and in practice, but both have the potential of supporting great changes in the learning culture.

Many of the challenges of portfolio assessment as we saw them in a Norwegian portfolio study in teacher education (Dysthe & Engelsen, 2004) were related to what Shepard called 'the emergent paradigm'. Both teachers and students have educational experiences rooted in the 'old' learning culture, and the change from traditional assessment to portfolio assessment challenged many of the taken-for-granted ideas and practices. A number of dilemmas were experienced, some of them common dilemmas in teaching-learning environments that became more visible with the change to portfolio assessment. Dilemmas are contradictions or problems that cannot be solved, and therefore efforts have to be made to balance competing demands. One of the major dilemmas that teachers experienced was how to integrate assessment and learning. Another was how to balance control and freedom.

The major challenges at the three sites of our portfolio study were the following:

Balancing formative and summative assessment

Portfolio assessment lends itself particularly well to formative assessment, but institutional demands and students' needs for grades made teachers seek various compromises that tried to take care of both summative and formative assessment. It was particularly difficult for teachers in disciplines with a traditional strong testing culture, and often this resulted in final grades being given primarily on the basis of sit-down exams, while the portfolios counted little. Since students had put a lot of time and effort into the portfolios, this caused dissatisfaction and such practices could undermine students' willingness to engage in portfolio work. Forms of summative assessment that tried to balance the formative aspect included:

- Grading the portfolio alone. The dilemma was then primarily related to the amount and the timing of the feedback to students' work.
- Oral exam based on the portfolio, where the student would present the portfolio and discuss it with the exam commission. This reduced the dilemma for the teacher because the portfolio was not directly assessed, but used as a resource for the students during the exam. Students liked this assessment model because they had a lot of freedom in the design of the portfolio as well as being able to showcase their work orally and demonstrate deep knowledge gained in the portfolio process. Interviews with students indicated that they felt empowered by the oral assessment format. From an institutional point of view the problem was the high cost of this model.
- A written exam based in different ways on the portfolio work

Balancing teacher and student control—new roles

Portfolio assessment provides space for students to take a greater responsibility in finding ways of creating and demonstrating their knowledge. Where the old traditions prevailed, portfolios might end up just as a collection of very traditional assignments. Giving over control to students is a difficult process because it involves new roles for both parties. It takes time to find the right balance.

Balancing individual and collaborative work

Traditional assessment focuses on individual performance. Portfolio assessment often encourages extensive collaborative learning processes around portfolio assignments, and this was the case in many of the disciplines in our study. The portfolios, however, were most often individual, maybe with documentation of a group project included, but the portfolios rarely mirrored the extent of collaborative efforts. A major challenge is how to handle the dilemma of collaborative work and individual assessment.

Portfolios—'filing cabinet or learning arena?'

Portfolios in all our sites were digital, but in many cases the specific learning potentials in the digital medium were not utilized. They were sometimes used only as filing cabinets for individual students' work, while in other cases the technology was used to facilitate collaborative cross-institutional projects where students produced collective analytic hypertexts and published their joint portfolios on the web. The latter, however, brought to the fore the dilemma of transparency versus protection of individual students' privacy.

In general portfolio assessment makes new demands both on the institution, the teachers, and on the students. The point of the short glimpses of dilemmas that I have presented is to underline that unless these are explicitly dealt with, the learning potential in portfolio assessment may not be utilized.

Summing up challenges for the institution, for the teachers and for the students

The potential of portfolio assessment to bridge theory and practice depends on the extent of participation by the students in all phases of development of a portfolio culture. It also depends on whether there is institutional support for integrating portfolios in the community of practice, and not just tolerance for individual teachers' innovative practice. Some practical challenges for the institution are:

- To establish clear frameworks and guidelines for portfolio assessment;
- To be clear about organizational details and procedures, including procedures when students fail;
- Grading practices and how to deal with reliability and validity issues;
- How to develop an interpretative community for assessing portfolios.

For teachers:

- How to balance control and freedom in the portfolio process;
- How to integrate process and product in the assessment;
- How to deal with the dilemma of formative versus summative assessment;
- How to assign and assess reflective texts;
- How to involve students in criteria discussions;
- How to promote self-assessment;
- How to utilize the particular potential in the digital medium;
- How to develop new teacher and student roles.

For students the most needed competences relate to the following issues:

- Written and oral communication;
- ICT competence;
- Collaboration;
- Time management;
- Peer review skills/feedback competence;
- Explicit criteria;
- Metacognitive stategies;
- New roles in the learning and assessment process;
- Freeriders;
- Plagiarism.

The introduction of portfolio assessment highlights the need to develop many of the competences or skills that Birenbaum (1996) identified as crucial for the 21st century. But we draw the conclusion from our empirical material that such competences should not be taught or assessed in isolation, but have to be integrated into disciplinary content work. This is also in accordance with a sociocultural perspective on the deeply contextualized nature of all activities.

THE CHALLENGE FROM GLOBAL TRENDS TOWARDS TESTING AND ACCOUNTABILITY SYSTEMS

The California story, from its introduction and the change towards more contextual and authentic writing assessment, did not have a happy ending (Murphy, 2003).

The story of writing assessment in California revisited in 2004

A radical change has taken place in assessment policy in California and the progressive assessment practices which were in place in the mid-1990s have been reversed. High stakes testing was introduced to monitor individual student learning, to control and compare schools. California's new high stakes STAR program (Standardized Testing and Reporting) introduced in 1998 a multiple-choice test of students in Grades 2 through 11 in reading, writing, and mathematics. The primary means for assessing writing in high school was once more multiple-choice.

It is a very rare situation that assignment paradigms change so dramatically in such a short time. Murphy has documented that while teachers in 1988 were concerned with students' overall ability to write good texts in a variety of genres, in 2001 teachers emphasized the teaching of isolated skills and grammar. Eighty-eight percent of the teachers in 1988 said that they put a lot of emphasis on genre characteristics when responding to student writing, while only 56% did so in 2001. It actually seems that the new test has managed to destroy much of the progress that was made in writing pedagogy over the last 20 years. Murphy's study shows the importance of creating tests worth teaching to.

This is just one example of the global trend toward increasing beliefs in testing and accountability systems, disregarding the findings from educational research about what are necessary conditions for productive learning.

Some challenges for research

If the new modes of assessment are going to survive, research is needed both in order to improve the quality of the assessment practices and to investigate their consequences. High claims are being made at the moment about their positive influence on learning. Research is needed to:

- Document the learning effects of alternative assessment forms and to reveal the critical factors for student learning;
- Understand how both teacher and peer feedback can be improved;
- Investigate the constructive use of quality criteria;
- Improve self- and peer assessment;

- Learn about how students can internalize standards for good performance;
- Assess learning intervention in virtual learning environments;
- Implement quality assurance of the *methods: from psychometrics to edumetrics;*
- Expand traditional concepts of validity and reliability that can be used for the complex teaching–learning process

CONCLUSION

A main message in this chapter has been that the learning culture and assessment are so dependent on one another that we cannot change one without the other. I also want to remind us all that assessment has always been a political issue, and that educators and researchers should not be naïve or complacent about what drives the political agenda when it comes to education. In this day and age accountability, effectiveness, and quality management are key concepts in most countries. There is a strong tendency to think and act as if quality equals what can be measured, and the backlash in assessment policies, which we have witnessed take place in the United States, should be a warning. National tests vary in quality, and I have shown the importance of creating tests worth teaching to, as well as the importance of alternative forms of assessment. For educational research to influence decision-making processes a solid research base is needed.

REFERENCES

Birenbaum, M. (1996). Assessment 2000: Towards a pluralistic approach to assessment. In M. Birenbaum & F. J. R. C. Dochy (Eds.), *Alternatives in assessment of achievement, learning processes and prior knowledge*, 3–29. Boston, MA: Kluwer.

Dysthe, O. & Engelsen, K. S. (2004). Portfolios and assessment in teacher education in Norway: A theory-based discussion of different models in two sites. *Assessment and Evaluation in Higher Education*, 29(2), 239–258.

Gardner, H. (1984). *Frames of mind: the theory of multiple intelligences.* New York: Basic Books.

Gipps, C. (1994). *Beyond testing: Towards a theory of educational assessment.* London: Falmer Press.

Gillespie, C, Ford, K., Gillespie, R., & Leavell, A. (1996). Portfolio assessment: Some questions, some answers, some recommendations. *Journal of Adolescent & Adult Literacy*, 39, 480–491.

Greeno, J., Collins, A., Resnick, L. (1996). Cognition and learning. In D. Berliner & R. Calfee, (Eds.), *Handbook of Educational Psychology*, 15–46. New York: Macmillan

Immerwahl, J. (2000). *Great expectations: How Californians view higher education.* San Jose, CA: National Center for Public Policy and Higher Education and Public Agenda, Table 3, National column.

Lave, J. & Wenger, E. (1991). *Situated learning: Legitimate peripheral participation*. New York: Cambridge University Press.

Murphy, S. (2003). That was then, this is now: The impact of changing assessment policies on teachers and the teaching of writing in California. *Journal of Writing Assessment, 1*(1), 23–45. (Hampton Press Inc.)

Murphy, S. & Underwood, T. (2000). *Portfolio practices: Lessons from schools, districts, and states*. Norwood, MA: Christopher-Gordon.

Packer, M. J. & Goicoechea, J. (2000). Sociocultural and constructivist theories of learning: Ontology, not just epistemology. *Educational Psychologist, 35*(4), 227–242.

Shavelson, R. J. & Huang, L. (2003). Responding responsibly to the frenzy to assess learning in higher education. *Change*, Jan./Feb., 11–19.

Shepard, L. A. (2000). The role of assessment in a learning culture. *Educational Researcher, 29*(7), 4–14.

Shepard, L. A. (2001). The role of classroom assessment in teaching and learning. In V. Richardson (Ed.), *Handbook of research on teaching* (4th ed.). Washington, D.C.: American Educational Research Association.

Wenger, E. (1998). *Communities of practice: Learning, meaning, and identity*. Cambridge: Cambridge University Press.

Wenger, E, McDermott, R., & Snyder, W. M. (2002). *Cultivating communities of practice*. Boston, MA: Harvard Business School Press.

Part II

Connecting education and society through assessment

Education is often characterized as a sector that has an established a rationale of its own and can operate and develop within its own boundaries as if it were somewhat detached from society. But through the effects of assessment, education operates at the boundaries of its own contexts. Assessment represents an interface (but not the only one) to the wider society and serves to link education to participation in professional practice and, in its widest meaning, citizenship. There are stakeholders 'out there' who have interests in the outcome of education, and through assessment results they receive information about both the learners and the educational institution. The chapters in this section address various aspects of assessment as it forms a link between education and society.

Education is a social institution that cannot legitimately be self-referencing. Its orientation and its mandate points outside of itself, and this outward orientation is particularly made manifest through assessment. This creates tensions around assessment and generates a need to balance resulting dilemmas; for example, the mandate that education is given by external stakeholders and the ideals and priorities valued within educational institutions are not always congruent. Murphy's and Hertzberg's chapters both demonstrate this issue from the point of view of secondary education in California and Norway, respectively. They both tell success stories about the ways that assessment supports learning to write in secondary schools, but they also illustrate how assessment becomes a tool for diverse priorities; those dominant among teachers and those held by the political authorities. Assessment is also a lever mediating the relationships between educational priorities and the accountability concerns advocated by political authorities. Murphy discusses how changes in the assessment policies impacted on teaching practices in secondary education in California. There was a change from emphasising creative writing and teaching of diverse types of writing genres in the 1980s, to the recent implementation of multiple-choice scholastic achievement tests, which were used for accountability purposes. Murphy shows how political authorities exert power on educational practice through assessment policies. She clearly demonstrates the backwash effect of assessment on teaching, and consequently on learning.

Policies overrule the teachers' own priorities concerning what is important to teach.

In both the Californian and the Norwegian cases, it is shown that new assessment policies, focusing on high stake tests, accountability and, in its consequence, comparison of assessment results between institutions, tend to constitute educational practices that work contrary to the priorities and values of teachers and researchers. In the Norwegian case, the researchers became aware of the development of new assessment policies and volunteered to become involved in the development of new tests. They saw it as an opportunity to influence the assessment policy and try to use assessment both to reinforce the strengths in the ongoing practice and to improve on its weaknesses. In the teaching of writing, the balancing of emphasis on basics like spelling and grammar, and valuing the use of writing genres and expression of experiences, ideas and values, is problematic. In their educational practice, teachers also need to balance their professional priorities and the students' need to succeed in the tests that they are obliged to take. But they can, together with researchers, try to make an impact on the assessment policies.

In higher education the interests and dilemmas of assessment, and consequently what should be taught and learned, are somewhat different. The other chapters in this section address how assessment connects professional education and work. A recurring theme in discussions about assessment is whether the competence required for success in education matches what is valued in work life. Gulikers, Bastiaens and Kirschner, taking nursing as an example, ask: What is authentic to school and what is authentic to the real world of work? How do we ensure that what students learn is what is demanded of them in the workplace? Lindström has studied the variation in qualities of knowing in art and design between experts (craft teachers and artisans) and novices (students in vocational craft education). He demonstrates how experts and novices approach problem solving differently, and how they talk about what they have been doing in different ways. The divergence depicts not only the difference in levels of expertise between experts (artisans) and novices (students). In addition to differences in the competence of the agents in this vertical mode, Lindström also describes the diverse expertise of practising artisans and craft teachers. The cultures of education and work are different; there are contextual differences between them. Generally speaking education is process-oriented, while work is product-oriented. Havnes also describes education and work as different social worlds. Assessment certifies individuals to move on from education to professional practice, but it is also highlights the commonalities and the discords between education and work.

Falchikov and Boud question the extent to which current assessment practices connect with learning after graduation. As lifelong learning is becoming an aspect of work, there is a need for education to align assessment practice to the requirements for learning in the workplace. It implies a new function for assessment; that is, assessment for lifelong learning, in addition to formative and summative assessment. Falchikov and Boud expand, both in time and space, the horizon within which we view assessment. Gulikers et al. take as their starting point that authenticity of assessment depends on the resemblance of what is assessed and how it is structured with what they call 'the professional real world'. Five dimensions of authenticity are identified; the task, the physical context, the social context, the result/form of assessment (the product or performance that students produce to demonstrate their competence), and criteria and standards. There is a continuum of degree of authenticity in each of these dimensions, and some dimensions seem to be more crucial than others. Another point that is strongly argued is that authenticity is understood within multiple relations. Neophyte students and more advanced students may have different perceptions of authenticity. Students and teachers have different perceptions. Authenticity is, thus, both objective and subjective. When assessment is designed for authenticity, these different perspectives lead to problems and dilemmas which need not be resolved.

The complexity of the relationship between education and work is further discussed by Falchikov and Boud. In developing an agenda for assessment they encounter a series of problems. One is that the notion of lifelong learning is problematic; it needs to be developed if educators are to design curricula that prepare students for lifelong learning and assessment. In common with Gulikers et al., they ask what characteristics of learning and assessment in the 'professional real world' assessment in education should resemble. Falchikov and Boud particularly point to the tendency to focus on lists of individual dispositions when lifelong learning is conceptualized, the problematic notion of transfer that dominates formal education, and the undeveloped understanding of the relationship between formal and informal learning. Another problem is the role of assessment in formal education. Summative assessment of the students' performance within the educational setting dominates and certification is at the core of mainstream assessment. There is a strong institutional resistance to uptake of new modes of assessment, and Falchikov and Boud call for an agenda for development of lifelong assessment.

Gulikers et al. argue that the relationship between learning in professional education and workplace practice is not a direct relationship, but one that is mediated through what are termed *criterion situations*. A criterion situation reflects a realistic work situation, but it is 'an abstraction from professional practice' constructed for learning and assessment purposes to meet students' competence at diverse levels of expertise. In the course of an educational programme, authentic assessment may be partial and limited in the early stages and more complex as the competence of the learner develops. There is also a movement from unidisciplinary to interdisciplinary tasks. Havnes discusses how learning tasks for students in nursing education can also serve as learning tasks for professional nurses. Students go out into the professional real world and construct learning tasks together with professionals. The outcome that is included in the student portfolio for assessment purposes is also distributed in the workplace to support professional learning and workplace development. In this way the relationship between education and work takes a more concrete and material form.

The example of portfolio assessment in nursing education illustrates assessment as a tool for student learning as well as for the purpose of learning and development of workplace practices. This shows assessment operating as a boundary structure that both creates boundaries between social worlds and bridges them. Assessment bridges the social worlds of teachers and students, of diverse groups of teachers within an educational programme, and the social worlds of education and work. The stark differences between education and work, within the context of lifelong learning, demand a focus on this perspective on assessment.

3 Some consequences of writing assessment

Sandra Murphy

In the last several decades, the educational field at large has grown much more aware of the social aspects of learning, of literacy, and of assessment (see for example, the work of Broadfoot, 1996; Cope & Kalantzis, 1993; Gipps, 1999; Street, 1995). While learning was once viewed as the acquisition of knowledge and skills, it is now viewed as socially derived and situated, constructed and developed in interactions with others (Vygotsky, 1978, 1986). Learners, in turn, are seen as motivationally, behaviourally, and metacognitively active constructors of knowledge (American Psychological Association, 1993; National Research Council, 2000). Social perspectives have also transformed the way we think about literacy, and in particular, writing. Writing was once viewed as if it were a set of discrete skills, but contemporary theories characterize it as a socially mediated process that varies in important ways across different cultures and across different contexts and purposes for writing.

In the assessment field, a good deal of work has been done to create new assessment theory and new models for assessment to accommodate these emerging social perspectives (Camp, 1993b; Frederiksen, Mislevy & Bejar, 1993; Frederiksen & Collins, 1989; Linn, Baker & Dunbar, 1990). What the new measurement theory suggests is that assessments should be congruent with the kind of learning and with the theoretical constructs they purport to measure. For the assessment field this presents a dilemma, because some traditional forms of assessment appear incompatible with new theories of learning and literacy. Yet traditional forms of assessment are well entrenched in practice, and established practices are notoriously resistant to change.

In part, this resistance stems from the competing agendas of stakeholders in the assessment process. Seen as a continuum, the stakeholders' agendas vary from individual students using learner centred techniques such as writing portfolios to learn and to represent themselves and their abilities to others at one end of the continuum, to government agencies looking for efficient ways to inform decisions about policy and the distribution of resources at the other (Murphy &Camp, 1996). And as White (1996) notes, teachers want assessments that acknowledge the complexity of writing and their expertise in teaching it, while testing firms and their clients want cost-effective assessments.

What has often been overlooked as a part of the 'cost' of an assessment is the impact it has on students, and in particular, on the kind of education they receive. However, assessment scholars are now redefining the concept of validity to include the social consequences of assessments—their impact on curriculum and participants (Frederiksen & Collins, 1989; Linn, Baker & Dunbar, 1990; Messick, 1989a, 1989b, 1994; Moss, 1992, 1994). And in recent years, researchers have begun to investigate this impact.

The discussion that follows reviews research on ways that statewide assessments of writing in the United States have impacted its educational environment. For the most part the scope of the discussion is limited to studies of assessments occurring in the last years of secondary school or at the point of transition from secondary school to college (or work). It is important to note at the outset that the role played by writing in assessment in this transitional secondary context in the United States is very different from its role in most other countries. In most national systems, extended written examinations serve as gatekeepers for university admission. The tests are designed to assess what students have learned from the secondary curriculum. In contrast, extended writing plays a marginal role at best in postsecondary admissions decisions in the United States. To be sure, tests are used as gatekeepers to postsecondary education, but not ones that aim to measure what has been learned through extended writing. Instead, as Foster and Russell (2002) point out, 'Multiple-choice tests are the primary bases for access decisions in the United States: the SAT, ACT, GRE, MedCAT, LSAT, GMAT—all the familiar exam acronyms for U.S. students—require little or no writing' (Foster & Russell, 2002, p. 330).[1] The SAT, the ACT, the GMAT, and the MedCAT now have components that require actual writing, but those components are generally of minimal consideration in the overall performance rating of the student. They consist of brief essays designed to measure writing competence itself rather than knowledge in a particular area of study.

Other assessments at the secondary level in the United States are used to monitor school progress in writing, to hold schools accountable for that progress, and to ensure that students who graduate possess minimum writing competencies. And in recent years, U.S. policymakers have been turning more frequently to using tests as levers for reforming curriculum, for defining, in effect, what should be taught. For instance, a survey of statewide assessment practices in 1997 showed that 46 of the 50 states had some kind of statewide writing assessment. The purpose most frequently identified by respondents (43 states) was the 'improvement of instruction' (Roeber et al., 1997 cited in Mehrens, 1998). Many of these tests carry high stakes.

Stakes, as scholars have explained, are the consequences associated with test results (Heubert & Hauser, 1999; Madaus, 1988). Selection exams carry high stakes for students, because their consequences are more or less immediate and important: they determine who is qualified to study at college and university. Stakes are similarly high for U.S. students who are in danger of failing the high school exit exams because such exams act as gatekeepers for graduation. But because such exams set standards for minimum competency, as opposed to selection for college entrance, they may have little, if any impact on students who actually plan to attend college.[2] On the other hand, stakes are low for all students taking the statewide exams that are used to monitor school improvement; these exams have no immediate consequences for the students themselves. For teachers and administrators, however, the stakes are high.

The consequences of tests used to monitor school performance affect teachers, schools and districts in very real material ways. By 1996, at least 23 states in the United States reported attaching explicit consequences to state test results including funding, assistance from outside consultants, warnings, and loss of accreditation (Bond, Braskamp, & Roeber, 1996). More recently, the U.S. Department of Education (2006) indicated that schools that fail to make adequate yearly progress, as determined by assessments and other factors, will undergo 'corrective action,' which can include replacing school staff, instituting a new curriculum, significantly decreasing management authority in the school, extending the school year or school day, restructuring, or takeover by the state. The high stakes for teachers and administrators attached to such tests help to ensure their impact (sometimes called backwash) on curriculum. Research suggests that tests that carry high stakes have greater impact on curriculum and instruction than tests with low stakes (Pedulla et al., 2003). Other studies suggest that educators will sometimes respond as if stakes are high, even when the results are used only to convey information (Corbett & Wilson, 1991; Madaus, 1988).

Evidence in the research literature indicates that when high stakes are attached to tests (or perhaps when educators perceive them as high) districts deemphasize their own objectives in lieu of those the tests reflect (Dorr-Bremme & Herman, 1986). Teachers, in turn, are influenced to 'teach to the test' (Smith & Rottenberg (1991). However, whether this is seen as good or bad depends in part on the agenda of the stakeholder and in part on the nature of the construct underlying the test. Diverse approaches to assessing writing are employed in the United States, including multiple-choice tests, impromptu writing sample tests, and portfolios. They each imply a different view of writing and how it should be taught; they each have detractors and advocates.

MULTIPLE-CHOICE TESTS OF WRITTEN EXPRESSION

Instead of requiring actual writing, multiple-choice (sometimes called indirect) tests of writing estimate *probable* writing ability through observations of specific kinds of knowledge and skills associated with writing. They demand passive recognition of error and selection of best examples. Critics of such tests have argued that they lead to negative consequences: among other things, that they narrow and fragment curriculum, discourage higher-order learning, and undermine teacher professionalism and expertise (Bracey, 1987; Corbett & Wilson, 1991; Madaus, 1988; Madaus & Kellaghan, 1993; Pearson & Valencia, 1987; Resnick & Klopfer, 1989; Shepard, 1991; Smith, 1991; Wells, 1991). In regard to writing in particular, scholars charge that multiple-choice tests fail to address the cognitive and reflective processes involved in actually producing a text (Camp, 1993b). These processes include making plans for writing, generating and developing ideas, making claims and providing evidence, organizing, establishing connections within the text, finding a tone and rhetorical stance appropriate to the audience and the subject matter, evaluating generated text, and revising, all of which require higher order skills. Ironic as it may seem, although there has been a call for rigorous standards and increased attention to writing in recent years, the most common format used in large-scale accountability systems is the multiple-choice format (Hamilton, 2003).

Yet U.S. policy makers value such tests as levers for reform, to move schools and teachers, so to speak, 'back to basics.' Some view the impact of such tests as a positive development—see, for example, J. Murphy's (1990) review of reform efforts. As Corbett and Wilson (1991) explain, some policy makers view narrowing of the curriculum as 'a focusing of the instructional program, ridding the curriculum of the distractors that have prevented schools from doing the job of providing all students with essential learning skills' (p. 133). And, in the measurement community, well-designed multiple-choice tests have been widely supported for many years because they are reliable and demonstrate concurrent validity (see for example, Godshalk et al., 1966).

BACKWASH FROM MULTIPLE-CHOICE TESTS OF WRITING

Research on backwash from large scale, high stakes multiple-choice tests of writing suggests that they tend to influence writing curriculum in two ways: (1) actual writing begins to disappear from the curriculum; (2) the curriculum begins to take the form of the test. For example, in case studies of two public schools in Arizona, Smith (1991) observed that teachers shifted from a writing process curriculum to 'worksheets covering grammar, capitalization, punctuation, and usage' when their district's test date neared, because those activities were better aligned with the test (p. 10). In a study of two districts, Shepard and Dougherty (1991) reported that teachers of writing had begun to ask students to look for errors in written work instead of producing their own writing, because of the format of the writing test used in those districts. Teachers also reported increasing the amount of time they allocated to basic skills and vocabulary.

Results of a more recent investigation complement findings in these earlier studies. In an investigation of the effects of changing assessment policies in California, surveys were distributed to random samples of high school English teachers in 1988 and 2001 (Murphy, 2003). When the first survey was distributed in 1988, the state assessment plan included multiple-choice tests of written expression, but students were also required to compose a sample of writing. Using a matrix sampling plan, the state assessed a variety of genres, although individual students generated single samples of writing. When the second survey was distributed in 2001, a very different accountability system was in place. Instead of asking students to write, the assessment system at the secondary level relied entirely on multiple-choice tests to assess writing. At the time, the California Standards Tests collected actual writing samples, but only at grades 4 and 7 (California Department of Education, 2002).

Analysis of the results of the two surveys indicated that teachers who responded in 2001 when the multiple-choice test was in place spent less time teaching actual writing and more time teaching grammar and usage than teachers who responded in 1988 when actual writing samples were collected. Teachers in 2001 also reported putting more emphasis on grammar and usage and less emphasis on the features of genre in their comments on student work than teachers in 1988. The findings in this study thus support those of other studies that have investigated the consequences of assessment, namely that teachers shape instruction to match the form and content of tests.

BACKWASH FROM DIRECT ASSESSMENTS OF WRITING

In contrast to indirect, multiple-choice tests, in direct assessments of writing, students produce single (or sometimes multiple) impromptu samples of writing under timed, controlled conditions, or multiple samples of writing in a 'natural' context (the classroom) supported by instruction and feedback (for example, portfolios). Such assessments treat writing as a generative process in which a variety of skills are orchestrated. In recent decades their use in accountability systems has been growing. By 1997, 37 states in the U.S. had mandated assessment systems that included a writing component (Hillocks, 2002 p. 17).

Advocates of direct assessment argue that the best way to assess an individual's ability to perform a task is to elicit and evaluate an actual performance of that task. Diederich (1974) put the argument this way:

> People who hold the view that essays are the only valid test of writing ability are fond of using the analogy that, whenever we want to find out whether young people can swim, we have them jump into a pool and swim. (p. 1.)

Assessment scholars also defend direct assessments on the grounds that they send the message that it is important for students to learn composition skills and for teachers to teach them (e.g., White, 1995).

However, measurement experts have challenged direct forms of assessment such as essay tests because they can be unreliable (e.g., Breland, 1983). Moreover, not all direct assessments are seen as equally valid. For example, assessment scholars have raised questions about using a single, timed, impromptu writing sample to assess writing ability. Camp (1983), claimed that arguments about the validity of this approach rest on questionable assumptions:

1. Impromptu writing is representative of all writing
2. 'Writing is writing'—the skills involved in writing are the same, whatever its purpose or circumstances.(p. 6).

Camp (1993b) also criticized timed, impromptu assessments because they are not well-aligned with contemporary U.S., process-oriented views of effective writing instruction. Other scholars have argued that a single sample cannot adequately represent the variety of types of writing that examinees will be expected to employ in the contexts for which most assessments are designed. For example, research has demonstrated that the writing that students do in college varies on a number of rhetorical and practical dimensions (e.g., Bridgeman & Carlson, 1983; Hale et al., 1996). Many tests given at the transition to college in the United States sample a single type of writing; however, it is one that may not align in important ways with the kinds of tasks that students in college may be asked to do.

BACKWASH FROM IMPROMPTU WRITING TESTS

Evidence on the impact of impromptu writing tests is mixed. Some research suggests that teachers are likely to increase the time students spend writing when an assessment includes this kind of writing component (Almasi et al. 1995; Koretz, Mitchell et al. 1996; Koretz & Hamilton, 2003; Murphy, 2003; Stecher, Barron, Kaganoff & Goodwin, 1998). For instance, in a study of the effects of the Maryland School Performance Assessment Program (MSPAP) by Almasi et al. (1995) teachers said they altered instructional tasks 'to give more writing opportunities, to emphasize personal response to reading, and to include student choice in such literacy tasks.' In a later study of MSPAP conducted by Koretz, Mitchell et al. (1996), these findings were reaffirmed. Teachers reported an increase in emphasis on writing for a variety of purposes, including analysis and evaluation of text and literary comprehension, along with a corresponding decrease in emphasis on spelling, punctuation, and grammar.

In contrast, other studies of the impact of such tests demonstrate a narrowing effect on the curriculum (Wallace, 2002; Scherff & Piazza, 2005), a turn toward formulaic teaching (Loofbourrow, 1994; Johnson, Smagorinsky, Thompson & Fry, 2003; Hillocks, 2002), and a negative effect on student attitudes (Ketter & Poole, 2001; Loofbourrow, 1994). In a case study of the influences of the now defunct California Assessment Program's genre-based assessment in a junior high school, Loofbourrow found that teachers narrowed their teaching to the types, length, and forms of the test. She also found that teachers resorted to 'formulaic' teaching and that students were often frustrated with the test format, either because they were prompted to write about something that wasn't important to them or because they didn't have enough time.

Results of Hillocks's more recent study of the impact of statewide assessment programs on instruction in writing suggest that the trend toward formulaic teaching and writing observed in Loofbourrow's study may be fairly widespread. After an in-depth analysis of multiple kinds of data from five states, including interviews with teachers and administrators and document reviews, Hillocks concluded that state-wide assessments will 'engender formulaic writing and the thinking that goes with it' if they have the following characteristics:

> ...(1) prompts providing a specific topic and subject matter with no or highly limited accompanying data, (2) one limited session for writing, and (3) criteria that call only for 'developing ideas' without specifying the nature of development much beyond a request for detail. (p. 201)

When Hillocks began his research, 37 of the 50 U.S. states had some sort assessment that required actual writing. He identified 12 states that had programs with these characteristics. In states with more effective assessment programs, criteria called for evidence, and benchmark papers displayed their use. In states where students had more time (e.g., Kentucky, where portfolios were collected) they were able to find information and develop evidence for their writing. Hillocks's study suggests that the consequences of some assessments are better than others.

Whether the impact is good or bad, however, it seems clear that the formats of writing assessment do influence curriculum and instruction. For instance, Oneill, Murphy, Huot, and Williamson (2006) found that what teachers taught and how they taught it influenced test formats in three states. The assessment formats in the three states were very different. The 'writing' test in California was a multiple-choice test. In Georgia, the test asked for a single sample of persuasive writing produced under controlled, timed conditions. In Kentucky, students were required to produce portfolios of writing under normal classroom conditions with a focus on 'writing for authentic audiences' and 'situations' (Kentucky Department of Education, 1999).

Questions on the surveys distributed in the three states asked teachers about the influence of tests on curriculum and about their teaching practices. The results indicated significant differences across the three states in the types of writing that were assigned most frequently, the length of assignments, the number of drafts, and the amount of time allowed for the writing assignments. In California, where there was no actual writing sample collected, 72% of the teachers assigned response to literature, a form of writing that most frequently aligned closely with the typical content of their English courses. In Kentucky 52% of the teachers assigned response to literature most frequently, but 48% of them assigned a variety of other kinds of writing instead, including types of writing such as short story and autobiographical narrative. In Kentucky, the assessment system called upon students to choose pieces that addressed a variety of audiences for a variety of purposes, using a variety of forms. In Georgia 48% of the teachers assigned response to literature most frequently, but 52% of them assigned other types of writing and those types aligned in important ways with the type of writing on the state test.

In California and Kentucky, where writing was collected under 'natural' classroom conditions, teachers were more likely to allow three or more days for writing, to require three or more drafts, and to require assignments of greater length. Teachers in Georgia, on the other hand, were more likely to assign single-draft, short pieces of writing and to require that the writing be turned in the same day than teachers in California and Kentucky, a finding that was consistent with the 90 minutes allowed for writing on the Georgia state test. The results of the survey thus support the idea that test formats influence not only what types of writing are taught, but how. Evidence from other research suggests that teachers not only focus on the types of writing covered in a test, they shift their instruction and evaluation strategies to match the rubrics used to score the assessments (Mabry, 1999).

BACKWASH FROM PORTFOLIOS

As an assessment method, portfolios appear to address many of the concerns held by U.S. assessment scholars about the validity of using timed, impromptu, single sample assessments to assess writing ability. Because portfolio samples are collected under more natural and authentic conditions and embedded in instruction, expectations can be made transparent. Further, when a portfolio approach is used, writing can be treated as a recursive process and revisited for revision. Moreover, evidence from research shows that time and instructional support for writing give students a better chance to do their best (Hillocks, 2002; Herman et al., 1993). As noted above, Hillock's analysis suggests that students in Kentucky, where portfolios were assessed instead of impromptu samples of writing, students had time to find information and develop evidence for their writing. Herman et al. (1993) found that raters' scores for portfolio collections of classroom work were higher than those for a standard writing assessment in which students were given 30 to 40 minutes to write. Portfolios also offer opportunities to broaden the assessment construct by sampling a range of genres and to engage students more directly in the assessment process in ways that give them responsibility for evaluating their own learning (Camp, 1992, 1993a).

However, the emphasis here is on the word *can*. Because they reflect curricula and the web of beliefs, goals, and assumptions that underpin education, portfolio programs vary widely in ways that are theoretically and educationally important (Murphy & Underwood, 2000). In some assessment programs, portfolio contents are highly standardized. In others, students are encouraged to choose what the portfolios will contain. In some programs, students submit only final, polished versions of work; in others they submit drafts, notes, and other evidence of the processes they engaged in as they produced their work. In some programs, students are asked to reflect on their work, their learning, or their processes, in others, not. All of these basic differences in assessment design reflect at some level different views about the construct of writing that the assessment purports to measure and the role of the student in the process. Not surprisingly, like other approaches to assessment, the results of research on the consequences of portfolio assessment programs are mixed.

Some studies of large-scale portfolio assessment programs have demonstrated positive effects on the educational environment. Nearly three-fourths of the principals interviewed in a study of Vermont's portfolio assessment program reported that the portfolio program produced positive changes, including 'an increased emphasis on higher order thinking skills', 'lessened reliance on textbooks and worksheets; an increase in writing overall and more integration of writing with other subjects; more work in cooperative groups...' (Koretz, Stecher, Klein & McCaffrey, 1994, p. 31).

Evidence in the literature also suggests that participation in scoring sessions for this kind of curriculum-embedded assessment contributes to teachers' knowledge and expertise and to curricular reform (Gearhart & Wolf, 1994; Sheingold, Heller & Paulukonis, 1995; Storms, Sheingold, Nunez & Heller, 1998). For example, Storms et al. (1998) found that teachers learned about the qualities of student work from the conversations that occurred during scoring sessions. Teachers surveyed in a study by Sheingold et al. (1995) reported substantial changes in their teaching and assessment approaches. In particular, they indicated changes in the sources of evidence they used for assessing student performance, in their expectations for students' responsibility for their own learning and assessment, in their goals for instruction, and in their use of explicit performance criteria to evaluate student work. Finally, using and triangulating a number of data sources, Gearhart and Wolf (1994) found that teachers increased their understanding of the narrative genre and their capacity to provide focused genre-based comments about children's narratives.

Portfolio assessments, however, have not exerted uniformly positive effects, in part because the design of portfolio assessment systems can work against instructional reform goals. One study, in which a highly standardized portfolio was employed, found that because so many different types of writing were required, students had few opportunities to practice and refine any one type, had few decisions to make about the relative quality of different pieces of their work, and were thus unable to reflect on individual progress and goals (Murphy, Bergamini & Rooney, 1997). Similarly, while Kentucky with its statewide portfolio system fared much better overall than other states in Hillocks's (2002) study of the impact of statewide assessments on writing instruction, other research suggests that the system has had negative consequences. Callahan (1999) found that some high school English teachers in Kentucky see the portfolios 'primarily as a stressful administrative task...imposed from outside, introduced as a high-stakes accountability task, and embedded in a massive top down reform effort'. In her view the pressure of the assessment situation also encouraged 'a form of dishonesty among both teachers and students' when some portfolios were accepted despite questions about the origin of some of the texts they contained (pp. 34–35). Spaulding and Cummins (1998) found that many students at the University of Kentucky who had completed the portfolios said that compiling them was not a useful activity (p. 191). Concerns have also been raised by measurement experts about the cost and the difficulties of obtaining reliable scores for portfolios (Nystrand, Cohen & Dowling, 1993), although some assessment programs have overcome those obstacles (LeMahieu, Eresh & Wallace, 1992; Herman et al., 1993).

CONCLUSION

Although direct cause and effect relationships cannot be demonstrated, taken together the findings of the studies reviewed here suggest that the content and format of statewide accountability writing tests influence curriculum and instruction. When policy-makers make decisions about the design of such assessments, they will necessarily be making choices about what kinds of writing or writing skills will be tested, and in the process they will be privileging some curricular content represented in the assessment and ignoring other content that is not. They will also be privileging particular instructional approaches. In the present high stakes environment in the United States, it is likely that their choices will prompt changes in teaching.

Given the powerful interplay between curriculum and assessment, it is all the more important to design assessment systems that enhance learning. Although there are no guarantees that authentic assessments will do so (Mehrens, 1998), they are certainly more likely to enhance learning than assessments that are inauthentic. Authenticity refers to 'the degree of correspondence of the characteristics of a given language test task to the features of a target use... task' (Bachman & Palmer, p. 23). For writing assessment this means the test writing tasks should represent the types of writing that examinees will be expected to employ in the context for which the assessment is designed. Unlike multiple-choice tests, authentic assessments engage students as active constructors of meaning. Thus they are in line with current views of learning. When assessment is authentic, and when the activities involved in building and conducting the assessment also contribute to the professional development of teachers, some would argue, the assessment itself can become an effective means for promoting the kinds of learning it addresses (Eresh, 1990; Camp, 1992, 1993a; LeMahieu, Gitomer & Eresh, 1995; Moss, 1994).

It is also clear there is a need for a more integrated, systemic approach to assessment, one that takes into account the impact that assessment necessarily has on curriculum. When assessments are systemically valid, they 'induce curricular and instructional changes in education systems (and learning strategy changes in students) that foster the development of the cognitive traits that the tests are designed to measure' (Frederiksen & Collins, 1989, p. 27). Arguments against authentic assessment often rest on the grounds of technical adequacy and cost. An important challenge for measurement experts and policy makers in the future, then, one that is especially relevant to the consequential validity of assessments, will be to balance the demands of technical adequacy and cost with the development and validation of assessments that enhance learning and the educational environment. Frederiksen and Collins (1989) point out that, 'the efficiency in current testing practices is greatly outweighed by the cost of using a system that has low systemic validity—one that has a negative impact on learning and teaching' (p. 32).

However, determining whether the impact of an assessment is negative or positive is a problematic issue. Assessments of writing necessarily embody different priorities and views of learning because they are typically structured around particular content, a particular taxonomy of discourse, or a particular curriculum for writing. As the research reviewed here reveals, whether consequences of an assessment are viewed as good or bad depends on the values and beliefs of the stakeholder. While some curriculum and assessment experts value new modes of assessment because they are in line with current views on learning and because they assess higher-order skills as opposed to rote reproduction of knowledge, not all stakeholders hold the same beliefs and values. Herein lies an intractable problem for large-scale assessments. Although assessments can be designed to further particular instructional goals, the goals themselves remain matters of public debate. Another intractable problem for the developer of a large-scale assessment, then, is how to balance the competing curricular agendas of its stakeholders.

To address this problem, small-scale alternatives to large-scale writing assessments have been proposed by some assessment experts (see for example, Broad, 2003; Huot, 2002). For instance, Huot (2002) believes assessments should be site-based, locally controlled, context-sensitive, rhetorically based, and accessible. A '*site-based*' assessment, Huot explains, 'is developed in response to a specific need that occurs at a specific site', and that is based on the 'resources and concerns' of its constituents. In a '*locally controlled*' assessment, the individual institution would be 'responsible for managing, revising, updating and validating the assessment procedures, which should in turn be carefully reviewed…to safeguard the concerns of all those affected by the assessment process'. In a '*context-sensitive*' assessment, the procedures would 'honor the instructional goals and objectives as well as the cultural and social environment of the institution or agency and its students, teachers and other stakeholders.' In a '*rhetorically based*' assessment, 'All writing assignments, scoring criteria, writing environments and reading procedures' would 'adhere to recognizable and supportable rhetorical principles integral to the thoughtful expression and reflective interpretation of texts'. In an '*accessible*' assessment, all 'procedures and rationales for the creation of writing assignments, scoring criteria and reading procedures, as well as samples of student work and rater judgment' would 'be available to those whose work is being evaluated' (p. 105).

Were such principles to be enacted, the resulting assessments would be much more likely to accommodate the interests and curricular goals of their particular stakeholders. But Huot speaks from the perspective of a college writing program administrator and teacher. Given the widespread use of large-scale assessments to monitor U.S. educational programs and their popularity with policy makers and the public at large, it is unlikely that locally-controlled, site-based alternatives will ever be considered outside of the college environment. Indeed, policy-makers want large-scale measures that allow them to compare individual sites to one another, using, so to speak, the same yardstick. For public education then, at least at the K-12 level, the dilemma remains: how to balance the need for efficient, cost-effective assessments with the need for assessments that are aligned with contemporary views on literacy and that enhance the educational environment.

NOTES

1. The admission test acronyms stand for the Scholastic Achievement Test, the Graduate Record Exam, the Medical Colleges Admission Test, the Law School Admission Test, and the Graduate Management Admission Test.
2. For example, a recent study of high school exit exams in six states conducted by the Achieve Foundation revealed that the questions on these exams reflect 'modest expectations' and test 'material that most students study early in their high school years' (Achieve, 2004). States give students multiple opportunities to pass exit tests and most college-going students will have passed them long before their senior year. Unlike the Norwegian exam described in this volume, the U.S. high school exit exams do not use writing to examine what was learned from the curriculum about subjects other than writing.

REFERENCES

Achieve, Inc. (2004). *Do graduation tests measure up? A closer look at state high school exit exams*. Washington, D.C.: Achieve.

Almasi, J., Afflerbach, P. Guthrie, J., & Schafer, W., (1995). *Effects of a statewide performance assessment program on classroom instructional practice in literacy* (Reading Research Report 32). College Park, MD: National Reading Research Center, University of Maryland.

American Psychological Association. (1993). *Learner-centered psychological principles: Guidelines for school redesign and reform*. Washington, D.C.: Presidential Task force on Psychology in Education.

Bachman, L. F. & Palmer, A. S. (1996). *Language testing in practice*. Oxford: Oxford University Press.

Bond, L. A., Baskamp, D., & Roeber, E. (1996). *The status report of the assessment programs in the United States*. Washington, D.C.: The Council of Chief State School Officers and Oak Brook, IL: North Central Regional Educational Laboratory.

Bracey, G. (1987). Measurement-driven instruction: Catchy phrase, dangerous practice. *Phi Delta Kappan, 68*, 683–686.

Breland, H. M. (1983). *The direct assessment of writing skill: A measurement review*. College Board Report no. 83–6 (ETS Research Report no. 83–32). New York: College Entrance Examination Board.

Bridgeman, B. & Carlson, S. (1983). *Survey of academic writing tasks required of graduate and undergraduate foreign students*. TOEFL Research Report No. 15; ETS Research Report No. 83–18. Princeton, NJ: Educational Testing Service.

Broad, B. (2003). *What we really value: Beyond rubrics in teaching and assessing writing*. Logan, Utah: Utah State University Press.

Broadfoot, P. (1996). *Education, assessment and society*. Buckingham, UK: Open University Press.

California Department of Education (2002). *Standardized testing and reporting program: Help about STAR 2001*. Retrieved 11–18–02 from http://star.cde. ca.gov.

Callahan, S. (1999). All done with best of intentions: One Kentucky high school after six years of state portfolio tests. *Assessing Writing, 6*(1), 5–40.

Camp, R. (April, 1983). *Direct assessment at ETS: What we know and what we need to know.* Paper presented at the National Council on Educational Measurement.

Camp, R. (1992). Assessment in the context of schools and school change. In H. H. Marshall (Ed.), *Redefining student learning: roots of educational change,* 241–263. Norwood, NJ: Ablex.

Camp, R. (1993a). The place of portfolios in our changing views of writing assessment. In R. E. Bennett & W. C. Ward (Eds.), *Construction versus choice in cognitive measurement: Issues in constructed response, performance testing, and portfolio assessment,* 183–212. Hillsdale, NJ: Lawrence Erlbaum.

Camp, R. (1993b). Changing the model for the direct assessment of writing. In M. Williamson & B. Huot (Eds.), *Validating holistic scoring for writing assessment,* 45–78. Cresskill, NJ: Hampton Press.

Cope, B. & Kalantzis, M. (1993). *The powers of literacy: A genre approach to teaching writing.* Pittsburgh: University of Pittsburgh Press.

Corbett, H. D. & Wilson, B. L. (1991). *Testing, reform, and rebellion.* Norwood, NJ: Ablex.

Diederich, P. (1974). *Measuring growth in English.* Urbana, IL: National Council of Teachers of English.

Door-Bremme, D. & Herman, J. (1986). *Assessing student achievement: A profile of classroom practices.* Los Angeles, CA: Center for the Study of Evaluation.

Eresh, J. (1990, November). *Balancing the pieces: Content, teachers, tests, and administration.* Paper presented at the annual meeting of the Conference for Secondary School English Department Chairpersons, Atlanta, GA.

Foster, D. & Russell, D. R. (2002). Conclusion. In D. Foster & D. R. Russell (Eds.), *Writing and learning in cross-national perspective: Transitions from secondary to higher education,* 319–339. Mahwah, NJ: Lawrence Erlbaum.

Fredericksen, J. & Collins, A. (1989). A systems approach to educational testing. *Educational Researcher, 18*(9), 27–32.

Frederiksen, N., Mislevy, R., & Bejar, I. (Eds.) (1993). *Test theory for a new generation of tests.* Hillsdale, NJ: Lawrence Erlbaum.

Gearhart, M. & Wolf, S. (1994). Engaging teachers in assessment of their students' narrative writing: The role of subject matter knowledge. *Assessing Writing, 1,* 67–90.

Gipps, C. (1999). Socio-cultural aspects of assessment. In P. D. Pearson & A. Iran-Nehad (Eds.), *Review of Research in Education, 23,* 335–393.

Godshalk., F., Swineford, E., & Coffman, W. (1966). *The measurement of writing ability.* New York: College Entrance Examination Board.

Grant, S. G. (2000, February). Teachers and tests: Exploring teachers' perceptions of changes in the New York State-mandated testing program. *Education Policy Analysis Archives* [On-line serial], 8(14). Available: http://epaa.asu.edu/epaa/v8n14.html.

Hale, G., Taylor, C., Bridgeman, B. Carson, J., Kroll, B., & Kantor, R. (1996). A study of writing tasks assigned in academic degree programs (TOEFL Research Report #54). Princeton, NJ: Educational Testing Service.

Hamilton, L. (2003). Assessment as a policy tool. In R. Floden (Ed.), *Review of Research in Education, 27,* 25–68. Washington, D.C.: American Educational Research Association.

Heubert, J. P. & Hauser, R. M. (Eds.). (1999). *High stakes: Testing for tracking, promotion, and graduation.* Washington, D.C.: National Academy Press.

Herman, J., Gearhart, M., & Baker, E. (1993). Assessing writing portfolios: Issues in the validity and meaning of scores. *Educational Assessment, 1*(3), 201–224.

Hillocks, G., Jr. (2002). *The testing trap: How states writing assessments control learning.* New York: Teachers College Press.

Huot, B. (2002). *(Re) articulating writing assessment for teaching and learning.* Logan, Utah: Utah State University Press.

Johnson, T. S., Smagorinsky, P., Thompson, L., & Fry, P. G. (2003). Learning to teach the five-paragraph theme. *Research in the Teaching of English, 38,* 136–176.

Kentucky Department of Education (1999). *Kentucky writing portfolio: Writing portfolio development teacher's handbook.* Frankfurt, KY: Author.

Ketter, J. & Pool, J. (2001). Exploring the impact of a high-stakes direct writing assessment in two high school classrooms. *Research in the Teaching of English, 35,* 344–393.

Koretz, D. & Hamilton, L. S. (2003).*Teachers' responses to high-states testing and the validity of gains: A pilot study* (CSE Tech.Rep. 610). Los Angeles: Center for Research on Evaluation, Standards, and Student Testing.

Koretz, D., Mitchell, K., Barron, S., & Keith, S. (1996). *Final report: Perceived effects of the Maryland School Performance Assessment Program.* (Tech. Rep. No. 409). Los Angeles: University of California, Center for Research on Evaluation, Standards, and Student Testing.

Koretz, D., Stecher, B., & Deibert, E. (1993). *The reliability of scores from the 1992 Vermont portfolio assessment program* (Tech. Rep. No. 355). Los Angeles: University of California, Center for Research on Evaluation, Standards, and Student Testing.

Koretz, D., Stecher, B, Klein, S., McCaffrey, D., & Deibert, E. (1993). *Can portfolios assess student performance and influence instruction? The 1991–1992 Vermont Experience.* (CSE Technical Report 371). Los Angeles: National Center for Research on Evaluation, Standards, and Student Testing, University of California, Los Angeles.

LeMahieu, P. G., Eresh, J. T., & Wallace, R. C. (1992). Using student portfolios for a public accounting. *School Administrator, 49*(11), 8–13.

LeMahieu, P., Gitomer, D., & Eresh, J. (1995). Portfolios in large scale assessment: Difficult but not impossible. *Educational Measurement: Issues and Practice, 14*(3), 11–28.

Linn, R. L., Baker, E., & Dunbar, S. B. (1990). Performance-based assessment: Expectations and validation criteria. *Educational Researcher, 20*(8), 15–21.

Loofbourrow, P. (1994). Composition in the context of the CAP: A case study of the interplay between composition assessment and classrooms. *Educational Assessment, 2*(1), 7–49.

Mabry, L. (1999). Writing to the rubric: Lingering effects of traditional standardized testing on direct writing assessment. *Phi Delta Kappan, 80,* 673–679.

Madaus, G. F. (1988). The influence of testing on the curriculum. In L. Tanner (Ed.), *Critical issues in curriculum, eighty-seventh yearbook of the National Society for Study of Education,* 83–121. Chicago: University of Chicago Press.

Madaus, G. F. & Kellaghan, T. (1993). Testing as a mechanism of public policy: A brief history and description. *Measurement and Evaluation in Counseling and Development, 26*(6), 10–21.

Mehrens, W. (1998). Consequences of assessment: What is the evidence? *Education Policy Analysis Archives, 6*(13). Retrieved from http://epaa.asu.edu/epaa/v6n13/

Messick, S. (1989a). Meaning and values in test validation: The science and ethics of assessment. *Educational Researcher, 18*(2), 5–11.

Messick, S. (1989b). Validity. In R. L. Linn (Ed.), *Educational measurement* (3rd. ed.), 13–104. New York: American Council on Education and Macmillan.

Messick, S. (1994). The interplay of evidence and consequences in the validation of performance assessments. *Educational Researcher, 23*(2), 13–23.

Moss, P. (1992). Shifting conceptions of validity in educational measurement: Implications for performance assessment. *Review of Educational Research, 62*(3), 229–258.

Moss, P. (1994). Can there be validity without reliability? *Educational Researcher, 23*(2), 5–12.

Murphy, J. (1990). *The educational reform movement of the 1980's: A comprehensive analysis. In J. Murphy (Ed.), The reform of American public education in the 1980s: Perspectives and cases.* Berkeley, CA: McCutchan.

Murphy, S. (2003). That was then, this is now: The impact of changing assessment policies on teachers and the teaching of writing in California. *Journal of Writing Assessment, 1*(1), 23–45.

Murphy, S. & Camp, R. (1996). Toward systemic coherence: a discussion of conflicting perspectives on portfolio assessment. In R. Calfee & P. Perfumo (Eds.), *Writing portfolios in the classroom: Policy and practice, promise and peril.* Hillsdale, NJ: Lawrence Erlbaum.

Murphy, S., Bergamini, J., & Rooney, P. (1997). The impact of large-scale portfolio assessment programs on classroom practice: Case studies of the New Standards field-trial portfolio. *Educational Assessment, 4*(4), 297–333.

Murphy, S. & Underwood, T. (2000). *Portfolio practices: Lessons from schools, districts, and states.* Norwood, MA: Christoper-Gordon.

National Research Council. (2000). *How people learn: Brain, mind, experience, and school.* Washington, D.C.: National Academy Press.

Nystrand, M., Cohen, A., & Dowling, N. (1993). Addressing reliability problems in the portfolio assessment of college writing. *Educational Assessment, 1*(1), 53–70.

Oneill, P., Murphy, S., Huot, B., & Williamson, M. (2006). What high school teachers in three states say about different kinds of mandated state writing tests. *Journal of Writing Assessment, 2*(2), 81–108.

Pearson, P. D. & Valencia, S. (1987). *Assessment, accountability, and professional prerogative. Research in literacy: Merging perspectives; Thirty-sixth yearbook of the National Reading Conference.* Rochester, NY: National Reading Conference.

Pedulla, J., Abrams, L., Madaus, G., Russell, M., Ramos, M., & Miao, J. (2003). *Perceived effects of state-mandated testing programs on teaching and learning: Findings from a national survey of teachers.* Chestnut Hill, MA: National Board on Educational Testing and Public Policy.

Resnick, L. B. & Klopfer, K. (1989). *Toward the thinking curriculum: Current cognitive research. 1989 yearbook of the Association for Supervision and Curriculum Development.* Alexandria, VA: The Association for Supervision and Curriculum Development.

Roeber, E., Bond, L. A., & Braskamp, D. (1997). *Trends in statewide student assessment programs, 1997.* North Central Regional Educational Laboratory and the Council of Chief State School Officers.

Scherff, L. & Piazza, C. 2005. The more things change, the more they stay the same: A survey of high school students' writing experiences. *Research in the Teaching of English, 39*(3), 271–304.

Sheingold, K., Heller, J., & Paulukonis, S. (1995). *Actively seeking evidence: Teacher change through assessment development* (MS#94–04). Princeton, NJ: Educational Testing Service.

Shepard, L. A. (1991). Will national tests improve student learning? *Phi Delta Kappan, 73*, 232–238.

Shepard, L. A. & Dougherty, K. C. (1991, April). *Effects of high-stakes testing on instruction.* Paper presented at the annual meeting of the American Educational Research Association, Chicago.

Smith, M. L. (1991). Put to the test: The effects of external testing on teachers. *Educational Researcher, 20*(5), 8–11.

Smith, M. L. & Rottenberg, C. (1991). Unintended consequences of external testing in elementary school. *Educational Measurement: Issues and Practice, 10*(4), 7–11.

Spaulding, E. & Cummins, G. (1998). It was the best of times. It was a waste of time: University of Kentucky students' view of writing under KERA. *Assessing Writing, 5*(2), 167–200.

Stecher, B. M., Barron, S. I., Kaganoff, T., & Goodwin, J. (1998). *The effects of standards-based assessment on classroom practices: Results of the 1996–97 RAND survey of Kentucky teachers of mathematics and writing* (CSE Tech. Rep. 482). Los Angeles: Center for Research on Evaluation, Standards, and Student Testing.

Street, B. (1995). *Social literacies: Critical approaches to literacy in development, ethnography and education.* London: Longman Group.

Storms, B. A., Sheingold, K., Nunez, A., & Heller, J. (1998). *The feasibility, comparability, and value of local scorings of performance assessments* (Technical report). Princeton, NJ: Educational Testing Service, Center for Performance Assessment.

U.S. Department of Education. (2002). No child left behind: Executive summary. http://www.ed.gov/nclb/accountability/schools/accountability.html.

Vygotsky, L. S. (1978). *Mind in society: The development of higher psychological processes* (M. Cole, B. John-Steiner, S. Scribner & E. Souberman, Eds.). Cambridge, MA: Harvard University Press.

Vygotsky, L. S. (1986). Thought and language (A. Kozulin, Ed. & Trans.). Cambridge, MA: MIT Press.

Wallace, V. L. (2002). Administrative direction in schools of contrasting status: Two cases. In G. Hillocks Jr. (Ed.), *The testing trap: How state writing assessment control learning*, 93–102. New York: Teachers College Press.

Wells, P. (1991). Putting America to the test. *Agenda, 1*, 52–57.

White, E. (1995). An apologia for the timed impromptu essay test. *College Composition and Communication, 46*(1), 129–139.

White, E. (1996). Power and agenda setting in writing assessment. In E. M. White, W..D. Lutz, & S. Kamusikiri (Eds.), *Assessment of writing: Politics, policies, practices.* New York: The Modern Language Association of America.

4 Assessment of writing in Norway
A case of balancing dilemmas

Frøydis Hertzberg

FROM TRUST TO ACCOUNTABILITY?

The Norwegian school system has a long tradition for relying on teachers'
continuous assessment. Students meet their first exam at the end of lower
secondary school (grade 10), and only in one written subject. The exam
itself is a day-long exam because Norway has no tradition for multiple-
choice tests or two-hour exams. In the subject of Norwegian this means
that students are expected to produce a lengthy essay during a period of
five hours, on a topic selected from a generous repertoire of assignments.
However, only one-fifth of the cohort sit for Norwegian, which implies that
the majority of students will leave lower secondary without having ever
had their writing assessed by an external assessor. Another consequence is
that most of the marks on the students' final diploma have been given by
their own teachers. The marks are of importance for the students' choice
of course in upper secondary, although all students are guaranteed admit-
tance to the school in general.

The high degree of trust in teachers' judgment and in assessment through
school-leaving exams has been a leading principle in Norwegian primary
and secondary education for more than two centuries. However, with the
recent introduction of national tests this situation is changing radically. In
spring 2004 there were centrally given tests in English, math and reading,
and in 2005 writing was included. As testing is felt to be an alien element
in Norwegian schools, it has created considerable turbulence.

My article will aim at analyzing this situation in the light of different
perspectives on assessment of writing in the Norwegian context. I will
make no easy judgments, but discuss the pros and cons of both the traditional and the new system. I will start with the school leaving exam. This
exam can be seen as the real proof of the pudding: what have the students
actually learnt during their 10 years in school?

THE SCHOOL-LEAVING EXAM AS
EVALUATED BY THE QAL PROJECT[1]

The QAL project has two main objectives:

1. To study the acquired level of competence in written Norwegian at the end of lower secondary (What do they accomplish and what do they not accomplish?)
2. To examine this assessment as a national quality assurance system (To what degree can the assessment be trusted as a reliable measure for students' writing competence?)

For the four of us who have undertaken this study, an important motivation has been the knowledge of how deeply the exam influences day-to-day writing instruction. It does so by establishing a norm for the kind of writing tasks students are expected to master, and a norm for how such tasks are to be assessed. Thus, by examining the exam we can get a part of a picture of the teaching and learning that takes place in Norwegian classrooms.

The study is based on representative samples of students' essays from four consecutive years (1998–2001). Our total corpus consists of more than 3300 essays, with information about marks and evaluation, as well as a few background variables. All texts have been marked by two experienced teachers, and in addition about one third of them (928 texts) have been randomly selected to be marked by three additional assessors. Earlier studies have shown that the number of five assessors is optimal for obtaining reliable grades on essays of this category (Berge, 1996). Whenever we relate findings to text quality, it is these 928 texts we are talking about. However, quantitative measures have been calculated using the total corpus.

The project is an umbrella for several independent studies, ranging from topics like assessor reliability and quantitative measures of text quality to 'risk takers' (students who seem to challenge conventional norms of content and style) and students' preference of topics, genres and writing styles. The final report is Berge et al. (2005).

WHAT DID WE FIND?

A widespread notion of exam writing is that it is instrumental, narrow and inauthentic. This is not what we found. Our investigation shows that Norwegian students are offered a wide range of possibilities as to topics, genres and writing styles, to which they respond by writing creative, personal and often independent essays. The best essays are of very high quality even judged by literary criteria. There is a tendency for all students, even the most low-performing, to master basic textual traits like the use of a beginning and an end, the development of a plot with its resolution, chronology, and cause/effect. The assessors, for their part, are willing to accept the students' own premises, although not uncritically. They are very capable of identifying weak and strong parts of each text, and they are loyal to the instruction from the national board saying that shortcomings at one text level should be balanced against strong aspects at another level. They do not react negatively when conventional genres are challenged, and they seem to take 'rude' language or provocative attitudes without moralizing. In other words, the picture is a great deal brighter than one could have expected.

Also the correlation between the assessors is higher than expected; it varies from .65 to .72, with .70 as a mean. This is not high enough to satisfy test standards in general, but higher than for the upper secondary exam in Norwegian and higher than for similar writing studies. A survey of international writing tests in Berge (2002) shows only two tests with higher reliability than the Norwegian exam, and in both cases the assessors were selected and trained for that particular task. The difficulties involved in reliable assessment of writing proficiency are well known in the research literature (see for instance Lehman, 1993, 1994; Weigle, 2002). This is not only because each assignment can be answered in a number of different ways, but also because syntax, text structure, and genre traits are not standardized as is, for example, spelling. To assess the kind of very individualistic and creative texts written in this exam the assessors need to develop a shared norm of what constitutes text quality of students' writing at that level of the school system, and this common norm will typically be based on a mixture of explicit criteria and holistic judgment. The relatively high correlation between our assessors is probably the result of years of in-service training both among the assessors and among writing teachers in general.[2]

All this seems very positive. But the study has definitely identified some problems, of which the most important are (1) the gender differences and (2) the overwhelming dominance of personal narratives at the expense of argumentative and expository genres. For the cohorts that include information on gender,[3] it is evident that girls strongly outperform boys. In 2002, on a scale from 6 (excellent) to 1 (fail), 28% of the girls and only 12% of the boys obtained 5 or 6, whereas 29% of the boys and only 5.5 % of the girls obtained 1 or 2. In other words, there are many girls and few boys at the top, and many boys and few girls at the bottom. Also, in the middle group the girls do better than boys. In its turn, this gender gap is related to the next problem, the dominance of narrative writing. When the material is explored more deeply, there is an indication that the difference between girls and boys is most clear-cut in creative writing. The one task in the 2001 set that asks for an article or essay has a different distribution of marks from the other six; the mean grade is the same for girls and boys, and both the strongest and the most low-performing writers are to be found among the boys.[4] In other words, with a better balance between narrative and non-fictional writing we have reason to believe that the gender gap would become smaller.

We consider the dominance of narrative writing as a problem in itself, independent of the gender gap,. The curriculum demands both fictional and non-fictional writing, and the exam assignments offer opportunities for both. A large majority of students, however, seem to avoid non-fiction tasks. Only about 20% choose such tasks, and among these the preferred types are texts written in a humorous and often ironic style, in other words not the most typical argumentative genre. This certainly means that Norwegian students do not get sufficient experience with the kind of writing demanded of them in higher education, not to say in a future job.

We interpret this situation in the light of what we call *the characteristic writing culture* in primary and secondary school in Norway. The teaching of writing has undergone great changes during the last two decades, due in great part to the introduction of creative writing in the seventies and process writing in the eighties. The striving for *a personal voice* and the idea of *the student as an author* has gone deep into Norwegian classrooms, and texts that have fictional qualities are encouraged and highly appreciated by the teachers. In such a writing culture, there may be a slight undervaluing of expository and argumentative writing by both students and teachers. This may be the explanation for why students tend to avoid argumentative writing, combined with the fact that narratives dominate children's leisure reading and the deep-rooted belief that narratives are easier to write. In fact, there is considerable research evidence that argumentation actually *is* more demanding. Whereas oral narratives may serve as structural models for written ones, the structure of written argument differs so much from spoken argument that it offers very limited support for writing. In addition, systematic argument seems to involve a demand on cognitive processes which may not be fully developed in young people (Freedman & Pringle, 1988, 1989; Andrews, 1995).

The exam is not capable of changing this bias towards fictional writing; in effect it may even reinforce it. Since an important underlying premise is to meet the students 'where they are', the assignments chosen for the students will predominantly offer opportunities for creative writing, with the natural consequence that more of the students will choose such tasks. In fact, the girls' favourite exam genres—stories, letters, and diary entries—are always to be found among the assignments.

However, these problems must not be allowed to overshadow the positive findings of the study. Through the QAL project we identified a writing culture that encourages creativity and allows experiment, a culture where students have reason to be confident that their texts are met with respect and tolerance. Otherwise students with obvious spelling problems would not write vivid and lengthy essays, and the most skilled writers would not want to experiment with linguistic style and genre traits on the day of the exam. All in all, we think the exam mirrors a classroom culture that is worth cherishing.

A NEW REGIME

The object of our investigation, the school leaving exam, appeared in a new light in 2003, when a unanimous parliament passed a bill mandating national tests in math, English, reading and writing. Such tests were to be taken by all students at grades 4, 7, 10, and 11, the intention being that the tests may replace the school leaving exams altogether.

At an early stage of the process, the QAL project group reacted strongly against the idea of writing tests. As mentioned above there is solid research-based evidence for arguing that large-scale testing of writing beyond the level of spelling and punctuation is connected with serious problems of validity and reliability. We also feared the possible consequences of such tests, as they might undermine the *writing as process* ideology that under-lies our national curriculum and tend to make writing a purely instrumental activity. Such effects would certainly be accentuated with web publishing of the results, which would obviously result in league tables. Consequently we wrote a letter to the Minister of Education arguing against her plans, drawing upon our experience as researchers, and relating our arguments to international literature on assessment of writing (Berge et al., 2003).

Our initiative was met with an immediate response. Evidently there was no question of going back on parliament's decision, but as researchers we were asked to participate in the process of constructing acceptable tests. Three of the project members accepted this challenge, and in the following year these three formed the core of a working group which also included experienced practitioners and a specialist in dyslexia.

The obvious reason for accepting the challenge from the Minister of Education lies in the Norwegian proverb: 'Having said A, you have to say B'. The concern of the group was also to avoid the worst possible conse-quences of parliament's decision, such as limiting the assessment to mere spelling and punctuation or testing writing performance on the basis of predictive validity only. In the latter case writing is assessed not through the students' own writing, but through their ability to detect errors, clumsy syntax, incoherent text structure, or inadequate vocabulary in texts writ-ten by others. Such tests may well predict writing competence to a certain degree, but as shown in Sandra Murphy's contribution to this book, they may have a serious backwash effect on writing instruction. When the Cali-fornia Department of Education replaced writing assignments with multi-ple-choice tests, it resulted in teachers spending less time teaching actual writing and more time teaching grammar and usage, as discussed by Mur-phy (chapter 3, this volume)

However, national tests also offer some possible pedagogical gains. As revealed by the QAL study, Norwegian writing instruction has resulted in an unintended bias toward personal narrative writing and a perturbing gender gap. There are also obvious problems connected to the fact that neither students nor teachers are provided with what Somerset (1996: 280) calls 'a common yardstick' until 10th grade. This places too heavy a burden on teachers' own judgment and a lack of clear information to the students about what is expected of them. In short, Norwegian writing instruction may rely too much on free, spontaneous writing and the idea that 'form will come by itself'. We are here at the very core of the criticism that has been raised against the *writing as process* ideology in general, especially from the Australian *genre school* (Reid, 1987; Cope & Kalantzis, 1993), but also from George Hillocks's comprehensive meta-analysis of writing research studies (Hillocks, 1984, 1986). Hillocks's study shows that writing instruction based on clear goals and a blend of teachers' guidance and students' active participation is more effective than the free writing strategy advocated by, for instance, Donald Graves (1983). The same principles underlie the writing pedagogy introduced by the genre school, which included a much increased emphasis on factual writing, particularly writing in science (Martin, 1985; Halliday & Martin, 1993; for brief introductions to the genre pedagogy see Cambourne & Brown, 1989; Beard 2000: 118 ff).

Inspired by the genre school, the research group sees the national tests as an opportunity to reform Norwegian writing at its weakest points. By including topics and genres from natural science and social science they intend to broaden the students' writing repertoire and make writing a useful tool for enhancing learning in these disciplines. This is very much in accord with the ideology of the forthcoming National curriculum, where writing is considered one of the basic skills to be made explicit in the curricula of all school subjects. ('Basic' in this case must be interpreted as something much more than 'elementary'.) In other words, the backwash effect of such tests might benefit rather than damage the positive and creative writing culture revealed by the QAL project.

A PERIOD OF TENSION AND TRANSITION

The first round of writing tests was carried out in spring 2005. The entire cohorts of 4th, 7th, and 10th grades were tested (grade 11 being voluntary), and in all cases the tests combined factual and fictional writing. The test at grade 10 consisted of two tasks connected to the topic *Mars—The Red Planet*. The students had been preparing for the topic days beforehand together with their teacher, and the test itself took one whole day. The first task was to discuss the question of life on Mars, the other to reflect upon a philosophical question. The tests had been graded by the students' own teachers in accordance with criteria developed by the research group, and some of the tests were randomly drawn for an additional external assessment.

The reactions from the teachers were mixed. On the one hand many of them reported to have obtained new and useful knowledge about assessment criteria, on the other hand they claimed that the tests did not provide information about their students that they did not have already. They complained about the amount of time being spent on the whole process, but most of all they reacted against the publicizing of the results on the web. This, in fact, is the real root of the controversy. About 10% of the students boycotted the tests, often supported by their parents and even their teachers. In some cases groups of activists published the tests on the web in advance. The opponents got unexpected support as it became known that OECD warned the Norwegian government against publicizing the results. Furthermore, a national evaluation report brought severe criticism of the tests, particularly on the ground of the unacceptably low reliability of the scores.

In view of this turbulence, national testing became a political issue before the parliamentary election in the autumn 2005. The election led to a change from a right-wing to a left-wing coalition, with the immediate result that the new government decided to freeze the whole testing system for at least one year. After approximately half a year it was proclaimed that the tests were to be taken up in 2007, but with some changes: the results are not to be reported on the *Skoleporten* website[5]; the time for the testing has been moved in order to make the tests more useful for teachers; third, the *writing tests* are no longer to be included in the battery of national tests. Only a sample of each cohort will be selected every year.

From one perspective the writing researchers behind the tests can draw a sigh of relief because they had been advocating smaller scale testing since the very beginning. But the new government policy is fragile in many ways. First and foremost it is not in accordance with the unanimous parliament bill from 2003. Second, the fate of the testing system lies in the hands of a left-wing coalition that may be replaced by a different coalition at any time.

What, then, will happen if or when the national writing tests are taken up again? Following the line of thinking in the IEA study presented above, the combination of the school leaving exam and the national tests ought to meet the vital need for high validity assessment of writing (Lehman, 1993). Each student will be assessed through a variety of tasks requiring writing that differs in genre, writing style, and length, and answers will be written at different stages and in different contexts. Together with the teachers' continuous assessment, the two should make a solid base for assessing Norwegian students' writing performance. But in the long run the combination of the two systems will be considered too expensive to maintain, and the school leaving exam is likely to be reduced or even abolished.

At this point it is necessary to widen the perspective. Apart from the fact that both the exam and the tests are meant to assess writing, they differ strongly in their purpose. The school leaving exam is a traditional assessment for selection, whereas the national tests—besides providing teachers with a tool for supporting teaching and learning—are intended to serve the goal of accountability. In the latter case there is also an expectation about comparisons between provinces, rural and urban areas, boys and girls, minority and majority language students, but first of all between different cohorts. In other words, whereas exams serve the purpose of selecting students for further education or future jobs, assessing for accountability purposes provides data for policy makers and for monitoring quality over the years.

If the exam is removed from secondary education, the national tests will have to take on both the assessing-for-selection and the assessing-for-accountability purposes. However, the tests are not intended to fulfil the function of discriminating between individual students. It is even questionable whether they can meet the expectations of accountability. The idea of monitoring changes over time is connected with severe methodological problems; because the tasks are new every year, it is not possible to make reliable comparisons from one year to another. What *will* be possible, however, are horizontal comparisons between schools and regions. A change of government may also mean a reintroduction of the publicizing of the results on *Skoleporten*, which inevitably will result in league tables. From a rich body of research literature we know the damaging ethical and pedagogical incidental effect of this (see for instance Murphy's contribution in this book, and Gipps 1994: 144 ff., 1996; Stobart & Gipps, 1997: 25 ff; Hillocks, 2002).

In the case of writing instruction there are several possible negative outcomes. One is a bias towards instrumental, factual writing at the expense of creative writing, the exact opposite of the present situation. In the long run one might expect more frequent testing, and since this means higher expenses, the relatively ambitious framework developed by the present research group may be replaced by tests that are easier both to develop and to score. A possible future scenario could be a reintroduction of writing tests on a national scale, based on multiple-choice and standardized text structures. Such tests would come out with more reliable scoring tables but would mean a giant step backwards for Norwegian writing instruction. They would be contrary to the view of assessment that Caroline Gipps states in clear and unqualified terms: Assessment for selection, monitoring, and accountability purposes where 100% sample is used, she says, 'can *and must* be based on a model of assessment which will enhance and support good learning' (Gipps 1996: 252). In the case of Norwegian writing instruction 'good learning' can be interpreted as enhancing teachers' and students' competence in factual writing and writing across the disciplines, but without abolishing the creative writing culture that has been documented by the QAL project.

CONCLUSION

On a macro level the Norwegian case is an illustration of the consequences of politicians taking control over assessment systems. The rationales for the shift of strategies have been rooted in politics, not in education, and in the ongoing discourse educationalists have had difficulties making themselves heard. In fact, researchers have had the choice between two alternatives: staying out of it or trying to make the best of it.

The writing research group chose the last alternative, interpreting the new situation as a possibility to promote the kind of writing that needed enforcement. However, from the very beginning the group was confronted with serious dilemmas that are still unsolved. One is to turn a system primarily constructed for accountability purposes into a system for enhancing learning. Another is the risk connected to the possible abolishment of a well-functioning school leaving exam that also serves as selection for further education. A third dilemma lies in having to contribute to a regime opposed by most teachers and researchers by the publicizing of the results. Even if the most recent political step has made such negative outcomes less plausible, we are probably dealing with a temporary time-out rather than a stable situation.

NOTES

1. The QAL project (QAL=Quality Assurance of Learning Outcome in Written Norwegian) is a part of the evaluation of a recent curriculum reform (Evaluation of Reform 97). Project members are Professor Lars Sigfred Evensen, Professor Kjell Lars Berge, researcher Wenche Vagle, senior advisor Sissel Anderson, and myself. The project has been financed by the Norwegian Research Council.
2. Disagreement between the assessors is in itself interesting, and our qualitative corpus includes a sample of essays where the assessors strongly disagree. This is most typically the case with unconventional essays, often essays that do not directly conform to the assignment given.
3. The QAL corpus includes information of gender only in the 2001 cohort, but we have summary statistics of the grade distribution also from the 2002 cohort.
4. However, only 7% of the cohort chose that task, so one should not generalize on the basis of these results
5. 'Skoleporten' (The School Gate) is the name of the website 'for quality assessment and development in primary and secondary education', administrated by the Directorate for Primary and Secondary Education, http://www.skoleporten.no. An English version of the website is in progress.

REFERENCES

Andrews, R. (1995). *Teaching and learning argument*. London: Cassell.

Andrews, R. (Ed.) (1998). *Narrative and argument*. Milton Keynes: Open University Press.

Beard, R. (2000). *Developing writing*, 3–13. London: Hodder & Stoughton.

Berge, K. L. (1996). *Norsksensorers tekstnormer og doxa: En kultursemiotisk og sosiotekstologisk analyse*. Dissertation, Trondheim: NTNU.

Berge, K. L. (2002). Hidden norms in assessment of students' exam essays in Norwegian upper secondary schools. *Written Communication, 19*, 458–492.

Berge, K. L., Evensen, L. S., & Hertzberg, F. (2003). Utvikling av nasjonale skrivetester—noen motforestillinger. *Norsklæreren, 3*, 50–53.

Berge, K. L., Evensen, L. S., Hertzberg, F., & Vagle, W. (2005). *Ungdommers skrivekompetanse*. Vol. 1 & 2. Oslo: Universitetsforlaget.

Cambourne B. & Brown, H. (1989). Learning to control different registers. In R. Andrews (Eds.), *Narrative and argument. Milton Keynes: Open University Press, 43–54*.

Cope, B. & Kalantzis, M (1993). *The powers of literacy: A genre approach to teaching writing*. London: Falmer Press.

Freedman A. & Pringle, I. (1988). Why students can't write arguments. In N. Mercer (Ed.), *Language and Literacy from an Educational Perspective*. Vol. 2, 233–242.

Freedman, A. & Pringle, I. (1989). Contexts for developing argument. In R. Andrews (Ed.), *Narrative and argument*. Milton Keynes: Open University Press, 73–84. Milton Keynes: Open University Press.

Gipps, C. (1994). *Beyond testing: Towards a theory of educational assesment*. London: Falmer Press.

Gipps, C. (1996). Assessment for learning. In A. Little & A. Wolf (Eds.), *Assessment in transition: Learning, monitoring and selection in international perspective*, 251–262. Oxford: Pergamon.

Graves, D. (1983). *Writing: Teachers and children at work*. London and Exeter, NH: Heinemann Educational Books.

Halliday, M. A. K. & Martin, J. R. (1993). *Writing science: Literacy and discursive power*. London: Falmer Press.

Hillocks, G. (1984). What works in teaching composition: A meta-analysis of experimental treatment studies. *American Journal of Education, 93*(1), 133–170.

Hillocks, G. (1986). *Research on written composition: New directions for teaching*. National Conference on Research in English. ERIC Clearinghouse on Teaching and Communication Skills, National Institute of Education.

Hillocks, G. (2002). *The testing trap: How state writing assessments control learning*. New York: Teachers College Press.

Lehman, R. (1993). Rating the quality of student writing: Findings from the IEA study of achievement in written composition. In A. Huhta, K. Sajavaara, & S. Takala (Eds.), *The international encyclopedia of education*. Oxford: Pergamon, 169–198.

Lehman, R. (1994). Essays, scoring of. In T. Husén & T. N. Postlethwaite (Eds.), *The international encyclopedia of education*, 2018–2025. Oxford: Pergamon.

Martin, J. R. (1985). *Factual writing: Exploring and challenging social reality*. Oxford: Oxford University Press.

Reid, I. (Ed.) (1987). *The place of genre in learning: Current debates*. Typereader Publications No. 1, Centre for Studies in Literary Education, Deakin University.

Stobart, G. & Gipps, C.(1997). *Assessment: A teacher's guide to the issues* (3rd ed.). London: Hodder & Stoughton.

Weigle, S. C. (2002). *Assessing writing*. Cambridge: Cambridge University Press.

5 Assessing craft and design
Conceptions of expertise in education and work

Lars Lindström

The aim of the present study is to articulate implicit criteria used by teacher educators and professional artisans to assess expertise in craft and design. The research questions are these: (1) How do two teacher educators and an artisan assess portfolios in metalwork consisting of finished products, sketches, and interviews about the working procedure? (2) In the view of these assessors, what distinguishes novices from experts (including professional craftspeople) with regard to how they address their tasks (processes) and succeed in them (products)? (3) To what degree do the two professions (educators, artisans) agree in their assessment of what constitutes expertise? (4) What dilemmas are there to be balanced in the assessment of craft and design?

METHODS

Three craftspeople, acknowledged to be highly skilled in the field of metalwork, were recruited for the study. Two of these, Metal Designer D (male) and Silversmith E (female), were assigned a free design task in metal, which took 10 weeks or more. Five trainee craft teachers, Students F–J (3 males, 2 females), having volunteered to participate in the study, were assigned the task of interpreting the concept of a chandelier; they had five weeks at their disposal. In comparison with the expert craftspeople engaged, the trainee craft teachers were regarded as novices; that is, they were solving problems in a domain that they had not yet mastered. The study nevertheless showed that even *within* the group of students there were considerable differences as to where the participants were deemed to belong on a continuum from novice to expert.

Portfolio assessment

Metal Designer D, Silversmith E, and Students F–J were asked to use a *portfolio* to document steps in the process leading from an idea to a final product. They should preserve *journal notes*, *sketches*, and *drafts* and be attentive to *sources of inspiration* (one's own previous works, works by col-leagues and peers, works which are part of the cultural heritage, etc.).

After completion of the assignments, the two craftspeople and the five trainee craft teachers were interviewed about their working process and how they evaluated their work. These *portfolio interviews* were conducted by the author, by two craft-and-design experts from teacher training (Edu-cators A and B, both males), and by the third craftsperson (Artisan C, male), who was engaged as an *external co-assessor*. The interviews lasted about an hour each and were held in a room where all the portfolios were exhibited.

Repertory grids

A few days later, the teacher educators and the external co-assessor were interviewed themselves by the author, articulating the qualities of know-ing that they perceived in the works of craft and design. All the portfolios were available in the room for closer examination if necessary. The sub-jects' implicit criteria of expertise were explored by using the *repertory grid technique* (Alban-Metcalf, 1997; Cohen, Manion & Morrison, 2000). This is a technique that originates from George Kelly's (1955) psychology of *personal constructs*, a theoretical framework for studying how human beings make sense of their experiences of the world.

The interviews were conducted using RepGrid (Shaw & McKnight, 1992), a Macintosh program, with the interviewee placed in front of the computer screen. The program presented the portfolios three at a time, in randomly chosen combinations. The interviewee was asked to say how two of the portfolios—any two—resembled each other and differed from the third one. The similarities and differences made up two poles seen as end points on a continuous scale. In RepGrid the scale runs from one to nine. The interviewees were asked to drag the symbol for one portfolio at a time and drop it at the point on the scale where the portfolio was believed to belong. The ratings of all the portfolios on each scale resulted in a repertory grid for each interviewee, with bipolar constructs in the rows and portfo-lios in the columns.

The procedure was repeated twice for the entire set of seven portfo-lios (two craftspeople, five students). The first time the focus was on the product, while the second time it was on the process. A total of 33 bipolar constructs were elicited in this way. In addition to the constructs generated by means of the repertory grid technique, the pairs of 'novice-expert' and 'bad-good' were included. The former pair aimed at an objective assess-ment of the individual's performance; the latter pair was a wholly subjec-tive judgement.

Immediately after the interviewee had elicited a construct and placed the portfolios on the scale between the similarity pole (X) and the contrast-ing pole (Y), the interviewer asked questions intended to 'generalize' and 'anchor' the meaning of the construct. This technique is called *laddering*, a metaphor referring to climbing up or down a few rungs in the interviewee's meaning system, which is assumed to be hierarchically structured. Laddering can be done by asking the interviewee which pole of the pair he or she prefers and then putting the question: 'Why do you prefer X to Y?' (*laddering up* to a more abstract or general level). Or one can take the opposite course and ask: 'Looking at each individual portfolio, how did you know where to place it on the scale between X and Y' (*laddering down* to a more concrete or specific level).

Each interview, both parts (product, process) included, lasted about three hours. Half of this time was devoted to laddering. This part of the interview was tape-recorded, transcribed, and analyzed, following a phenomenological approach. The aim was to find the best approximation of the novice–expert dimension for both 'processes' and 'products.' Here it was possible to use the quantitative property of repertory grids; after cluster analysis they yielded percentages which described how much each bipolar construct overlapped the novice–expert dimension. The higher the overlap, the more equivalent is the meaning and the more central will the position be in the overall hierarchical structure. Only bipolar constructs that show 80% or more overlap with the novice–expert dimension was included in the continued analysis. It was assumed that other bipolar constructs are more descriptive and therefore less likely to increase our understanding of how the interviewee construes the differences between a novice and an expert.

RESULTS AND DISCUSSION

The combination of quantitative processing of data (hierarchical cluster analysis of repertory grids) and qualitative methods (the laddering technique and a phenomenological approach to the analysis of interview data) made it possible to address the research questions on which the study focuses. The first two questions concern how teacher educators and artisans assess craft portfolios and how they distinguish between a novice and an expert in the field of metalwork. It was found that the implicit criteria used by Educators A and B and Artisan C (external co-assessor) could be categorized in five themes. Three of these distinguish the expert from the novice based on properties in the working process (Table 5.1); the other two constitute an evaluation of the qualities of the finished product (Table 5.2).

The process criteria are contained under three thematic headings, which coincide with the different phases of the design process as described in the most recent Swedish curriculum for the comprehensive school, Lpo 94 (Skolverket, 1996). Similar categorizations of the working procedure, from idea to finished product, have been presented ever since the preparatory outlines of the 1969 curriculum for the comprehensive school, Lgr

TABLE 5.1 Novice–expert matrix for metalwork: Process criteria

	Process criteria	
	Expert ← -------------------- *Novice*	
Idea and design	The expert has a goal or an idea in mind. He has a clear view of what he is going to do, what he has done, and the consequences of his actions. He controls the result by being 'in the process', that is, he is not controlled or distracted by external factors.	The novice enters the process fumbling. He has no clear idea of what he is looking for or how to get there; he is forced to resort to makeshift solutions in the course of the work, since the material causes problems.
Realisation	The expert has worked through the process before starting, often by doing detailed sketches. He is aware of the problems that may arise and has considered how to address these.	The novice embarks on the work unprepared; he is forced to search for solutions to technical and design problems whilst working with the material. He does not control the process; he is rather controlled by the material and its properties.
Evaluation	The expert is involved and close to his product. He is absorbed by the process and can describe it in words to other people. He is active, distinct, and detailed in his presentation. He takes responsibility for his work.	The novice describes the working process in an impersonal and detached way. He is passive and uninvolved in relation to the product. He finds it difficult to comment upon his work, to express himself.

69 (Skolöverstyrelsen, 1969). In the follow-up of Lgr 69 it was stated that pupils 'have hitherto devoted themselves too much to the production, while the teacher has devoted himself to the first two steps [idea, design]'(after Borg, 2001, p. 121). In the last 30 years the planning phase has been the subject of intensive discussion among craft teachers (Borg, 2001, p. 138). Up to now, however, the students' ability to describe and evaluate their working process and the finished product has received less attention.

In analysing those interviews that focused on the process, two observations are conspicuous. The first one concerns the way in which the interviewees (i.e., Educators A and B and Artisan C), describe the interaction between *idea, design,* and *realisation.* The expert, they say, 'has a goal or

TABLE 5.2 *Novice–expert matrix for metalwork: Product criteria*

Product criteria	
Expert ← - Novice	

	Expert	Novice
Craft	The expert does not compromise quality. He is able to successfully predict how the material will behave when shaped by forging, bending, planishing, etc. He possesses the know-how enabling him to get the desired form and expression.	The novice allows himself to be controlled by the material. Uncertainty in the treatment of the material obstructs his potential to express what he wants to.
Form	The expert is attentive to the properties of the material and consciously chooses the material that will provide the desired function and expression. He also possesses the required craft skill.	The novice does not know which material would be the most appropriate in terms of form. He may perhaps unconsciously mix two idioms that counteract each other. He has little feeling for how different parts of the product interact through weight, balance, etc.

an idea in mind'. He or she 'has worked through the process before start-ing, often by doing detailed sketches. He is aware of the problems that may arise and has considered how to address these'. As a consequence, he rec-ognizes problems as they appear and is able to solve them 'in the process'. The novice, on the other hand, 'has no clear idea of what he is looking for' and 'embarks on the work unprepared'. Thus he or she is 'forced to search for solutions to technical and design problems whilst working with the material'. Since he does not master the process, he will be 'controlled by the material and its properties'.

This description of expertise in the domain of craft and design is strik-ingly similar to Donald Schön's (1983) portrait of the *reflective practitio-ner*. The latter not only recognizes situations but is able to reflect upon how these are similar to and different from those that he already encountered. He has also built up a repertoire of alternatives of action, from which he can select the one that is most appropriate to the current situation. The selection is facilitated by using a sketchpad and other aids, which will allow the practitioner to experiment with qualities and relations in manners that are not possible whilst working with the authentic materials. Like-wise, Kimbell et al. (1991) emphasize the role of *modelling* in the design process. One interviewee's expression of solving problems 'in the process' aptly describes the *automatized performance* of the expert, according to the brothers Dreyfus (1986), as opposed to 'the detached, deliberative, and sometimes agonizing selection among alternatives' (p. 28), which characterizes the novice.

Another observation concerns the way in which the interviewees describe the expert's approach to *evaluation*. There is an obvious difference between the criteria of expertise that were generated by this study and those checklists that are often found in textbooks, which list components that should be present in a product or during performance. The interviewees in this study, however, tried to define a set of more general dispositions or key competencies. The typical textbook items are, at best, indicators of such 'habits of mind'. The interviewees' process criteria, in particular, add up to a culture of learning rather than a list of specific skills. The image of the expert, envisioned by the interviewees, stands out as an involved craftsperson who is able to describe his work in a distinct and detailed manner, a person who is proud of what he has achieved. This image drastically differs from the traditional one of an anonymous craftsperson whose knowing is 'silent' and inaccessible. In the present study, the expert craftsperson's attitude to his work resembles that of experts in any other profession.

Borg (2001) suggests that craft knowledge may be 'silent' for the novice but not for the expert. Taking lace making as an example, she rejects Dormer's (1994) opinion that the knowledge-base of this craft 'is in principle unrecoverable' and that 'its presence can only be demonstrated, not described' (p. 23). The thinking in crafts such as lace making, Dormer (1994) concludes, 'resides not in language, but in the physical processes involving the physical handling of the medium' (p. 24). Being an expert in the craft, Borg (2001) denies the validity of Dormer's conclusions. Lace making is definitely not a speechless activity, she claims. The professional vocabulary of lace making and the demonstration of lace making are mutually supportive. In order to learn the craft, the novice must both see and comprehend.

The product criteria can be summarized under the headings *craft* and *form*. Craft criteria such as 'craftsmanship' (Educator A), 'conscious treatment of the material' (Educator B), and 'good craft' (Artisan C) showed 95% or more agreement with the placing of products along the novice–expert dimension. It was also clear from the interviews that it is the craftsmanship that allows a connoisseur to see whether someone is an expert or not. Importance is also ascribed to good form, but this criterion takes second place. When asked why craftsmanship is so important, Educator B answers that this is what conveys the artistic expression. Craftsmanship makes it possible to achieve the form to which one aspires, in the opinion of Educator A. Without solid craft knowledge, an appealing form rarely arises, according to the interviewees in this study.

The interviewees' respect for the craft also emerges under the headings of idea, design, and realisation in Table 5.1. Educators and artisan all agree that a person who lacks knowledge of the craft has little potential for monitoring the design process. He does not grasp the opportunities hidden in the material; he fumbles his way, and is controlled by the material and its properties instead of controlling the work process himself. To sum up, the craft teachers and the artisan have not fallen victim to the devaluation of practical skills that is common in the art world. They seem rather to share design theorist Peter Dormer's (1994, p. 9) view that craft is 'the crucial, the only link between intention and expression'.

The emphasis on craftsmanship gives the Swedish subject of craft and design (*sloyd*) its special character. Another feature that used to distinguish craft from other visual arts is the importance attached to the *function* and *utility* of the object. Craftspeople produced utility objects, i.e. things that can be used and that fulfil specific, not just aesthetic functions in an envisaged or predetermined context. Functional aspects were mentioned repeatedly during the interviews, but it is worth noticing that they did not coincide with the assessment in terms of novice-expert. There may be several explanations for this; one is surely the fact that students had been given a rather free design assignment, in which evidently the utility of the product was given secondary importance.

However, the kind of assignment given, as well as the hesitation to include function and utility into the definition of expertise, probably also reflect the profound change of the meanings of craft objects that has taken place during the last century. Today, we respect or even envy the craftsperson primarily for his or her ability to direct the whole of the work process as well as the design of the artefact. We admire the skillful process and the unique design, even if we do not want the craft objects for use in our everyday life (Dormer, 1990). Thus it would be unfair to apply the standards of lighting design to a lamp project in metal work.

The low priority attached to the utility of objects may also be associated with the traditions of craft as a school subject. Otto Salomon's famous series of exercises in woodwork was aimed to get the boys to make simple, practically useful objects with an increasing degree of difficulty, from, for example, flower sticks and baseball bats, via nesting boxes and bootjacks, to toolboxes and cupboards. Up to and including the 1962 curriculum for comprehensive school, Lgr 62 (Skolöverstyrelsen, 1960) progression was ensured by having the pupils in each year make certain prescribed objects. In the mid-1960s, however, the focus shifted from the object to the process.

Kajsa Borg (2001), researcher in craft education, indicates that this degrading of the product in favour of the process may also have brought about certain undesired consequences. In her study of craft teachers and former pupils she found that, whereas the teachers emphasized the design process, the pupils tended to remember the objects. The work was pleasurable if the pupils understood the purpose and thought that they had some use for the finished product. It is probably still important to emphasize these *utility values* (associated with the *functions* of objects) and reflect upon these in craft teaching, if pupils are to feel that the subject is meaningful.

CULTURES OF EDUCATION AND WORK

The term *learning culture* denotes the assumptions that are made and the attitudes that prevail in an environment where learning takes place. In this study I was particularly interested in the relationship between the learning culture of formal education and that of working life. The first two research questions focus on those who are assessed. This group included both students training to become craft teachers and professional craftspeople. The criteria used to distinguish the expert from the novice were explored. The third research question focused on the assessors themselves. The differences and similarities between different professions (teacher educators, craftspeople) in the assessment of what constitutes expertise in craft were investigated.

The main impression is that there were large, recurrent similarities in the way that the teacher educators and the artisan assessed craft portfolios. However, a difference in the way the two groups viewed the working process also emerged. The craftsperson was found to be more product-oriented, while the teacher educators were more process oriented. For Artisan C it was important and a sign of expertise that '*one can achieve the desired result without mishaps in a short time*'. He often worked under pressure of time himself. If the product was not finished in time or became too expensive, there was a risk that the customer was not willing to pay for it. The customer then went to another craftsperson instead, who could offer a lower price or faster delivery. As a professional practitioner the craftsperson must consider the basic need of making a living. It is then safest to rely on what one has already mastered.

At the same time, Artisan C admits that he would be glad to devote more time to experimenting during the work process. If the aim was to acquire new experience and knowledge, he said, '*experiments and mistakes can also be a good working process*'. For the craftsperson—a person who 'himself is responsible for the idea/sketch for his products' (Ziemelis, 1984, p. 16)—it is essential to find the right balance between utilitarian production and personal development. Without utilitarian production he has no income; without personal development he risks running out of ideas or suffering burnout. The former jeopardizes his income in the short term, the latter in the long term. This can also be formulated as a balance between tradition and innovation.

The conflict between social utility and personal development has a long history in the school subject of craft and design. In the early days of craft teaching, from 1877 onwards, the main justification for the subject was from an economic point of view. It was mainly a matter of early vocational training in crafts such as carpentry, ironworking, tinsmithing, bookbinding, basket making, brush making, turning, and coach building (Luhr et al., 1887). A tour in 1882 to the more famous craft schools showed that in several of them the pupil

> makes things to sell for a profit, confines himself to such articles as can most easily be sold, and lets the work be governed by the demand. Sometimes the boy makes a multitude of things which are well below his level of development, while sometimes he is busy with things that are equally far above it, in which case, as they say, he 'does as much as he can' and lets the teacher do the rest. (after Berg, 1932)

'Under such conditions', as Hjalmar Berg (1932) comments in retrospect, 'craft must essentially lose its educational influence; the economic planning makes pedagogical planning impossible'.

Otto Salomon eventually made Swedish craft education well-known internationally, but he did not content himself only with criticizing this encouragement of 'jacks of all crafts'. He adapted craft teaching to the child's own potential by developing a series of exercises and suggesting a set of models ordered in increasing degrees of difficulty. The standard method that he designed at Nääs Craft School (later a training college for craft teachers) was to serve as a model for the rest of the country. To borrow the pithy wording of Salomon (1882), it had the effect that 'the attempts to use school as a means for the training of craftspeople gave way to the efforts to use crafts as a means to educate human beings'.

Salomon's methodology helped to separate learning from production. But since Salomon stuck to the principle that craft objects should have a utility value, there was still a connection to the original and more primary activities of which craftwork was once a part. In the 1960s, inspired by curriculum development in Britain (Eggleston, 1976), the Swedish teacher educator Thorsten Lundburg introduced the design process as the core of the subject. As a result, the utility value of the craft object took second place. The product did not necessarily have to be finished, whether in a functional or an aesthetic sense. The aim might have been achieved anyway, so long as the students had entered a learning process. Educator A is the interviewee who most clearly expresses this view of the subject when he discusses the students' work in terms of involvement in the 'metalwork process', 'drawing the bow', and 'going the whole way'.

The development of the subject of crafts is a good illustration of the *decontextualisation* that characterizes pedagogical activities, from a socio-cultural point of view (Säljö, 2000): Learning is freed from more everyday practices and becomes the very goal of the activities. There is a great difference, for example, between making utility objects for sale and making a bootjack according to Salomon's model, as an exercise in various craft techniques such as sawing, planing, filing, and so on. The distance to the social practice from which the assignments were once taken becomes even greater when the purpose is no longer to make a useful object but to enter a design process (Borg, 2001, pp. 117 ff.).

The separation between the learning cultures of the school and of the practising craft involves both potentials and risks. One of the potentials of formal education is manifested by the wider scope for self-generated creating, experimenting, and risk taking. These are valuable abilities in a society that is in a state of constant change. The same applies to the capability to design, realize, and evaluate one's own chosen work. The risks include the possibility that the school's learning culture distances itself too far from other social practices and learning cultures. Teaching can then be experienced to be irrelevant, antiquated, and divorced from reality. The result can be an anachronistic 'school craft' that is said to rear human beings, but is lacking a clear connection to the more developed craft cultures that exist outside school.

CONCLUSION

The teacher-educators and the artisan in this study evaluated craft portfolios by criteria that are very reminiscent of Donald Schön's portrait of the reflective practitioner. This practitioner not only has a rich repertoire of alternative solutions to a problem. He or she also tends to invent a virtual world, often by using the sketchpad, where various solutions may be tried out before they are applied to the actual situation of his or her practice. Thus expertise, as construed by the interviewees, is related to a particular culture of learning and practice, including a disposition to use experience, knowledge, and skills in certain ways.

This general approach to problem solving, however, is not in opposition to the need of a sound knowledge of the craft, as one would sometimes be inclined to think when listening to advocates of the 'process' versus the 'craft'. On the contrary! No other trait of the craft portfolios agreed more with the interviewees' conception of expertise than the demonstration of good craftsmanship. Sound knowledge of the craft, according to the teacher-educators and the artisan, is a necessary prerequisite of a good working process. The expert, who is attentive to the properties of the material, solves problems 'in the process' in contrast to the novice, who is controlled or distracted by external factors, which force him or her to makeshift solutions.

Finally, there were large similarities in the way that the teacher educators and the artisan assessed craft portfolios. However, the artisan did not allow himself as much leeway for trial and error as the educators did. The difference can be explained by the circumstances in which the two professions work. This discrepancy is important to keep in mind when debating the relationship between society and craft education or formal education in general. Ambitions to make schoolwork more 'authentic' or 'real', if carried too far, can reduce the freedom and tolerance for failures that are requirements for thoughtful learning.

That is, with too severe 'real-life' pressures and restrictions, education will not be able to prepare for lifelong learning. With too much autonomy, on the other hand, learning will become disconnected from the everyday contexts in which people live and work. The juxtaposition of learning cultures in education and work thus exemplifies an overall theme of this book, stating that the solution of one dilemma will constantly bring us to another that has to be dealt with.

REFERENCES

Alban-Metcalf, R. J. (1997). Repertory grid technique. In J. P. Keeves (Ed.), *Educational research, methodology and measurement: An international handbook (*2nd ed.), 315–318. Oxford: Elsevier Science.

Berg, H. (1932). *Införandet och ordnandet av slöjdundervisning för gossar vid Stockholms folkskolor.* Stockholm.

Borg, K. (2001). *Slöjdämnet: Intryck—uttryck—avtryck.* Linköpings Universitet, Filosofiska fakulteten. (Diss.)

Cohen, L., Manion, L., & Morrison, K. (2000). Personal constructs. In L. Cohen, L. Manion, & K. Morrison, *Research methods in education (*5th ed.), 337–348. London: Routledge/Falmer.

Dormer, P. (1990). *The meanings of modern design.* London: Thames & Hudson.

Dormer, P. (1994). *The art of the maker: Skill and its meaning in art, craft and design.* London: Thames & Hudson.

Dreyfus, H. L. & Dreyfus, S. E. (1986). *Mind over machine.* New York: Free Press.

Eggleston, J. (1976). *Developments in design education.* London: Open Books.

Kelly, G. A. (1955). *The psychology of personal constructs.* New York: Norton.

Kimbell, R., Stables, K., Wheeler, T., Wosniak, A., & Kelly, V. (1991). *The assessment of performance in design and technology.* London: School Examinations and Assessment Council (SEAC).

Luhr, R. et al. (1887). *Utlåtande och förslag afgifvet till Göteborgs Allmänna Folkskolestyrelse rörande undervisning i slöjd för gossar i stadens folkskolor.* Göteborg.

Säljö, R. (2000). *Lärande i praktiken: Ett sociokulturellt perspektiv.* Stockholm: Prisma.

Salomon, O. (1882). *Slöjdskolan och folkskolan, Del 4: En pedagogisk studie.* Göteborg.

Schön, D. A. (1983). *The reflective practitioner: How professionals think in action.* New York: Basic Books.

Shaw, M. L. G. & McKnight, C. (1992). *Think again: Personal decision-making and problem-solving.* Centre for Person-Computer Studies, Calgary, Alberta.

Skolverket (1996). *Grundskolan: Kursplaner, betygskriterier.* Stockholm: Fritzes.

Skolöverstyrelsen (1960). *Läroplan för grundskolan, allmän del* (Lgr 62). Stockholm: Liber Utbildningsförlaget.

Skolöverstyrelsen (1969). *Läroplan för grundskolan, allmän del* (Lgr 69). Stockholm: Liber Utbildningsförlaget.

Ziemelis, M. (1984). *Konsthantverk och konsthantverkare.* Stockholm: Statens kulturråd. (Rapport från Statens kulturråd 1983: 4).

6 Defining authentic assessment

Five dimensions of authenticity[1]

Judith T. M. Gulikers, Theo J. Bastiaens and Paul A. Kirschner

INTRODUCTION

In 1990, Boud argued that a major problem for education is the fact that there are gaps between teaching and professional practice and between assessment tasks and what occurs in the world of work. In the years thereafter, the educational culture changed to competency-based education that focused on developing competent students and future employees (Segers et al., 2003), which makes the issue of bridging the gaps between learning and working even more salient. To meet the educational goals, a constructive alignment between instruction, learning and assessment (ILA) is necessary (Biggs, 1996). A changed educational goal that focuses on competency development requires changes in the instructional phases, but requires new modes of assessment as well.

The need to contextualize assessment in interesting, real-life and authentic tasks is described as *one of the crucial elements* of new modes of assessment (Birenbaum & Dochy, 1996). Dochy (2001) describes the assessment of the application of knowledge to actual, real-life (authentic) cases as the core goal of alternative assessments. Gielen et al. (2003) even argue that authenticity of the assessment tasks is an imperative condition to achieve the expert level of problem solving. Moreover, increasing the authenticity of an assessment is expected, and experienced by students, to have a positive influence on student learning and motivation (e.g. Herrington & Herrington, 1998; McDowell, 1995). Authenticity, however, remains a vaguely described characteristic of assessment, because it is thought to be a familiar and generally known concept that needs no explicit definition (Petraglia, 1998). Because authenticity is seen as such an important element of new modes of assessment on the one hand, while authenticity is only vaguely described on the other hand, this chapter focuses on defining authenticity for the purpose of guiding future research as well as describing guidelines for developing and evaluating authentic assessments in educational practice. Based upon an extensive literature study, a theoretical framework consisting of five dimensions of assessment that can vary in their degree of authenticity is presented. In addition, a short overview is given of an exploratory study that gives insight into vocational education students' and teachers' perceptions of what assessment characteristics determine its authenticity. In the end, we will reflect on how this work can be used in issues concerning the balancing of dilemmas in new modes of assessment.

THE REASONS FOR AUTHENTIC COMPETENCY-BASED ASSESSMENT

The two most important reasons for using authentic competency-based assessments are their construct validity and their impact on student learning, also called consequential validity (Gielen et al., 2003). *Construct validity* of an assessment is related to whether an assessment measures what it is supposed to measure. With respect to competency assessment this means that tasks must appropriately reflect the competency that needs to be assessed, that the content of an assessment involves authentic tasks that represent real-life problems of the knowledge domain assessed, and that the thinking processes that experts use to solve the problem in real life are also required by the assessment task (Gielen et al., 2003). Based upon these criteria, authentic competency-based assessments are expected to have higher construct validity for measuring competencies than so-called objective or traditional tests. Messick (1994) argues that construct under-representation is one of the major threats to construct validity, which is countered by increasing the authenticity of the assessment. Authenticity, he argues, deals with not leaving anything out of the assessment of a certain construct, leading to minimal construct under-representation.

Consequential validity describes the intended and unintended effects of assessment on instruction or teaching (Biggs, 1996) and student learning (Dochy & McDowell, 1998). The expected positive influence of authentic assessment on student learning is twofold (Gielen et al., 2003). First, it is expected to stimulate the development of professional competencies, and second it is likely to increase students' motivation to learn through the fact that students experience authentic assessments as more interesting and meaningful, because they realize the relevancy and usefulness of it for their future lives.

DEFINING AUTHENTIC ASSESSMENT

What is authenticity? Different researchers have different opinions about what constitutes authenticity. Some see authentic assessment as a synonym for performance assessment (Hart, 1994; Torrance, 1995), while others argue that authentic assessment puts a special emphasis on the realistic value of the task and the context (Herrington & Herrington, 1998), thereby indicating that every authentic assessment is performance assessment, but not vice versa (Meyer, 1992).

The criterion situation

Messick (1994) focuses our attention on the fundamental ambiguity that pervades all authentic assessment practices, namely, *authentic to wha?* Messick argues that the authenticity of something can only be defined in relation to something else. For example, an assessment task can be authentic with respect to school problems, but inauthentic with respect to everyday life, because school problems do not relate to everyday life. The point taken in this study is that the authenticity of an assessment is defined by its resemblance to the real world, specifically, to the professional real world. Because current educational goals stress the importance of developing competent professionals, we argue that it is important to design assessments that resemble situations that starting professionals can be confronted with in the working life *or* situations that students have to deal with during their work placements. The situation, according to which the authenticity of an assessment in this chapter is defined, is called the *criterion situation*. A criterion situation reflects a real-life situation that students can be confronted with in their work placement or future professional life, which serves as a basis for designing an authentic assessment. The fact that we argue that a criterion situation reflects a professional practice situation incorporates a very important idea: it takes into account the educational level of the student. Students who are at the beginning of their studies possibly cannot deal with the authenticity of a real complex professional situation. If they are forced to do this, it will result in cognitive overload and in turn will have a negative impact on learning (Sweller et al., 1998). As a result, a criterion situation will sometimes be an abstraction of real professional practice in order to be attainable for students at a certain educational level. However, we should not lose sight of making the criterion situation resemble real life as much as possible. Van Merriënboer (1997) argues that an abstraction of real professional practice (i.e. the criterion situation) can still be authentic as long as the abstracted situation requires students to perform the whole competency as an integrated whole of constituent parts (knowledge, skills, and attitudes). The more students reach the end of their studies, the more the criterion situation will be exactly the same as the real professional practice situation. Thus, a criterion situation is a reflection of a professional practice situation at the students' educational level. In this light, criterion situations are the bridge between learning and working.

Another issue in defining authentic assessments that logically follows from the previous section deals with *what* students need to learn or develop from working with authentic assessments. Savery and Duffy (1995) define authenticity of an assessment as the *similarity* between the cognitive demands—the thinking required—of the assessment and the cognitive demands in the criterion situation on which the assessment is based. In other words, students need to develop professional thinking skills. Darling-Hammond and Snyder (2000) argue that dealing only with the thinking required is too narrow, because real life demands the ability to integrate and coordinate knowledge, skills, and attitudes, and the capacity to apply them in new situations. In their view, authentic assessment includes opportunities for the development and examining of students' thinking *and* actions. This implies that authentic assessment requires students to *demonstrate* their learning. Birenbaum (1996) deepens this idea of assessing thinking *and* action by emphasizing that students not only need to develop cognitive competencies such as problem solving and critical thinking, but also meta-cognitive competencies such as reflection and social competencies such as communication and collaboration. In other words, real life (reflected in the criterion situation) involves different kinds of competencies, all of which should be taken into account in designing authentic assessments for developing competent future employees.

Another crucial point in defining authenticity is the operationalisation of authenticity as a continuum. It is a misconception that something is either authentic or not authentic (Cronin, 1993). An assessment can be more or less authentic by resembling professional practice to a greater or lesser extent.

The definition of authentic assessment used in this study is an assessment requiring students to demonstrate the same (kind of) competencies, or combinations of knowledge, skills, and attitudes, that they need to apply in a criterion situation derived from professional practice. The level of authenticity of an assessment is thus defined by its degree of resemblance to the criterion situation. This idea is extended and specified by the theoretical framework describing that an assessment can resemble a criterion situation along a number of dimensions.

Subjectivity of authenticity: The role of perceptions

A problem that arises here is that authenticity is subjective (Honebein et al., 1993; Huang, 2002) and is dependent on perceptions. Entwistle and Entwistle (1991) have already shown that students' perceptions of the learning environment influence how they learn, not necessarily the context itself. A literature review by Struyven et al. (2003) showed that this is also true for students' perceptions of alternative assessments. Honebein, Duffy, and Fishman argued that the perception of authenticity can change as a result of age, educational level, or amount of practical experience or schooling. This can imply that what students perceive as authentic is not necessarily the same as what teachers and assessment developers see as authentic. If they do indeed differ, then the fact that teachers usually develop authentic assessments according to their own view causes a problem. They may do their best to develop authentic assessments, but this may all be for

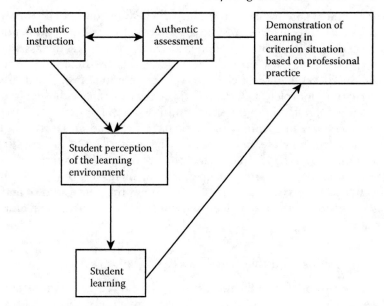

Figure 6.1 The general outline.

nothing if the learner does not perceive it as such. This process, known as *pre-authentication* (Huang, 2002), can be interpreted either as it being impossible to design an authentic assessment, or that it is very important to carefully examine the experiences of the *users* of the authentic assessments, before designing authentic assessments (Nicaise et al., 2000). Obviously, we chose the latter interpretation.

Figure 6.1 summarizes the important elements of the above discussion: to positively influence student learning authentic assessment should be *aligned to* authentic instruction; authentic assessment requires students to *demonstrate* their competencies in a situation that resembles professional practice; and authenticity is *subjective*, which makes it important to take students' perceptions into account when designing an authentic assessment.

The following section discusses five dimensions (a theoretical framework) that can vary in their degree of authenticity in determining the authenticity of an assessment. The purpose of this framework is to shed light on the concept of assessment authenticity and to provide guidelines for implementing authenticity elements into competency-based assessment.

AUTHENTICITY OF ASSESSMENT: A MULTI-FACETTED CONCEPT

For defining authentic assessment, we carried out a review of the literature on authentic assessment, on authenticity and assessment in general, and on student perceptions of (authentic) assessment elements. Many subconcepts and synonyms came to light, which were conceptually analyzed and divided into categories, resulting in five main aspects of authenticity, namely: the task, the physical context, the social context, the assessment form, and the criteria. We argue that these aspects are dimensions that can vary in their level of authenticity (i.e., they are continuums). The degree of authenticity is not solely a characteristic of the assessment chosen; it needs to be defined in relation to the situation in real life. For example: carrying out an assessment in a team is authentic *only* if the chosen assessment task is also carried out in a team in real life. The main point of the five-dimensional framework (5DF) is that each of the five dimensions can resemble the criterion situation to a varying degree, thereby increasing or decreasing the authenticity of the assessment. Figure 6.2 shows the dimensions of authentic assessment and their sub-elements, which will be further explained in the rest of this chapter.

Five dimensions of authenticity

As our definition for authentic assessment showed, we argue that the authenticity of all five dimensions is defined by its resemblance to the criterion situation and, to recapitulate, a *criterion situation* reflects a real-life situation at students' educational level that students can be confronted with in their internship or future professional life. This sets the frame for the argumentation of the five dimensions of authenticity.

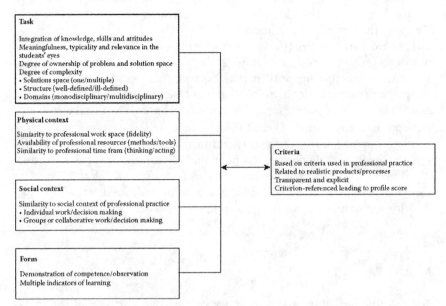

Figure 6.2 The Five-Dimensional Framework (5DF) for authentic assessment.

Task

An authentic task is a problem task that confronts students with activities that are also carried out in professional practice. This means, first of all, that an authentic assessment should always require students to *integrate knowledge, skills, and attitudes* as professionals do (Gielen et al., 2003; Darling-Hammond & Snyder, 2000). Moreover, we argue that the assessment task should *resemble the complexity* of the criterion task (Petraglia, 1998; Uhlenbeck, 2002). This does not mean that every assessment task should be very complex, as is often argued by most advocates of authentic assessment (e.g., Herrington & Herrington, 1998; Wiggins, 1993). Even though most authentic problems are complex, involving multi-disciplinarity, ill-structuredness, and having multiple possible solutions, real-life problems can also be simple, well-structured, with one correct answer, and requiring only one discipline (Cronin, 1993). Thirdly, the ownership for students in the assessment task should *resemble the ownership* for professionals in the real-life task. Savery and Duffy (1995) argue that giving students ownership of the task and the process to develop a solution is crucial for engaging students in authentic learning and problem solving. On the other hand, in real life, assignments are often imposed by employers and professionals often use standard tools and procedures to solve a problem (Resnick, 1987), both decreasing the amount of ownership for the employee. Therefore, the theoretical framework argues that in order to make students competent in dealing with professional problems, the assessment task should *resemble* the complexity and ownership levels of the real-life criterion situation.

Up to this point, task authenticity appears to be a fairly objective dimension. This objectivity is confounded by Messick (1994) and Stein et al. (2004), who argue that students' perception of *meaningfulness* of the assessment is at the heart of authenticity. They stress that merely providing assessment tasks representative of the professional discipline is not enough for creating an authentic experience, as long as students do not perceive the assessment as meaningful. Furthermore, Sambell et al. (1997) showed that it is crucial that students *perceive* a task as *relevant*. This is more likely to happen when they see the link to a situation in the real world or working situation, or when they regard the object of the assessment as a valuable transferable skill.

Physical context

Where we are, often if not always, determines how we do something, and often the real place is dirtier (literally and figuratively) than safe learning environments. Think, for example, of an assessment for auto mechanics for the military. The capability of a soldier to find the problem in a non-functioning jeep can be assessed in a clean garage, with the availability of all the possibly needed equipment, but the future physical environments will possibly involve a war zone, inclement weather conditions, less space, and less equipment. Even though the task itself is authentic, it can be questioned whether assessing students in a clean and safe environment really assesses their capacity to wisely use their competencies in real-life situations.

An important element of the authenticity of the physical context is that the *number and kinds of resources available*, which mostly contain *relevant* as well as *irrelevant* information (Herrington & Oliver, 2000), should resemble the resources available in real life (Arter & Spandel, 1992; Segers et al., 1999). For example, Resnick (1987) argues that most school tests involve memory work, while out-of-school activities are often intimately engaged with tools and resources (calculators, tables, standards), making these school tests less authentic. Another important characteristic crucial for providing an authentic physical context is the *time* students are given to perform the assessment task (Wiggins, 1989). Tests are normally administered in a restricted period of time, for example two hours, which is completely devoted to the test. In real life, professional activities often involve more time scattered over days or on the contrary, require fast and immediate reaction in a split second. Wiggins (1989) says that an authentic assessment should not rely on unrealistic and arbitrary time constraints.

Social context

Resnick (1987) emphasizes that learning and performing out-of-school mostly takes place in a social system. Therefore, a model for authentic assessment should consider social processes that are present in real-life contexts. What is really important in an authentic assessment is that the social processes of the assessment *resemble the social processes* in an equivalent situation in reality. At this point, this framework disagrees with literature on authentic assessment that defines collaboration as a characteristic of authenticity (e.g., Herrington & Herrington, 1998). Our framework argues that if the real situation demands *collaboration*, the assessment should also involve collaboration often combined with the possibility to ask for assistance, but if the situation is normally handled *individually*, the assessment should be individual as well.

Assessment form

Boud (1990) argued that it is not only the assessment content that influences student learning, but also the kind of assessment, independent of the content. The authenticity of assessment form depends on the degree to which students need to observably *demonstrate* (Wiggins, 1989) their professional competences by creating a *quality product or performance* that they can be asked to produce in real life (Wiggins, 1993). The rationale behind requiring students to demonstrate their learning in a real-life situation is that this makes it more valid to make inferences about underlying competencies and to predict future functioning in professional careers (Darling-Hammond & Snyder, 2000). Their performance needs to be *observable* (Wiggins, 1989). Since a fair conclusion about (professional) competence is often not possible in one single test, an authentic assessment should involve a *full array of tasks and multiple indicators of learning* (Darling-Hammond & Snyder, 2000). Uhlenbeck (2002) showed that a combination of different assessment methods adequately covered the whole range of professional teaching behavior.

Results and Criteria

Criteria are those characteristics of the assessment result (output) that are valued (Arter & Spandel, 1992). The result can be a *product or a process* so long as it is a realistic outcome, valued in professional life. The criteria should directly *relate to this realistic outcome*. Moreover, criteria should *concern the development of relevant professional competencies* and should be *based upon criteria used in the real-life (i.e., criterion) situation* (Darling-Hammond & Snyder, 2000). Setting criteria and making them *explicit and transparent to learners* beforehand is important in authentic assessment (Darling-Hammond, 1994), because this guides learning (Sluijsmans, 2002) and after all, in real life, employees usually know on what criteria their performances will be judged. Moreover, this implies that authentic assessment requires *criterion-referenced judgment*.

Figure 6.2 shows that the criterion dimension has a special status in the 5DF. This dimension has a reciprocal relationship with the other dimensions. On the one hand, criteria based on professional practice, which is the starting point for developing authentic assessments, should guide the *interpretations* of the other four dimensions. On the other hand, criteria can also be based on the interpretation of another dimension of the framework. For example, if the physical context requires the use of certain resources and tools, the criteria should specify how these should be used in the demonstration of competence, as these criteria guide students' learning.

SUBJECTIVITY OF AUTHENTIC ASSESSMENT: A QUALITATIVE STUDY

The subjectivity of authenticity is an issue that should receive attention, since the effectiveness of assessments largely depends on the impact they have on students' learning and motivation. As argued before, the perception of what authenticity is can change as a result of age, amount of practical experience, or years of schooling. A qualitative study (for an elaborate description see Gulikers et al., 2004) examined, through focus group interviews, what neophyte and senior students and teachers of a vocational college for nursing see as authentic assessment and how their ideas agree with each other and with the five theoretical dimensions of authenticity. This study also gave information about the relative importance of the dimensions of the five-dimensional framework (5DF) in the eyes of students and teachers. All three groups were asked to discuss the elements that they experienced to be important in an authentic assessment that serves to assess students' capability of functioning in professional practice. Overall, all groups spontaneously discussed four of the five dimensions of the 5DF as parts of authentic assessments. The social context was not perceived as important, since all groups felt that in the end assessment is an individual activity. All groups agreed on the importance of a *task* that reflects professional practice. In addition, senior students and teachers stressed the importance of requiring students to demonstrate their competence (*form*) in a professionally relevant performance or product (*result*); and teachers also stipulated the importance of using assessment *criteria* that are used in professional practice as well. Concerning the physical context, students and teachers differed. Teachers argued for more assessment at the work floor instead of in school, while neophytes argued that a simulation could be just as good so long as the task is realistic and the assessment requires them to demonstrate professional competencies. This result is also corroborated by a study of Gulikers et al. (2005), which also showed the authenticity of the physical context as being of less importance for younger students, so long as the task and the assessment form were authentic.

Furthermore, another interesting aspect came to light. While all groups were asked to describe what elements of an assessment are important for assessing if a student is capable of functioning in professional practice, seniors and teachers mostly agreed with the ideas of the theoretical framework ('assessments should relate more to our work placements'—senior), whereas neophyte students focused on traditional, clear and straightforward knowledge testing ('easy and clear, with only one possible answer'). This might mean two things: (1) the neophytes are mostly guided by their previous (traditional) assessment experiences, and (2) having more experience in professional practice (as seniors and teachers have) does indeed change the way people look at authentic assessment (Honebein et al, 1993).

IMPLICATIONS FOR AUTHENTIC ASSESSMENT PRACTICES

Cummings and Maxwell (1999) argued that people feel that 'authenticity is the way to go' (p. 178), which resulted in many authentic assessment practices. However, a lack of understanding of what really makes an assessment authentic led to inadequate assessment practices. They showed, for example, that attempts to make an assessment look more like real life on the surface made the task more contrived and artificial in students' perceptions.

The purpose of this chapter was to unravel the construct of authenticity of assessments and to come up with a definition of what authentic assessment is and what characteristics should be taken into account when developing such an assessment. Besides a theoretical perspective, we also stipulated that authenticity is, at least, partly subjective, by addressing a qualitative study that showed that neophyte and senior students and teachers stress different things as very important for authentic assessment. This shows the relevance of examining authentic assessments as students see it, since this provides us with the most relevant information for developing assessments that are helpful for students' learning.

In the context of balancing dilemmas in (optimizing) new modes of assessment, this chapter offers some food for thought for developing (authentic) assessments. First of all, we have to deal with the goal of an assessment and its *predictive validity*. Predictive validity is the degree to which future performance can be predicted by current assessment performance. If the educational goal of developing competent employees is pursued, then increasing the authenticity of an assessment is valuable. More authenticity is likely to increase the predictive validity of the assessment because of the resemblance between the assessment and real professional practice. However, one should not throw the baby out with the bath water. Objective tests are very useful for certain purposes as knowledge testing or high-stakes summative assessment on an individual achievement, where predicting students' ability to function competently in future professional practice is not the purpose. Hence, the goal of the assessment partly determines the importance of increasing the authenticity of an assessment.

Second, we conclude that authentic assessment is an important step towards bridging the gap between learning and working. Professional practice should be the starting point for developing authentic assessments, since this defines what students should know and be able to do after graduation. Authenticity is therefore dependent on the degree of resemblance between the assessment and professional practice. But confronting inexperienced students with professional practice situations at the expert level seems unfair. There should be a balance between making the assessment resemble professional practice, while not making it too complex for students. Therefore, we argue that the relationship between learning (assessment) and working is mediated by what is called the *criterion situation*. This reflects a real professional practice situation, but at the educational level of the student. It is crucial that this criterion situation reflects the integration of knowledge, skills, and attitudes of the real professional practice situation, since this is what we define as authentic assessment, but it can be an abstraction of real professional practice on more complicating aspects of the situation (Van Merriënboer, 1997). This implies that in the course of an educational program, authentic assessment might be partial in the beginning and more complete as students develop. By splitting up the authenticity concept into several assessment aspects, the 5DF gives opportunities for developing assessments that resemble professional practice at crucial point while decreasing the authenticity at points that might not be important for (young) students.

Third, authenticity is only one of the (crucial) elements of alternative assessments. The framework, as it is described in the theoretical argumentation, shows an ideal picture of authentic assessment practices. In real educational practice, one has to deal with other quality criteria (e.g., reliability) and practical possibilities as well. Every educational assessment requires a compromise between different quality criteria, goals, and practical possibilities. When, for example, practical reasons make it impossible to assess in real professional practice, the 5DF shows possibilities to decrease the authenticity of the physical context dimensions, while keeping authenticity of other important aspects of the assessment. In other words, the 5DF helps to find a balance between authenticity and other important quality criteria for new modes of assessment.

Finally, the 5DF not only gives input for developing assessments, it can also be used to help develop authentic learning tasks (Gulikers et al., 2004). In line with Biggs's constructive alignment theory (1996), instruction and assessment should be directed towards the same kind of learning. The 5DF can be used to develop an educational program in which the assessment is in balance with the instruction, in which learning tasks have a certain degree of authenticity that helps students prepare for an authentic assessment.

In sum, this chapter argues that the authenticity of an assessment depends on five assessment dimensions that can be designed to resemble professional practice to various degrees, and that we should take students' educational level and their perceptions of authenticity into account. By considering these issues, this chapter helps to find ways to optimize new modes of assessment.

NOTE

1. This chapter is published in a more elaborate form in: Gulikers, J., Bastiaens, Th., & Kirschner, P. (2004). A five-dimensional framework for authentic assessment. *Educational Technology Research & Development, 52*(3), 67–85.

REFERENCES

Arter, J. A. & Spandel, V. (1992). An NCME instructional module on: Using portfolio of student work in instruction and assessment. *Educational Measurement: Issues and Practice, 11*(1), 36–45.

Biggs, J. (1996). Enhancing teaching through constructive alignment. *Higher Education, 32*, 347–364.

Birenbaum, M. & Dochy, F. J. R. C. (1996). *Alternatives in assessment of achievements, learning processes and prior knowledge.* Boston, MA: Kluwer Academic.

Birenbaum, M. (1996). Assessment 2000: Towards a pluralistic approach to assessment. In M. Birenbaum & F. J. R. C. Dochy (Eds.), *Alternatives in assessment of achievements, learning processes and prior knowledge,* 3–29. Boston, MA: Kluwer Academic.

Birenbaum, M. (2003). New insights into learning and teaching and the implications for assessment. In M. Segers, F. J. R. C. Dochy, & E. Cascallar (Eds.), *Optimising new modes of assessment: In search of qualities and standards.* Dordrecht: Kluwer Academic.

Boud, D. (1990). Assessment and the promotion of academic values. *Studies in Higher Education, 15(1),* 101–111.

Brown, J. S., Collins, A., & Duguid, P. (1989). Situated cognition and the culture of learning. *Educational Researcher, 18(1),* 32–42.

Cronin, J. F. (1993). Four misconceptions about authentic learning. *Educational Leadership, 50(7),* 78–80.

Cummings, J. J. & Maxwell, G. S. (1999). Contextualising authentic assessment. *Assessment in Education: Principles, Policy and Practice, 1(2),* 143–166.

Darling-Hammond, L. (1994). Setting standards for students: The case for authentic assessment. *The Educational Forum, 59,* 14–21.

Darling-Hammond, L. & Snyder, J. (2000). Authentic assessment in teaching in context. *Teaching and Teacher Education, 16,* 523–545.

De Bock, D., Verschaffel, L., Janssens, D., Van Dooren, W., & Cleas, K. (2003). Do realistic contexts and graphical representations always have a beneficial impact on students' performance? Negative evidence from a study on modelling non-linear geometry problems. *Learning and Instruction, 13,* 441–463.

Dierick, S. & Dochy, F. (2001). New lines in edumetrics: New forms of assessment lead to new assessment criteria. *Studies in Educational Evaluation, 27(4),* 307–329.

Dochy, F. (2001). A new assessment era: Different needs, new challenges. *Research Dialogue in Learning and Instruction, 10(1),* 11–20.

Dochy, F. J. R. C. & McDowell, L. (1998). Assessment as a tool for learning. *Studies in Educational Evaluation, 23(4),* 279–298.

Entwistle, N. J. & Entwistle, A. (1991). Contrasting forms of understanding for degree examinations: The student experience and its implications. *Higher Education, 22,* 205–227.

Gielen, S., Dochy, F., & Dierick, S. (2003). Evaluating the consequential validity of new modes of assessment: The influence of assessment on learning, including pre-, post- and true assessment effects. In M. Segers, F. Dochy, & E. Cascallar (Eds.), *Optimising new modes of assessment: In search of quality and standards.* Dordrecht: Kluwer Academic.

Gulikers, J., Bastiaens, Th., & Martens, R. (2005). The surplus value of an authentic learning environment. *Computers in Human Behavior, 21(3),* 509–521.

Hart, D. (1994). *Authentic assessment: A handbook for education.* Menlo Park, CA: Addison-Wesley.

Herrington, J. & Herrington, A. (1998). Authentic assessment and multimedia: How university students respond to a model of authentic assessment. *Higher Educational Research & Development, 17(3),* 305–322.

Herrington, J. & Oliver, R. (2000). An instructional design framework for authentic learning environments. *Educational Technology Research and Development, 48(3),* 23–48.

Honebein, P. C., Duffy, T. M., & Fishman, B. J. (1993). Constructivism and the design of learning environments: Context and authentic activities for learning. In T. M. Duffy, J. Lowyck, & D. H. Jonassen (Eds.), *Designing environments for constructive learning,* 88–108. Berlin: Springer-Verlag.

Huang, H. M. (2002). Towards constructivism for adult learners in online learning environments. *British Journal of Educational Technology, 33,* 27–37.

McDowell, L. (1995). The impact of innovative assessment on student learning. *Innovations in Education and Training International, 32*(4), 302–313.

Messick, S. (1994). The interplay of evidence and consequences in the validation of performance assessments. *Educational Researcher, 23*(2), 13–23.

Meyer, C. (1992). What's the difference between authentic and performance assessment? *Educational Leadership, 49*(8), 39–40.

Newmann, F. M., & Wehlage, G. G. (1993). Five standards for authentic instruction. *Educational Leadership, 50*(7), 8–12.

Nicaise, M., Gibney, T., & Crane, M. (2000). Toward an understanding of authentic learning: Student perceptions of an authentic classroom. *Journal of Science Education and Technology, 9,* 79–94.

Petraglia, J. (1998). *Reality by design: The rhetoric and technology of authenticity in education.* Mahwah, NJ: Lawrence Erlbaum.

Resnick, L. B. (1987). Learning in school and out. *Educational Leadership, 16*(9), 13–20.

Sambell, K., McDowell, L., & Brown, S. (1997). But is it fair? An exploratory study of student perceptions of the consequential validity of assessment. *Studies in Educational Evaluation, 23*(4), 349–371.

Savery, J. R. & Duffy, T. M. (1995). Problem based learning: An instructional model and its constructivist framework. In B. G. Wilson (Ed.), *Constructivist learning environments.* Englewood Cliffs, NJ: Educational Technology Publications.

Segers, M., Dochy, F., & Cascallar, E. (2003). *Optimising new modes of assessment: In search of qualities and standards.* Dordrecht: Kluwer Academic.

Segers, M., Dochy, F., & De Corte, E. (1999). Assessment practices and students' knowledge profiles in a problem-based curriculum. *Learning Environments Research, 2,* 191–213.

Sluijsmans, D. (2002). *Student involvement in assessment: The training of peer assessment skills.* Unpublished doctoral dissertation. Open University of the Netherlands, Heerlen.

Stein, S. J., Isaacs, G., & Andrews, T. (2004). Incorporating authentic learning experiences within a university course. *Studies in Higher Education, 29*(2), 239–258.

Struyven, K., Dochy, F., & Janssens, S. (2003). Students' perceptions about new modes of assessment in higher education: A review. In M. Segers, F. Dochy, & Cascallar E. (Eds.), *Optimising new modes of assessment: In search of qualities and standards,* 171–224. Dordrecht: Kluwer Academic.

Sweller, J., Van Merriënboer, J. J. G., & Paas, F. (1998). Cognitive architecture and instructional design. *Educational Psychology Review, 10*(3), 251–296.

Torrance, H. (1995). *Evaluating authentic assessment.* Buckingham: Open University Press.

Uhlenbeck, A. (2002). *The development of an assessment procedure for beginning teachers of English as a foreign language.* Unpublished doctoral dissertation. University of Leiden, Leiden.

Van Merriënboer, J. J. G. (1997). *Training complex cognitive skills: A four-component instructional design model for technical training.* Englewood Cliffs, NJ: Educational Technology Publishers.

Wiggins, G. (1989). Teaching to the (authentic) test. *Educational Leadership, 46*(7), 41–47.

Wiggins, G. P. (1993). *Assessing student performance: Exploring the purpose and limits of testing.* San Francisco, CA: Jossey-Bass/Pfeiffer.

7 The role of assessment in preparing for lifelong learning
Problems and challenges

Nancy Falchikov and David Boud

How does assessment in higher education connect with learning after graduation? Does assessment contribute to the process of preparing students for lifelong learning? How can assessment practices help equip students for their future learning? We wish here to argue that conventional ideas of assessment within higher education are inadequate to provide a foundation for the learning and assessment demands of a lifetime of learning beyond the academy. We also wish to identify issues and dilemmas that must be addressed if assessment is to help rather than hinder learning after graduation.

The structure of the chapter is as follows. We start by exploring the idea of lifelong learning, and identify problems associated with some current conceptualisations of it that have implications for assessment. We then review an earlier argument we made that assessment has an important role in the preparation of learners for long-term learning (Boud & Falchikov, 2006). We suggest that, as typically interpreted, neither key purpose of assessment—learning and certification—provides sufficient future-orientation for lifelong learning. A third purpose needs to be conceptualized: assessment for lifelong learning. We then describe some newer assessment initiatives that might contribute to preparation for long-term learning, but note that uptake and development of these seem slow. We explore some possible reasons for this: systemic barriers, barriers within learners, the problem of the unknown future, and lack of alignment between assessment and other elements of the curriculum and with future learning needs. Our conclusion focuses on some suggestions for directions for development.

THE CONCEPT OF LIFELONG LEARNING

Although the concept of lifelong learning may seem relatively new, many of the attributes it espouses are not new to higher education. For example, as Bennett et al. (2000, p. 2) pointed out, as long ago as 1853, Cardinal Newman advocated that the 'university man' should possess cognitive, communication and interpersonal skills and 'certain affective qualities'.

Such qualities are not too far removed from current conceptualisations of lifelong learning (e.g. Dearing, 1997). In recent years, lifelong learning has been seen in terms of skills development for future employment or participation in society. This implies that students need to be prepared for a wider range of outcomes and contexts than those traditionally encountered within the university.

Several contemporary writers on lifelong learning stress employment and employability (e.g. Knight & Yorke, 2003). In exploring the goals of higher education and their relation to assessment, Knight and Yorke (2003, p. 88) identified the requirement to contribute to knowledge economies by producing graduates 'steeped in new, research-driven ideas and techniques' or, given that knowledge decays fast, to produce flexible, open, and creative graduates with general achievements able to 'thrive in turbulent times'. While these goals are not incompatible, they argued that, although they supported the second view, there may be a tendency in UK higher education to focus on the former. Accompanying this emphasis on goals, there has been a general shift in many western countries towards specifying what students will be able to know and to do in terms of what have become known as 'learning outcomes'. These learning outcomes, it is persuasively argued, should be closely aligned with assessment activities (Biggs, 2003).

PROBLEMS WITH LIFELONG LEARNING

Lifelong learning presents a number of challenges. First of all, as Coffield (2002) noted, one characteristic of the literature on lifelong learning is that much of it is dominated by lists rather than by models or other conceptualisations. Secondly, if students within formal education are to be prepared for future learning and to develop skills within that setting to this end, we must assume that such skills will transfer to different settings in the future. Such an assumption may be unfounded. Finally, there is a deal of confusion over what exactly constitutes formal, non-formal, and informal learning.

Problems with lists

Although lists of lifelong learning skills are ubiquitous, we should note though that, as Carr and Claxton (2002) pointed out, any list reflects a particular set of culturally determined values. Similarly, Knight and Yorke (2003) indicated that lists of characteristics of highly employable graduates vary according to the particular stance of the compiler.

Knight and Yorke (2003, p. 89) summarized some objections to list making:

1. They typically come from middle and senior managers detached from operational realities;

2. As 'wish lists' they are over-idealized;
3. What employers say they want and what the business is able to use may differ;
4. Qualities, skills, and dispositions are included and many believe qualities and dispositions cannot be taught;
5. Self-presentation is included and it may not be appropriate for higher education to attempt to shape the self or colonize 'workers' identities';
6. There seem to be national variations which make difficult the promotion of international labour market mobility.

However, we do not need to be concerned with the cult of lists to acknowledge that whether lifelong learning is represented in such ways, or indeed whether an instrumental approach is adopted in the pursuit of skills development, there is a substantial challenge presented by it to what is expected of assessment now.

Problems with transferability

Carter (1993, p. 86) noted that modules or courses aiming to develop generic or key skills tend to rest on assumptions that they can be 'decontextualized', and that students will be able to apply them to other domains, 'including their lives'. However, transfer of generic or key skills from the context in which they were learned to other contexts is less frequently demonstrated (e.g. Laybourn et al., 2000). Bowden and Marton (1998), however, suggest that the concept of transferability as currently used in higher education is redundant. They argue that, 'transfer is involved in every instance of learning: questions of transfer are simply questions of learning' (1998, p. 25). They suggest that most difficulties identified as problems of 'transfer' occur because teaching and learning activities do not focus sufficiently on understanding concepts in the context of the variety of ways in which they are actually used. By implication, this suggests that too much is covered and assessed at too superficial a level for meaningful learning to take place. If learning is to be deployed in a variety of contexts, it needs to be established in a variety of contexts.

Problems of differences in perception of what constitutes formal and informal learning

Although learning can take place in a wide variety of settings, there is a pervasive belief, both inside and outside higher education, that it is restricted to the formal setting of college or university. For example, a textbook on development through the lifespan limits its discussion of lifelong learning to two short sections (Berk, 2004). In a section on career development, the author discusses *formal* job training, while a section on late adulthood, describes some *educational programs* offered to 'senior citizens' in various countries. Informal learning is not mentioned. In addition, Boud and Solomon (2003) found that, in the workplace, being identified as a learner does not seem to be compatible with acceptance as a competent worker.

Even when learning outside college or university is acknowledged, it can be perceived to be different from formal education. Colley et al. (2003), noted that formal learning in institutions whose primary raison d'être is education is associated with objective, 'vertical knowledge', while informal learning, acquired in locations such as the workplace or community, whose functions are wider than education and do not necessarily include it at all, is characterized by practical, useful 'horizontal knowledge'. Colley et al. point to the danger of polarising formal and informal learning, and acknowledge that there are many features common to both. As we have argued elsewhere (Boud & Falchikov, 2006), this encourages us to look to the ways in which formal higher education contributes to what has been previously regarded as informal lifelong learning.

Whatever the problems are with formulations of lifelong learning, for students to be lifelong learners, they need to be able to make judgements about (or assess) their own learning in order to adequately manage their own learning. Assessment in some form is intrinsic to learning of any kind. In addition, greater emphasis needs to be placed on the variety of contexts in which learning takes place in order to better facilitate greater transferability of skills learned formally, including self- and peer assessment skills, to future formal or informal contexts, and transferability from one future context to another.

THE ROLE OF ASSESSMENT

In formal educational settings, assessment traditionally has two main functions: summative and formative, both of which operate at or close to the time of delivery. Significant tensions for both learners and teachers are created when the same assessments are required to serve both functions. In addition, summative assessment is also 'used' by others, for their own purposes. Policymakers and administrators have a stake in assessment, as well as teachers and students. Employers, too, are very interested in student grades. Thus, we encounter a dilemma: much assessment seems to benefit others more than it benefits learners. Moreover, the influence of the grades that result from assessment persists beyond formal education, but its formative functions that benefit learners operate often only at the time of delivery. Thus, while many learners emerge unscathed, for some assessment may have enduring negative consequences. At what cost to learners do we assign grades?

As we have argued elsewhere (Boud, 2000; Boud & Falchikov, 2006), if we are to help prepare learners for lifelong learning, a third purpose of assessment is needed: assessment to promote learning outside formal education throughout life. This learning will necessarily occur within many different contexts. In order to fulfil this purpose, we need to acknowledge the tensions that already exist within assessment in higher education and the possibilities for damage to learners that can result from assessment. We also need to move beyond contextual and time-limited functions.

INDICATIONS OF CHANGE: STRAWS IN THE WIND?

We have argued that few activities undertaken by individuals in later life are characterized by the formality found within educational settings. We have also considered how informal aspects of formal education might contribute to later learning opportunities (Boud & Falchikov, 2006). Interestingly, some previously informal activities undertaken by students on a voluntary basis are increasingly being incorporated into formal structures, so that all have the opportunity to benefit. An example of this is peer learning (Boud et al., 2001; Falchikov, 2001).

There are some signs of change in assessment practices that may be seen to support future learning by preparing learners to become autonomous assessors of their own work (Boud & Falchikov, 2006). There are also more general changes in assessment that support what used to be seen as non-formal learning. For example, assessment is now no longer limited to terminal essay and examination-based events. It encompasses a wide variety of activities and creations. A number of initiatives such as 'authentic assessment', 'autonomous assessment', and 'devolved assessment' capture aspects of what we regard as appropriate assessment for lifelong learning in that they have a forward-looking focus, and are authentic representations of real-life problems. An overview of alternative assessments that are consonant with the ideals of assessment for lifelong learning is to be found in Falchikov (2005, pp. 68–80).

There appear to be few examples of institutional acceptance and implementation of the idea that assessment should fulfil the function of supporting long-term learning. Alverno College (2003, p. 1) is a notable exception to this, in that their philosophy, 'assessment as learning', represents an attempt to create 'learning that lasts'. Mentkowski et al. (2000) assert that for learning to be integrative and lasting, the educational system must be coherent, connecting teaching, learning and assessment. Stress is placed upon explicit criteria, diagnostic feedback, and reflective self-assessment. Similarly, the American Association for Higher Education (AAHE) Assessment Forum Guide (1997) contains principles of good practice for assessing students based on the Alverno premise. Prominent among these principles is the assertion that assessment is most effective when it reflects an understanding of learning as multidimensional, integrated, and revealed in performance over time. This development provides opportunities for educators to promote 'coherence and alignment' (Pearson et al., 2001, p. 176) among the key elements of education.

PROBLEMS OF UPTAKE OF ASSESSMENT STRATEGIES FOR LONG-TERM LEARNING

It may seem that, in higher education, we already have the means to encourage and develop assessment for lifelong learning in a variety of contexts, but a visit to any institution will quickly indicate few examples of implementation. Ideas are available, but they tend not to be applied to benefit learning within formal education, let alone beyond it. We must conclude that there are problems that are acting as barriers. We have identified four: barriers within the system, barriers within learners, the problem of the unknown future, and the lack of alignment both within the curriculum and between assessment and future learning. Addressing these barriers we suggest constitutes the new agenda for assessment.

Systemic barriers

Most systemic barriers within formal education are manifest through the actions of teachers and assessors, though they may not have prompted them originally. These include the dominance of summative assessment concerns that emphasize reproducibility, standardisation, conformity, and a norm-referencing reduction of complex outcomes to simple scores. External pressures on educational institutions—from professional bodies and government agencies—often cause institutions to react defensively and pay more attention to summative than to formative assessment. It is common to find an institutional resistance to seeing assessment in anything other than summative terms. It is assumed that students do not have a role other than as the subject of assessment. Lip service may be paid to the importance of assessment to promote learning, but policies and practice to support this are less widely discussed than are processes to guide summative decisions. In addition, there has been a lack of conceptualisation of long-term learning outcomes, though the key skills agenda has partially attempted to address this.

Areas in which academics have rather more direct influence also create barriers to assessment reform. These include the control of curriculum and assessment practices by groups that stress the integrity of academic disciplines over the increasingly complex world of transdisciplinary practice. Added to this there is also a lack of sophistication in assessment practice and limited range of assessment forms in use (e.g. examination, academic-style papers, etc.) as indicated by the critical remarks made about assessment practice in UK universities by the Quality Assurance Agency (QAA, 2003).

It may be that barriers also exist in informal education and in contexts other than higher education. Informal learning, by its nature, can occur in any context at any time. Its chameleon-like character may itself be a barrier to learning. Informal learning lacks transparency and some people may fail to identify learning when it is taking place. Active engagement and reflection is required if learning is to lead to development and change.

Barriers within learners

While barriers within learners have been little discussed in the literature on higher education, it appears to us to be an issue of such importance that it must be considered high on the agenda. In fact it can be argued that this is, perhaps, the most insidious barrier of all to having students accept assessment as a key element of their continuing learning. The greatest obstacle is the experience of being assessed in the past and the ways in which these experiences influence expectations and behaviour in the present. While phenomena such as maths phobia have been long associated with experiences of this kind, there is increasing evidence from new forms of testing that there is an adverse impact of the motivation and confidence of learners of lack of success at earlier stages of education. For example, the Assessment Reform Group (2002) found that, as pupils mature, their levels of resentment, anxiety, cynicism and mistrust of standardized achievement tests increases. It will come as no surprise that high levels of anxiety have been noted in undergraduates near to examination times (e.g. Martin, 1997). Ilott and Murphy (1997) noted distress and anger in students who failed courses. They also investigated the negative feelings of teachers charged with the task of communicating a failure to a student. In addition, James (2000) suggests that grades and inadequate feedback to students on specific work can negatively impact on students' overall self-perception and confidence.

Anecdotal evidence suggests that many students have been hurt and distressed by acts of assessment earlier in their assessment careers and this has a negative influence on their willingness to be assessed and their openness to assessment (Boud, 1995a). For example, many of the postgraduate students and academic colleagues we encounter (in master's courses or staff development workshops) have had extremely negative experiences associated with acts of assessment at many different stages of their educational experience, from their earliest days in school through to university courses. Even in the context of receiving feedback, studies suggest that students are concerned about being treated respectfully and personally (c.f. Higgins et al., 2002). The emotional impact of being humiliated on occasions of being assessed cannot be overestimated, and expectations derived from previous assessment experiences are very powerful and remain with learners for very long periods of time. There is often a weight of unresolved distress associated with these experiences which colours attitudes towards being assessed. In short, learners seek to avoid being assessed whenever possible and only subject themselves to it when there is no obvious alternative. They come to live with assessment, but not to relish it. Of course, the group we have observed have been those who on any measure are successes of the assessment system. If the experiences of those who are more typical products of higher education are any more negative than these, then the barriers to be confronted are substantial indeed. We have argued that traditional practices can not only undermine students' capacity to judge their own work in the present, but that they also constrain the agenda of lifelong learning (Boud & Falchikov, 2006). We also believe that newer forms of assessment may not be immune from these criticisms. For example, while providing students with criteria may be beneficial in terms of current learning, it may create the expectation that future learning depends on specification of standards by others.

However, not all affective responses to assessment need be negative. There are also positive indicators. Negative experiences tend to be associated with *being* assessed. While this spills over into the notion of assessment per se, there does not seem to be the same degree of emotion attached to making one's own assessments (except when these are denigrated by those in positions of power and authority). It may be necessary therefore to position the agenda of assessment for lifelong learning as far from connotations with assessment as possible. Notions of self-monitoring might help shift the focus, though this can create difficulties. It is simply not possible to rename what is essentially an act of assessment as something that is not assessment. Such a process would be transparently artificial. Nevertheless, it is necessary to acknowledge the negative baggage of assessment discourse and find ways of engaging productively with it.

In addition to emotional impacts, role expectations with regard to assessment and learning also have a strong influence. Students have expectations of what are legitimate roles for themselves in learning and being assessed and can be resistant to practices that might seek to alter these. In the context of lifelong learning, as we noted above, the concept of 'learning' does not lie easily within the workplace. Role expectations again are called into play and competent workers appear to see learning as undermining their status.

The problem of the unknown future

In addition to our reservations concerning conceptualising lifelong learning through individually constructed lists, we are also concerned that it has come to be too closely associated with the concept of employability. Employment needs in a rapidly changing world cannot be realistically forecast. This poses a further problem for lifelong learning and its assessment. Moreover, conceptions of lifelong learning give no prominence to affective aspects of learning that we consider to be vital.

The question has been posed as to whether, instead of aiming for a career, we should all be preparing for a lifetime of 'portfolio working'. Kerka (1997, p. 1) argued that individuals should consider themselves 'a collection of attributes and skills, not a job title'. Earlier, Handy (1989) also expressed the hope that we come to see the benefits of thinking of life as a portfolio of activities, some undertaken for payment, others for pleasure, and some for a cause. Not all share this rosy view. Karpf (2002), for example, sees portfolio working as 'a fancy name for exploitation'.

In a world characterized by uncertainty, unpredictability and what Barnett (2000) calls 'super-complexity', important questions arise about the nature of higher education. A vital role for education in such a context is to prepare students for an unknown future. If we are to prepare students to operate in an unpredictable and pluralistic world then old ideas about how they are to learn within the academy may need to be re-evaluated. Barnett (2004) asserts that acquisition of skills or accumulation of knowledge cannot accomplish learning for an unknown future. Instead, he advocates developing 'the right relationship between persons and the changing world' (Barnett, 2004, p. 259). Individuals need the 'capacity to live with the existential angst' that results from knowing that we often have insufficient grounds for our actions. In order to achieve these qualities, Barnett calls for 'a transformatory curriculum and pedagogy which are understood to be and practised as endeavours of high risk'. He does not, unfortunately, spell out what such a curriculum might look like, arguing that, as it does not constitute 'a set of practices that we readily understand' (Barnett, 2004, p. 260) we all need to go on learning.

Of course, an individual student's unknown future may be known to others. For example, a new graduate will need to discover how their chosen workplace or professional community 'works'. This may be known by experts who have worked there for some time, but they may have difficulty in communicating this to others who have not had their experience.

Lack of alignment

As we and others (e.g. Biggs, 2003) have argued, it can be desirable to bring learning outcomes, curriculum activities and assessment into alignment and design fully integrated programs. However, we appreciate that this may be difficult to achieve, due to the great diversity of interests involved in education, particularly when learning throughout the life span is considered. In order to maximize the potential of assessment to aid lifelong learning, it is not sufficient to limit one's horizons to the present nor is it sufficient to limit one's context to the familiar. Alignment with future needs is also required. This requirement poses further dilemmas and it adds to the complexity of the overall challenge of achieving alignment.

How might we begin to work towards a more forward looking alignment? Teaching methodologies, assessment strategies, a commitment to personal and professional development and awareness of context must all work in harmony. While practices such as portfolio building and construction of patchwork texts (e.g. D'Aoust, 1992; Winter, 1995) require integration within some elements of the learning context, alignment that includes these various elements is necessary. It becomes essential that teaching methods enable participation, scaffolding and peer interaction. Assessment strategies must entail decision making, synthesis and identification, and use of evidence. The commitment to personal and professional development essential to lifelong learning necessitates making visible the invisible, striving for transparency and awareness of the importance and influence of context. Specific illustrations of activities to these ends are given in Boud and Falchikov (2006), but worthwhile activities alone are insufficient, an overall coherence of desired outcomes, activities and assessment is needed.

While the new 'assessment culture' beginning to permeate higher education emphasizes alignment of assessment with other elements within the curriculum (e.g. Birenbaum & Dochy, 1996), this does not seem to be occurring in practice to a great enough extent. In addition, as we have suggested, preparing students for lifelong learning requires that we help them become lifelong assessors, and that alignment between present practices and future needs is also necessary.

SOME DIRECTIONS FOR DEVELOPMENT

We have argued that we must find ways of balancing some of the dilemmas that assessment for future learning presents and of incorporating the preparation of students for lifelong learning into all our teaching, learning, and assessment practices. Self and peer assessment skills have an important part to play in equipping learners for future learning. Given that some of our earlier work has focused on self- and peer assessment (e.g. Falchikov & Boud, 1989; Boud, 1995b; Falchikov, 2005), this might suggest merely that we wish to support the idea of student involvement in assessment. While it is true that self- and peer assessment are important parts of what is being considered here, they are far from all of it. To focus merely on particular aspects of assessment is to ignore the wider changes that are necessary. It is not simply a matter of adding self-assessment to the learning and assessment repertoire, but of rethinking learning and assessment from a new point of view and examining the consequences for future practice.

Similarly, for feedback to begin to address the issue of learner and assessor autonomy, it must do more than serve as a key component to formative assessment. Learners must locate feedback for themselves from a variety of sources, and, indeed, begin to see themselves as possible sources of feedback for others. While the seeds of such practice are discernible, for example, in cases where evidence of learning required by a jointly agreed learning contract is sought out and presented by the learner, we need to sow such seeds more widely and actively encourage their growth.

We have also advocated the benefits of peer learning and peer assessment in the past (e.g. Boud et al., 2001; Falchikov, 2001; Falchikov, 2005). Ideas of staging or 'expert scaffolding' (Vygotsky, 1978; Bliss et al., 1996) are integral to the development of expertise, whether it be in judgement and evaluation or relate to learning itself. Modelling and scaffolding characterize several examples of peer tutoring. These practices have an important part to play in developing assessment skills for lifelong learning, but, again, cannot solve the problem alone.

Although current assessment practice has some features that encourage longer-term learning, it also has many characteristics that undermine the ability of learners to equip themselves for a lifetime of continuing learning that is a necessary feature of most contemporary work. A new link needs therefore to be formed between assessment and lifelong learning. This can take the form of sustainable assessment in which preparation for future learning and assessment is incorporated into assessment practices at all levels (Boud, 2000). This will require learning for inter-contextuality. It requires a breaking down of the often rigid separation of pedagogy from assessment. Learning about assessment is a necessary part of the curriculum as much as learning through assessment tasks. Although we see assessment as crucial to this enterprise, as we have argued, it should not be expected to carry the whole burden itself. We support colleagues such as Mentkowski and her colleagues (e.g. Mentkowski et al., 2000; Rogers and Mentkowski, 2004) and Dochy et al. (2004) whose models work on the premise that learning must be integrative and lasting, and that the educational system must be coherent. Teaching, learning and assessment are partners. Each has a part to play; all must work in concert. However, as we argued before (Boud & Falchikov, 2006), assessment needs to be aligned not only with teaching and learning within formal education, but also with long-term formal, non-formal, or informal learning and in and between a variety of contexts.

REFERENCES

AAHE Assessment Forum (1997). *Learning through assessment: A resource guide for higher education*. L.F. Gardiner, C. Anderson and B.L. Cambridge (Eds.). Washington, DC: American Association for Higher Education.
American Association for Higher Education (AAHE). (2006). *American Association for Higher Education 9 principles of good practice when assessing students* http://online.bc.cc.ca.us/courseassessment/Section_7_Loop/Section7_6Principles.htm (accessed 25.5.6).
Alverno College (2003). http://www.alverno.edu/about_alverno/about_index.html (accessed 1.10.3)
Assessment Reform Group (2002). *Testing, motivation and learning*. Cambridge: Faculty of Education, University of Cambridge.

Barnett, R. (2000). *Realizing the university in an age of supercomplexity.* Buckingham: Society for Research into Higher Education and the Open University Press.

Barnett, R. (2004). Learning for an unknown future. *Higher Education Research and Development, 23*(3), 247–260.

Bennett, N., Dunne, E., & Carré, C. (2000). *Skills development in higher education and employment.* Buckingham: Society for Research into Higher Education and Open University Press.

Berk, L. E. (2004). *Development through the lifespan* (3rd ed.). Boston: Allyn & Bacon.

Biggs, J. (2003). *Teaching for quality learning at university* (2nd ed.). Buckingham: Society for Research into Higher Education & The Open University.

Birenbaum, M. & Dochy, F. J. R. C. (Eds.) (1996). *Alternatives in assessment of achievements, learning processes and prior knowledge.* Boston: Kluwer Academic.

Bliss, J., Askew, M., & Macrae, S. (1996). Effective teaching and learning: Scaffolding revisited. *Oxford Review of Education, 22*(1), 37–61.

Boud, D. (1995a). Assessment and learning: Contradictory or complementary? In P. Knight (Ed.), *Assessment for learning in higher education.* London: Kogan Page, 35–48.

Boud, D. (1995b). *Enhancing learning through self assessment.* London: Kogan Page.

Boud, D. (2000). Sustainable assessment: Rethinking assessment for the learning society. *Studies in Continuing Education, 22*(2), 151–167.

Boud, D. & Falchikov, N. (2006). Aligning assessment with long-term learning. *Assessment and Evaluation in Higher Education, 31*(4), 399–413.

Boud, D. & Solomon, N. (2003). 'I don't think I am a learner': Acts of naming learners at work. *Journal of Workplace Learning, 15*(7/8), 326–331.

Boud, D., Cohen, R., & Sampson, J. (Eds) (2001). *Peer learning in higher education: Learning from and with each other.* London: Kogan Page.

Bowden, J. & Marton, F. (1998). *The university of learning: Beyond quality and competence in higher education.* London: Kogan Page.

Carr, M. & Claxton, G. (2002). Tracking the development of learning dispositions. *Assessment in Education, 9*(1), 9–37.

Carter, D. (1993). Critical thinking for writers: Transferable skills or discipline specific strategies? *Composition Studies/ Freshman English News, 21*(1), 86–93.

Coffield, F. (2002). Skills for the future: I've got a little list. *Assessment in Education, 9*(1), 39–43.

Colley, H., Hodkinson, P., & Malcom, J. (2003). *Informality and formality in learning: A report for the Learning and Skills Research Centre.* London: Learning and Skills Development Agency.

D'Aoust, C. (1992). Portfolios: Process for students and teachers. In K. Blake Yancey (Ed.), *Portfolios in the writing classroom.* Urbana, IL: National Council of Teachers of English.

Dearing, R. (1997). *Higher education in the learning society: The report of the national committee of inquiry into higher education.* Norwich: Her Majesty's Stationery Office.

Dochy, F., Gijbels D., & van de Watering, G. (2004, June). *Assessment engineering: Aligning assessment, learning and instruction.* Keynote lecture at the EARLI-Northumbria Assessment Conference, Bergen, Norway.

Falchikov, N. (2001). *Learning together: Peer tutoring in higher education.* London: RoutledgeFalmer.

Falchikov, N. (2005). *Improving assessment through student involvement.* London: RoutledgeFalmer.

Falchikov, N. & Boud, D. (1989). Student self-assessment in higher education: A meta-analysis. *Review of Educational Research, 59*(4), 395–430.

Handy, C. (1989). *The age of unreason.* Boston: Harvard Business School Press.

Higgins, R., Hartley, P., & Skelton, A. (2002). The conscientious consumer: Reconsidering the role of assessment feedback in student learning. *Studies in Higher Education, 27*(1), 53–64.

Ilott, I. & Murphy, R. (1997). Feelings and failings in professional training: The assessor's dilemma. *Assessment and Evaluation in Higher Education, 22*(3), 307–316.

James, D. (2000). Making the graduate: Perspectives on student experience of assessment in higher education. In A. Filer (Ed.), *Assessment: Social practice and social product.* London: RoutledgeFalmer.

Karpf, A. (2002). Why 'portfolio working' is just a fancy name for exploitation. *Guardian,* April 30, http://www.guardian.co.uk/Archive (accessed 25.5.6)

Kerka, S. (1997). Will we all be portfolio workers? Trends and issues alert. http://www.cete.org/acve/textonly/docgen.asp?tbl=tia&ID=111 (accessed 6.9.4)

Knight, P. T. & Yorke, M. (2003). *Assessment, learning and employability.* Maidenhead: Society for Research into Education & Open University Press.

Laybourn, P., Falchikov, N., Goldfinch, J., & Westwood, J. (2000). Evolution of skills development initiatives. In S. Fallows and C. Steven (Eds.), *Integrating key skills in higher education: Employability, transferable skills and learning for life.* Kogan Page: London.

Martin, M. (1997). Emotional and cognitive effects of examination proximity in female and male students. *Oxford Review of Education, 23,* 4, 479 (accessed electronically, 10.3.4)

Mentkowski, M. et al. (2000). *Learning that lasts. Integrating learning, development and performance in college and beyond.* San Francisco: Jossey-Bass.

Newman, J. H. (1907). *The idea of a university.* London: Longmans Green.

Pearson, P. D., S. Vyas, Sensale, L. M., & Kim, Y. (2001). Making our way through the assessment and accountability maze. Where do we go now? *The Clearing House, 74*(4), 175–182.

Quality Assurance Agency (QAA) (2003). *Learning from subject review 1993–2001: Sharing good practice.* Gloucester: Quality Assurance Agency for Higher Education.

Rogers, G. & Mentkowski, M. (2004). Abilities that distinguish the effectiveness of five-year alumna performance across work, family and civic roles: A higher education validation, *Higher Education Research and Development, 23*(3). 347–374.

Vygotsky, L. S. (1978). *Mind in society.* Cambridge, MA: Harvard University Press.

Winter, R. (1995). The assessment of professional competencies: The importance of general criteria. In A. Edwards & P. Knight (Eds.), *Assessing competence in higher education.* London: Kogan Page in association with the Staff and Educational Development Association.

8 Assessment
A boundary object linking professional education and work?

Anton Havnes

The existence of schools and universities is justified by reference to the fact—or rather the hope—that they are enabling students to handle situations other than the ones which they are using to gain that capability.—Bowden and Marton (1997, p. 25)

INTRODUCTION

There are critical voices, particularly from socio-cultural, situated learning, and cultural-historical perspectives, questioning the power of formal education to prepare for future competent action outside of education. Professional education certifies, but does it qualify for independent professional practice? Lave (1988), for instance, argues that the dominant didactic structures of formal education rather tend to disconnect the students' learning from the context of application in society outside of education. In his analysis of schools as contexts of learning Engeström (1987, p. 101) concludes that reproduction of texts is typical of school learning. There is a danger that the 'text becomes a closed world, a dead object cut off from its living context.' Bereiter and Scardamalia (1989, p. 367) criticize traditional schooling for degenerating learning into schoolwork and consequently subverting future learning in wider social contexts. 'From the standpoint of the students, doing schoolwork is what school is about' (p. 377). In her analyzes of nursing students' learning in clinical placement Heggen (1995) identified a gap between the learning tasks that students were obliged to complete to fulfil the requirements of the educational program (e.g. assignments and procedures) and the demands in the work situation in the hospital context. Students experienced a dilemma concerning being loyal to the educational requirements or to the demands of the workplace. In their position as students they were situated within a hierarchical relationship between education and work, where the educational institution exerted power through its control of the assessment of students.

These are just a few of examples of research that criticize formal education for becoming a 'closed world'. Another aspect of this critique is that the traditional conceptions of transfer that formal education is grounded on are questioned. Is the problem of applying knowledge across contexts (transfer) basically a cognitive challenge for the individual? Is it about the capability of the individual to access what is previously learned and then apply it in new and upcoming contexts or tasks? Is transfer basically a matter related to the students' learning? Could it be that transfer is an aspect of learning across contexts, rather than bringing knowledge across contexts?

This discussion starts from the position that transfer is a phenomenon that includes, but extends beyond, students' learning. The theoretical starting point is recent contributions to the analysis of transfer (Lave, 1988; Greeno et al., 1996; Beach, 1999, 2003; Tuomi-Gröhn & Engeström, 2003). The emphasis is on learning as contextual practice, the situated character of knowing, and the relationships between contexts and contextually specific practices. These perspectives on learning and knowledge emphasize the situativity of knowledge and learning, but also the bridging of boundaries between the contexts. In this case the focus is on the relationship between professional education and professional practice. The challenges that individuals encounter when they move from education to work (which are often framed as problems of transfer) are analyzed as aspects of the relationship between the institutional practices of formal education and work. This starting point expands and reframes the core from which begin assessment practice and assessment research. It moves beyond the investigation of students' acquisition of knowledge and skills toward an analysis of knowledge and knowledge use across contexts, or, to put it in other words; the trans-contextuality of knowledge and knowledge use.[1]

ASSESSMENT RESEARCH

Assessment has a vital role to play in bridging the boundaries between education and work and the wider society. Knight and Yorke (2003), for instance, discuss the central role of assessment in preparing students for employment. Their argument is that there is a need to focus on designing what they call an *employability-aware curriculum*. They propose that such a curriculum would emphasize a set of core competences that will sustain learning beyond the educational setting: *understanding*; *skills*; *efficacy beliefs, self-theories and personal qualities*; and *metacognition*; the USEM model (p. 8). Boud (2000) argues for a parallel aspect of assessment that also relates to the transfer problem. What do students experience about assessment in higher education, and what competence do they develop through the way they participate in assessment? Assessment 'has to move from the exclusive domain of assessors into the hands of learners', Boud argues (p. 151). Students should learn to *do* assessment, not just *be* assessed. He introduces the notion of *sustainable assessment* which implies that students should learn to 'undertake assessment of the learning tasks they face throughout their lives' (p. 152). The dominant assessment practices in higher education, he argues, disqualify students from participation in assessing their own professional practice, their future colleagues' practices, or institutional (often taken for granted) practices that they will be involved in.

These critical voices connect to an ongoing debate about transfer: is it the case that when students have acquired a set of competences in the course of their education they will be able to apply it in new contexts, new tasks, and new societal practices? Transfer has usually been conceptualized as a challenge for the individual when he or she moves across contexts. It is commonly described as one-directional, from education to work; it is not commonly referred to as, for instance, the application of experience from work in the educational setting. There is an assumption that learning for transfer can be achieved by improving the curriculum. The problem mainly concerns organising student learning. It is also suggested that the required curriculum improvement can be managed within the context of the educational institution itself. The curriculum changes need to be informed by the world outside, but the institutional boundaries between education and work are basically maintained.

My argument is that analysing, re-thinking, and perhaps re-arranging the nature of the systemic relationship between education and work is another challenge that needs attention if we want to promote learning across contexts. The role of assessment in constituting this relationship is essential. At this level of socio-cultural analysis a series of new questions arises. What differences are there between the knowledge that dominates in formal education and the knowledge that dominates in work? What differences are there between the use of knowledge in formal education and at work? If we assume that there are significance differences to take into consideration, what implications would they have for assessment? This analysis is based on the assumption that the social world of education and the social world of work value knowledge and the use of knowledge in different ways (Eraut, 1994; Russel, 1997; Blakeslee, 2001). My suggestion is not that such differences should be abolished; rather, they need to be addressed and included as resources for learning. But the potential can only be fulfilled by continuously analysing the relationships between education and work, and by including the analysis of differences between academic and professional practice in students' learning. Such an analysis implies questioning how learning, teaching, supervision, and assessment operate on the boundaries between education and work, and openness to potential re-organization of the way learning and assessment operate on these boundaries.

LEARNING, KNOWLEDGE, AND BOUNDARIES

Studying student learning implies analysing its embeddedness in socio-cultural contexts.

Learning as practice in context

Taking the situatedness of learning as the starting point, assessment can be analyzed from the perspective that learning is relational to the constraints (Barwise & Perry, 1983) and affordances (Gibson, 1979) of the context in which it takes place. A distinction between the acquisition and application of knowledge is problematic. Students learn by applying knowledge.

Lave and Wenger (1991, p. 109) argue that formal education is grounded on the assumption that people learn *from* talking *about a practice*. A problem then occurs: the practice that students talk *about* is different from the (classroom) practice they talk *within*. Students learn to talk in a classroom context, for instance about nursing in a hospital context, but their talk is situated in the institutional context of the (increasingly academically oriented) classroom practice. What students (as well as professionals) in fact learn, Lave and Wenger argue, is the practice *to* talk *within the practice* of the socio-cultural context where they talk (or write). They learn 'classroom talk'. Consequently, the learning that in fact takes place in professional education is an aspect of the modes of knowledge use that are valued in the educational context. To learn is to become included in the socio-cultural practice of a community of practice; it is to learn a practice. Learning, then, is an aspect of doing (Dewey, 1938), learning in school is 'doing schooling' (Scribner &Cole, 1981). Professional education is, thus, mainly to be understood as a context of application of knowledge, and students' learning is fundamentally driven by how knowledge is applied in this setting. Assessment is the component of the educational system that more than anything defines what students should know, as well as what they should do with knowledge. But in professional education, students' learning is also situated in the context of work practice.

Contexts and boundaries

Contexts relate to each other, both through the fact that people move between them and in diverse other ways. Consequently, being 'inside' a community of practice, social world, or activity system also implies a relationship to 'the outside'. In spite of the fact that any social context has its particularities, they are not isolated islands. 'Joining a community of practice involves entering not only its internal configuration but also its relations with the rest of the world' (Wenger, 1998, p. 103). In the context of this discussion, entering the educational program of, for instance, nursing implies entering the relationship between the educational program and the nursing profession. Students' learning is situated within a given cultural context, but it is also inherent in poly-contextuality and boundary crossing (Engeström et al., 1995). In this respect, formal education can only be partially closed of from the outside world, and learning will have trans-contextual dimensions. The concern here is how assessment practices mediate the trans-contextual aspects of students' learning. The boundary relationship of the learning context to other contexts (e.g. professional education and professional practice) is an integral aspect of students' learning during pre-service training.

As I have argued, knowledge is applied differently in academia and in work life; it has different values and social meaning. A core question is whether assessment takes into account the values and requirements of both the educational program and what is expected of students in the professional field that they enter after graduation (Boud, 2000). In this respect the relationship between education and work emerges as an aspect of student learning. While they are students it is an integral dimension of education. Learning is multiply situated both in context and in relationships between contexts. Establishing institutional practices of assessment to meet the multiple situatedness of learning could generate two core educational challenges. One is to establish a knowledge base, learning and assessment that have relevance both in the educational context and in the professional context. The alternative would be to establish an educational program where students are trained in dealing with the diversity of knowledge use in education and work.

Boundary objects

The most essential dimension of assessment in professional education is that it certifies new professionals and communicates information about their qualifications across the boundaries between education, the professional field and society. A core question then is to what extent assessment bears meaning across context, or, to use Bowker and Star's characteristics of boundary objects, 'serves multiple communities of practice simultaneously, be these within a single organization or distributed across multiple organizations' (Bowker & Star, 1999, p. 313).

Boundary objects are defined by Wenger (1998, p. 105) as 'artifacts, documents, terms, concepts, and other forms of reifications around which communities of practice organize their interconnections'. Bowker and Star (1999, p. 297) define boundary objects as 'objects that inhabit several communities of practice and satisfy the informational requirements of each of them'. They are able to 'travel across borders and maintain some sort of constant identity' (p. 16).

Boundary objects are cultural artefacts that evolve from and in the next turn become included in human practice. They can be physical or psychological. They represent a sub-category of Vygotsky's (1978) notion of *tool* in that they are means that are used in different communities of practice and are able to communicate across communities. Drawings, for instance, are boundary objects that bridge the activities of architecture and construction work. A leaving certificate is a boundary object that conveys meaning across boundaries between education and work. A portfolio is a tool for learning and assessment within an educational context that can be developed further for learning purposes in work life and also provides information for promotion and application for new positions. Examples of psychological boundary objects are concepts, models and theories that in similar ways inhibit several communities of practice, social worlds or activity systems. They serve to bridge their practices, for instance the practices of professional education and professional practice. Like artefacts, boundary objects are collective and shared among members of a community. Concepts, for instance, have an existence beyond the conceptualization of individuals. They are cultural products available for individual use, because they are reified in texts, pictures, and stories. They provide meaning and guidance for prospective individual actions (Wenger, 1998; Wartofsky, 1979).

ASSESSMENT AND BOUNDARIES

When we view learning as an aspect of boundary crossing and assessment as a boundary object the commonalities and differences between the social practices of education and work are made the focus of analysis. The object of analysis, thus, goes beyond the transfer of knowledge and skills that happens when individuals (students, teachers, or practitioners) move between communities of practice. The social practice, knowledge, tools, and ways of using knowledge and tools in different contexts are included in the analysis. The study must include three main aspects. One is the embeddedness of student learning practice in the priorities and demands of the educational program, that is, the context-specific requirements of the curriculum and assessment practices. Another focus is the embeddedness of assessment in the institutional practice of higher education, for instance, the increasing requests that professional education should reach academic standards. A third focus is the embeddedness of students' agency in learning in the boundary relationships between education and work and, consequently, in the diversity of social practices and knowledge use typical of these contexts—students' meaning-making of their learning.

The analysis of assessment as boundary object does not reduce the significance of individual learning, fair and valid assessment of students' achievements, and the need to align teaching, learning and assessment within the educational program. But it goes further by recognising that assessment institutes academic and professional identities and maintains and bridges institutional boundaries. Student learning is embedded in these complexities at the system level.

The meaning of assessment goes beyond facilitating learning and certifying the students for their future role as professionals. It tells about more than the relationship between student learning and expected learning outcomes. It can be understood as a springboard for negotiation of meaning in many ways. Kvale (1993, 1996), for instance, argues that assessment is a system that serves to establish consensus among the academics about what is regarded as valid knowledge within the academic community. In addition to assessing students, assessment represents 'continual assessment of the knowledge of a discipline', it is a 'testing and confirmation of the value of the knowledge taught and acquired in a field'. Assessment 'contributes to establishing the valid knowledge of a discipline' (Kvale, 1996, pp. 219–220). This means that it is knowledge that is assessed, as much as students.

In the development of new modes of assessment there has been a strong focus on the use of (explicit) criteria. This is another example of how discussions about assessment address what counts as valid knowledge or knowledge use. Criteria define what is regarded as valid knowledge within a domain (and at a specific level of competence). For students a given set of criteria is a tool that directs their learning. Valuing what counts as knowledge also takes place when teachers give feedback to students, and when students are involved in discussing or suggesting criteria. Learning includes sorting out what counts as knowledge within a community of practice and what does not count. But the partners involved in the negotiations are not equal.

The assessment of students is basically in the hands of the higher education institution and the university teachers. Consequently, there is a risk that assessment mainly is grounded on values and priorities inherent in the activity system of higher education. The relevance or meaning that the products included in assessment in professional education (e.g. assignments, exam papers, presentations) have in professional practice becomes essential from the perspective of boundary crossing. Do these products serve as boundary objects? Do they convey meaning across contexts? Are the concepts, models, and tools that students labour with applied across the contexts of education and work? These questions address issues that are essential for students' learning.

TRANSFER—LEARNING—ASSESSMENT

Standard notions of transfer

Standard notions of transfer have mainly addressed the continuity in the learning trajectories of individuals as they pass from one situation to another or from one task to another. Knowledge is regarded as something possessed by the individuals in the form of mental representations or embodied skills. Transfer is about retrieval of the capacities that individuals have previously acquired in new contexts or tasks. This decontextualized concept of learning is based on the presupposition that knowledge is independent of the context of learning. Assessment will therefore address learning as achieved and 'stored' in individuals. The main function of assessment is to control the knowledge that a person has acquired during education and thus legitimatize the boundary crossing of new professionals from education to work. In other words, the problem of transfer of knowledge from education to work basically concerns how the students have processed and 'stored' the knowledge. One aspect of the 'storing' of knowledge is to make it retrievable in new contexts.

The situated learning paradigm and transfer

The situative perspective on learning (e.g. Lave, 1988; Lave & Wenger, 1991; Brown et al., 1989; Greeno et al., 1996) is based on the presupposition that learning is context-dependent social practice embedded in communities of practice. Students learn as they become participants in social practice. What is learned is practice, including talking, enquiring and reflecting, as well as doing.

> For a practice learned in one situation to transfer to another situation, the second situation has to afford that practice and the agent has to perceive the affordance. If a learned practice is to transfer, it has to be learned in a form that is invariant across changes in the situation [...] and transfer depends on an ability to perceive the affordances for the practice that are present in a changed situation. (Greeno *et al.*, 1993, p. 102)

'Afford' here means that the situation explicitly or implicitly 'demands' something to be done, what we could call the 'invitation' of the situation to act (Gibson, 1979). This view states that, for example, writing an assignment about a practical problem in the workplace basically implies learning to present and discuss it in writing within the context where the task is given, usually formal education. Learning to solve the problem in a practical work situation is fundamentally different. The context you talk *in* is dominant. This is the epistemological basis for the critique against didactically structured learning outside of the context of application. Transfer is primarily dependent of two main mechanisms. First, invariance in social practices across contexts, is what Barwise and Perry (1983) call *uniformities*—those aspects of a given real situation that connect it to other situations. Second, the competence of an individual to identify affordances of the new situation, involves, in Barwise and Perry's words, 'categorizing situations in terms of some of the uniformities that are present' (p. 10).

Apprenticeship learning is often used as model for analysing learning from a situated learning perspective. It is typically characterized by a close relationship (invariance) between the products that assessment of apprentices is based on and the products of the workplace. From this perspective learning to become, for instance, a nurse will have to involve using the tools and procedures that professional nurses apply in the workplace. The privilege of assessment of theoretical knowledge in professional education, and the dominant role of university teachers, is incongruent with the situated learning perspective. The institutional boundaries between education and work represent a threat to learning to become a professional.

The situated learning perspective on learning and human practice has been one of the grounds on which the notions of boundary crossing and boundary objects developed (Star & Griesemer, 1989; Wenger, 1998; Bowker & Star, 1999). The focus is on the diversities of the contexts, the characteristics of each context, and the establishment and maintenance of interaction between contexts. Individuals crossing boundaries between contexts can be seen as part of the relationships between the contexts, but the contact across contexts also takes many other forms. The authenticity of assessment tools, procedures and products and the (local) character of enquiry becomes an issue. Authenticity of assessment will increase with invariance of tools, procedures, products and frames of enquiry across contexts.

It is my argument that the dominant forms of assessment in professional education are linked to the standard notion of transfer. But the conventional concept of transfer is challenged in the development of new modes of assessment (Knight & Yorke, 2003; Boud, 2000; Guliker, this volume). These new approaches are to some extent aligned with the situated learning perspective. The attempt to develop new modes of assessment also gets support from representatives of the situated learning approach. For instance, Greeno et al. (1996, p. 39) states, 'many of the proposals for alternative assessments, such as evaluation of projects and portfolios [...] are relevant to the assessment of participation in inquiry practices'. Another dimension of assessment that is appreciated from a situated learning perspective is students' participation in assessing their own and other students' work—self and peer assessment (Greeno et al., 1996) because of its direct relevance to critical practice outside of education.

CULTURAL–HISTORICAL ACTIVITY THEORY

In cultural–historical activity theory the situatedness of human action and learning is essential. But the activity–theoretical argument does not view learning as context-bound to a specific situation in the same way as in the situated learning perspective. Transfer can be seen as an aspect of generalization across contexts. Generalization implies going beyond the level of direct relationships between situations. As Davidov (1990, p. 295) argues, 'generalization means to discover a principle, a necessary *connection* of the individual phenomena within a certain whole.' The whole can be more than a given context. Thus, invariance of knowledge use (practice) across contexts is not a prerequisite for transfer. Instead, the variance across contexts is a potential resource for learning when learning expands beyond one context and variance in the valuing and use of knowledge as a resource for learning. But the variance needs to be made an object of learning. From what we know about the relationship between assessment and learning, the variance needs to be integrated in the assessment structure. In this respect not only learners learn; diverse contexts can also be in a learning relationship to each other because assessment can include exploration of their relationship to each other's practice.

Tuomi-Gröhn and Engeström (2003) introduce the notion of *developmental transfer*. They expand the objectives of education to incorporate the development of the social practices in the institutions through inter-institutional interaction. They argue that the challenge of education is to develop the student into

> a collective change agent that works in partnership with local community organizations and workplaces. The school offers its expertise to work organizations going through transformations. This means that the school needs to prepare its teachers and students not just to do their assigned jobs but to work also as boundary-crossers between school and the work organization. (p. 32)

Developmental transfer is a model in which three parties learn in collaboration and dialogue: the academic institution, the student and the workplace (p. 33). The individual dimension is essential. But the institutional relationship between education and work is more fundamental, because it creates contexts and resources for students' learning. The multiple roles of education are emphasized; to educate new professionals, to play an active role in developing professional practice, and to develop the teaching, learning and assessment practices of the educational program. The role of learning as a joint endeavour for students and practitioners is addressed in the design of the learning environment and the curriculum. The unidirectional notion of transfer from education to work is replaced by a multidirectional notion of transfer across contexts—from education to work and from work to education. Transfer is seen as a dimension of the learning of individuals, but also as a collective endeavour and a joint enterprise between education and work, where it is the social practice of professionalism that is in focus more than the individual competence of a given professional.

ASSESSMENT, BOUNDARY CROSSING, AND TRANSFER

Professional institutions have a societal mandate to certify individuals and provide a basis for employers to select among candidates. This is a fundamental aspect of (summative) assessment. It has to be done with rigour. In the debate about new modes of assessment the role of assessment in driving learning (the formative functions of assessment) is emphasised. It also has to be done with rigour (but a different kind of rigour?). A third societal mandate of educational institutions is to play a role in developing ongoing professional practice in the workplaces. In this third task the role of assessment as boundary object is one essential component (research and partnership building are other examples of components). A third rigour might apply here, one addressing the relationships between academics/teachers and professionals as much as students.

My conception is that all modes of assessment can be analyzed as boundary objects and that this approach is particularly relevant to the development of new modes of assessment in professional education. If we want to generate student learning across the boundaries of education and work, the boundary-crossing role of assessment is essential. Learning across context is an aspect of (1) making brokering a dimension of students' learning practices; (2) conceptualising the products used to assess students in terms of their functions as boundary objects; (3) assessing the concepts and procedures that students use as tools in learning and assessment as boundary objects; and (4) assessing variance and invariance in the use of knowledge in education and in work. From this perspective the social meaning of assessment expands beyond the context of serving the purposes of summative and formative assessment, and includes critical enquiry of knowledge claims and priorities across contexts. It implies assessing knowledge in perspective of its situatedness and preparing for learning across contexts. Students need learning tasks that prepare them for learning tasks in the social world of work. But they also need learning tasks where the diverse ways of applying knowledge in academia and workplaces are confronted and analyzed—not just in theory, but in practice as well.

The work placement schemes of professional education do not necessarily meet these requirements of generating learning across contexts. In work practice students are easily immersed in the institutional practice of the workplace (Heggen, 1995). Back in professional education they are immersed in the institutional practice of the academic institution. There may be no brokering going on where 'translation, coordination, and alignment between perspectives' (Wenger, 1998, p. 109) across communities of practice take place. In such a case the managing of potential diversities between professional education and professional practice becomes a problem for the individual, not between social worlds and their preferences. It would then take the form of privatization of a social problem.

Assessment should include learning tasks that bridge the requirements of the educational institution and work practice. Transfer, thus, is a problem of student learning, but also of a relationship between education and work. There is a need to incorporate the transfer situation, which typically includes transition between contexts for students, teachers/researchers and professionals. A transfer situation is a learning situation with potential confrontations involving (1) people representing different social worlds; (2)

social practices; and (3) tools, procedures and priorities. Change within each context and in the relationship between the contexts is a potential outcome; learning is another, both for individuals and institutions. Such a learning practice is not contrary to appropriation of the standards of today; rather it is the opposite—a change agent must know what needs to be change.

CONCLUSION

To pursue an approach to assessment as a boundary object and learning as boundary crossing implies a critical review of institutional assessment practices in professional education. It implies re-framing and re-conceptualising ongoing practice and it is essential in the development of new modes of assessment. Recent policies and developments in assessment have had student learning and validity (authenticity of the learning and assessment tasks) as the main focus. But new modes of assessment are often linked to constructivist (Birenbaum, 2003) and co-constructivist (Klenowski et al., 2006) pedagogies, and to a contextual approach to learning and assessment. There is a need to sort out this mixed theoretical framework and clarify the relationship between the diverse theoretical positions that are currently associated with new approaches to learning and new modes of assessment. Assessment as a boundary object puts the institutional knowledge and practices in diverse contexts in focus. Assessment would go beyond qualifying new professionals for future professional practice, beyond constructivism and co-constructivism, and emphasize the confronting of institutional practices and knowledge of work and education, for students, professionals and teachers in professional education. Consequently, how to involve these three groups of agents as participants in the social practice in assessment is a challenge.

REFERENCES

Barwise, J. & Perry, J. (1983). *Situations and attitudes*. Cambridge, MA: MIT Press.

Beach, K. (1999). Consequential transitions: A sociocultural expedition beyond transfer in education. *Review of Research in Education, 28*, 46–69.

Beach, K. (2003). Consequential transitions: A developmental view of knowledge propagation through social organizations. In T. Tuomi-Gröhn & Y. Engeström, (Eds.), *Between school and work. New perspectives on transfer and boundary-crossing*. Amsterdam: Pergamon, 39–61.

Bereiter, C. & Scardamalia, M. (1989). Intentional learning as a goal of instruction. In L. B. Resnick (Ed.), *Knowing, learning, and instruction: Essays in honor of Robert Glaser*. Hillsdale, NJ: Lawrence Erlbaum, 361–363

Birenbaum, M. (2003). New insight into learning and teaching and their implications for assessment. In M. Segers, F. Dochy, & E. Cascallar (Eds.) *Optimising new modes of assessment: In search of qualities and standards*. Dordrecht: Kluwer.

Blakeslee, A. M. (2001). Bridging the workplace and the academy: Teaching professional genres through classroom–workplace collaboration. *Technical Communication Quarterly, 10*, 169–192.

Boud, D. (2000). Sustainable assessment: Rethinking assessment for the learning society. *Studies in Continuing Education, 22*(2), 151–167.

Bowden, F. & Marton, J. (1997). *The university of learning. Beyond quality and competence in higher education*. London: Kogan Page

Bowker, G. C. & Star, S. L. (1999). *Sorting things out. Classification and its consequences*. Cambridge, MA: The MIT Press.

Brown, J. S., Collins, A., & Duguid, P. (1989). Situated cognition and the culture of learning. *Educational Researcher, 18*, 32–42.

Davidov, V. V. (1990). *Types of generalization in instruction*. Reston, VA: National Council of Teachers of Mathematics.

Dewey, J. (1938). *Experience and education*. New York: Macmillan.

Engeström, Y. (1987). *Learning by expanding. An activity-theoretical approach to developmental research*. Helsinki: Orienta-Konsultit.

Engeström, Y., Engeström, R. & Kärkkäinen, M. (1996). Polycontextuality and boundary crossing in expert cognition: Learning and problem solving in complex work activities. *Learning and Instruction, 5*, 319–336.

Eraut, M. (1994). *Developing professional knowledge and competence*. London: RoutledgeFalmer.

Gibson, J. J. (1979). *The ecological approach to visual perception*. Boston: Houghton Mifflin.

Greeno, J., Collins, A., & Resnick, L. (1996). *Cognition and learning*. In D. Berliner & R. Calfee (Eds.), *Handbook of educational psychology*, 15–46. New York: Macmillan

Greeno, J. G., Smith, D. R., & Moore, J. L. (1993). Transfer of situated learning. In D. K. Detterman & R. J. Sternberg (Eds.), *Transfer on trial: Intelligence, cognition and instruction*. Norwood, NJ: Ablex.

Havnes, A. (2004). Examination and learning. An activity-theoretical analysis of the relationship between assessment and educational practice. *Assessment and Evaluation in Higher Education, 29*(2), 159–76.

Heggen, K. (1995). *Sykehuset som 'klasserom': praksisopplæring i profesjonsutdanninger*. [The hospital as 'classroom'. Work practice in professional education.]Oslo: Universitetsforlaget.

Knight, P. T. M. & Yorke, M. (2003). *Assessment, learning and employability*. London: Open University Press.

Kvale, S. (1993). Examination re-examined: Certification of students or certification of knowledge. In S. Chaiklin & J. Lave (Eds.), *Understanding practice. Perspectives on activity and context*. Cambridge: Cambridge University Press.

Kvale, S. (1996). Assessment as construction of knowledge. In R. Hayhoe & J. Pan (Eds.), *East-west dialogue knowledge and higher education*. New York: Sharpe, 117–140.

Lave, J. (1988). *Cognition in practice*. Cambridge: Cambridge University Press.

Lave, J. & Wenger, E. (1991). *Situated learning: Legitimate peripheral participation*. Cambridge: Cambridge University Press.

Russel, D. R. (1997). Rethinking genre in school and society. An activity theoretical analysis, *Written Communication, 14*, 504–554.

Säljö, R. (2003). Epilogue: From transfer to boundary-crossing. In T. Tuomi-Gröhn & Y. Engeström, (Eds.), *Between school and work. New perspectives on transfer and boundary-crossing.* Amsterdam: Pergamon, 311–321.

Scribner, S. & Cole, M. (1981). *The psychology of literacy.* Cambridge, MA: Harvard University Press.

Shepard, L. A. (2000). The role of assessment in a learning culture. *Educational Researcher, 56*, 411–436.

Star, S. L. and Griesemer, J. R. (1989). Institutional ecology, 'translational' and boundary objects. *Social Studies of Sciences, 19*, 387–420.

Tuomi-Gröhn, T. & Engeström, Y. (Eds.) (2003). *Between school and work. New perspectives on transfer and boundary-crossing.* Amsterdam: Pergamon.

Vygotsky, L. S. (1976). *Mind in Society: The development of higher psychological processes.* M. Cole, V. John-Steiner, S. Scribner & E. Souberman (Eds.). Cambridge, MA: Cambridge University Press.

Wartofsky, M. (1979). *Models: Representation and scientific understanding.* Dordrecht: Reidel.

Wenger, E. (1998). *Communities of practice. Learning, meaning, and identity.* Cambridge: Cambridge University Press.

Part III

The dilemmas of assessment practice in educational institutions

The chapters in this section address the practice or activity of assessment in learning contexts including schools, colleges, universities and workplaces. Assessment practice includes a range of activities: designing assessment appropriate for the learning context; developing or applying assessment tasks and criteria; managing the overall process of assessment; marking, grading, or otherwise judging the work presented for assessment; guiding, advising and providing feedback to learners; and, perhaps implicitly, determining or 'acting out' the purposes of assessment in the specific context.

Assessment practice is grounded in institutional and societal traditions, priorities and values. Although assessment has always been a contested field of activity, perhaps there have been periods of time when assessment practice has seemed stable and largely uncontroversial. Questions raised were mainly of a technical nature addressing how to do assessment well.

This is certainly not the case in current educational settings where, because of what has been identified as a shift in paradigm or culture, more fundamental or critical questions are frequently raised. Assessment practice operates under much less certain conditions but it must still go on. This brings us back to the dilemmas and tensions in assessment practice that arise in any setting and must somehow, through negotiation, trial and error, compromise, the development of procedures and regulations, be managed to enable day-to-day practice to go on and to evolve.

Assessment is fundamentally about enabling judgements to be made and making those judgements. Some dilemmas in practice centre on how and on what basis judgements about learning are made. One aspect illustrated here is the difference between what is espoused, or sometimes mandated by policy makers, and what happens in practice. Orr focuses particularly on societal and institutional demands for criterion-referenced assessment, entirely congruent with widely accepted definitions of the new assessment culture. She found that aspects of discredited norm-referencing approaches are used to create practical and shared definitions of standards or grade criteria which teachers can collectively implement. Norm-referencing, in the sense of comparing the performances of different students in order to understand and make explicit a 'standard' in a specific context, may be in the background rather than the foreground but it remains an ingredient in the mix alongside criterion-referenced judgements.

The work of Smith and Tillema in relation to portfolios for summative assessment in teacher education also highlights the variable and contested nature of assessment judgements. They found that some assessors prioritized the attainment of implicit or explicit professional standards of competence, and others the progress made by individuals or the need to make forward-looking judgements in order to enhance future learner development. Perhaps the portfolio, as a 'new' assessment tool, seems to teachers and to learners to afford, or even demand, different kinds of actions and judgements in comparison with established forms of tests and academic assignments. One of the dilemmas that has to be managed in practice is the locus and nature of authority in assessment judgements. Dysthe and colleagues suggest that portfolios as assessment tools support dialogic practice where understanding is developed through discussion, interaction and reflection involving teachers, students and others. This then implies a shared responsibility for judgement in contrast to a conventional test of 'given' knowledge where all the authority of judgement remains with the teacher.

A further aspect is the nature of the presentation, activity or performance which is required: the what rather than the how of assessment. Some of Dysthe's students asked for scope to exercise 'creativity' and determine in context what good practice in their profession was as teachers. Smith and Tillema noted that there was no general consensus about the standards defining professional competence in the field. Nevertheless, in practice, some benchmarks of appropriateness and quality must be used. They therefore suggest an audit process which can assure the quality of assessment use for high-stakes summative purposes. Educational institutions frequently look outside, to professional and work contexts, to determine benchmarks for learner attainments. Performance assessment, as discussed by Smits and colleagues in relation to nursing education, is based on making complex professional practice, which is a mix of skills, attitudes and understanding, the target for learning and assessment. They illustrate that whilst the principles of performance assessment are not difficult to understand and may be readily accepted, the practice of performance assessment raises many practical and theoretical difficulties. Students, educators and professionals in practice share a common goal in using assessment practices which mirror professional practice but fail to agree on how well specific instances of performance assessment achieve that common goal. Performance assessment looks different depending upon your position within it.

Whether we think about what is to be assessed or how it is to be assessed and, indeed, the two are often difficult to separate in practice and even at a conceptual level, problems of clarity, explicitness and communication emerge between those involved. Our new assessment culture very often sits alongside a rationalist, managerialist culture which regards assessment as a technology. From this perspective all that is required is to make explicit what the assessment requirements are and to describe in detail what standards learners need to attain. In higher education, lists and descriptions provided for students are deemed to ensure transparency. However, in the day-to-day practice of assessment it seems that lists and guidelines are not enough. Rules and requirements cannot simply be transferred and understood. Assessment is a social practice and needs to be treated as such. Dysthe and colleagues find that explicitness about assessment is essential but only useful so long as it forms the basis for dialogue amongst teachers and learners and is referenced to specific activities, products and processes which constitute the concrete manifestations of learning and assessment. Such processes foster a move from simply 'knowing about' assessment requirements and criteria towards understanding them and taking personal ownership of them. When assessment requirements are determined externally, outside the immediate educational setting, it may be teachers who experience most strongly the limitations of transparency. Gioka found that schoolteachers had difficulties in operating fluently and confidently with prescribed national curriculum standards in science. There were dilemmas to be managed in working to 'someone else's agenda' and, on the one hand, not wanting to jeopardize their students' chances of success in external tests and on the other hand following their own judgements and intuitions about what would help students learn and what was important for them to learn.

The dilemmas faced by the teachers Gioka studied, manifested themselves sharply in the form of real tensions between the formative and summative aspects of assessment. Some felt that they were 'not allowed' to help students with their course work by making suggestions or pointing out errors and inadequacies, when at the same time they were summative assessors of this work and thus accountable within a national system of testing. Balancing formative and summative assessment is something which emerges in all of the chapters here. It could be argued that in the 'old' testing culture we became aware of a gulf between learning and teaching practice and assessment practice with assessment often taking place at different times and contexts, with different procedures and requirements to those demanded throughout the course of learning. Perhaps now there is a better balance, even an alignment, between learning/teaching and assessment. However, what we have begun to notice more is the difficulty in bridging the gulf between formative and summative assessment. Even when learning, teaching and assessment are apparently integrated, teachers and learners feel the tensions of performing different roles at the same time. This demands new levels of awareness and capability and new strategies and techniques on the part of teachers which, as several chapters show, are still only emerging.

Feedback is the aspect of formative assessment which is most often discussed. Most models of learning place importance on feedback which helps learners to determine what they have achieved, how this differs from the goal they would like to achieve, and how they might achieve that goal. However, in practice, giving and receiving feedback is far from straightforward. As noted above, sometimes attempts to combine the roles of summative and formative assessment inhibit the giving and receiving of feedback. Simply giving explicit feedback, in the form of grades or qualitative comment, incurs similar problems to those discussed in relation to explicit assessment requirements. Feedback is not a transaction but a process in which teachers and learners need to participate. Kvale describes the feedback-rich nature of some craft-based workplaces where there is no formal teacher but apprentices receive feedback from a variety of more experienced staff and intrinsic feedback (Laurillard, 2002) from the 'products' of their work. Furthermore, they have in front of them models of the goals to be achieved in the form of the outputs of experienced workers. This contrasts with most school or college environments which are rather low in feedback. Practicalities, such as the role of a teacher who has responsibility for 30 pupils in school or one who teaches 200 students at university, often results in limited feedback. Such practicalities can be 'worked around'. For example Gioka shows how some teachers do implement effective feedback and formative assessment in classroom contexts similar to those of other colleagues who do not find this possible. Furthermore, practicalities are not inevitable 'givens' but reflect the underlying assumptions, values and purposes of education. It may be that some of the problems and dilemmas that teachers face in assessment are not to be overcome simply by better-skilled teachers but are actually due to fundamental disjunctions between the philosophies underlying educational systems and institutions and those of our contemporary assessment culture. A shift in perspective at the institutional level is needed.

Assessment is always to some extent about the exercise of power in order to serve certain interests and achieve specific purposes. This is not always explicit, especially when viewed from the perspectives of teachers and learners engaged in assessment practice in their own contexts. It seems that in Kvale's ideal workplace there is no conflict and everyone's interests are served by assisting the new apprentice to learn the trade effectively and achieve the required standards. In a school setting the teacher has to serve several masters. Assessment practice must meet the accountability demands of external moderators or examination boards so much so that some teachers feel that accountability overrides the purposes of accurate summative judgement or helpful formative feedback. Schools, colleges and universities also use assessment as a selection mechanism, often on behalf of others such as employers who may want the 'best' students identified, or professional bodies who want an assurance of professional competence. Assessment may simply be a means of disciplining and controlling learners and maintaining teacher authority. From another perspective, externally-controlled assessment can be a political means of controlling teachers and educational institutions. The dilemmas which teachers and learners need to balance, illustrated in the chapters here, may manifest themselves as practical problems, role conflicts or difficulties with communication, but stem from deeper contradictions and conflicts of a political nature.

REFERENCES

Laurillard, D. (2002). *Rethinking university teaching: A conversational framework for the effective use of learning technologies* (2nd ed.). London: RoutledgeFalmer.

9 A theory-based discussion of assessment criteria
The balance between explicitness and negotiation

Olga Dysthe, Knut Steinar Engelsen, Tjalve Gj. Madsen and Line Wittek

INTRODUCTION

In the international literature on assessment there seems to be common agreement that clear assessment criteria are necessary for an effective assessment strategy (Miller, 2003; Woolf, 2004). It has also been frequently observed in practice that the publication of explicit criteria is not sufficient to promote effective student engagement in assessment. In this chapter we explore this problematic issue of explicit criteria and transparency of assessment from a socio-cultural perspective, using dialogism and Wenger's concept of 'communities of practice' (1998).

To anchor our discussion in practice, we take our point of departure in two studies from Norwegian higher education. Student work in Norway has traditionally been evaluated by an exam commission consisting of one external and one or two internal assessors. Quality criteria have rarely been made explicit to students before the exam, and they have seldom been given any explanation afterwards. Students increasingly request explicit criteria. They see this as a way of achieving 'transparency', a key notion in educational rhetoric over the last decade (Orr, chapter 10). However, our research revealed stark differences in students' views on the usefulness and desirability of explicit assessment criteria. We have explored this by using the theoretical concepts of participation, reification, and negotiation from Wenger (1998) and Bakhtin's 'authoritative and inner persuasive word' (1981).

The recent introduction of new modes of assessment, such as portfolios, has widened the purposes of assessment and subsequently led to a new interest in criteria. Alternative assessment tends to emphasize learning rather than selection or certification and the responsibility for assessment is shifting to the student. Peer review and self-assessment are often included, the latter both as a means and goal (Taras, 2002; Topping, 2003). In addition, assessment is contextualized so that the formulation and use of criteria must reflect local priorities and values. A crucial question is then whether and how the criteria and standards are articulated, discussed, and negotiated. With this in mind we will discuss quality criteria primarily from a student perspective.

CONTRASTING STUDENT VIEWS ON CRITERIA FROM TWO STUDIES

Two research studies of student views on assessment criteria (Wittek, 2003; Engelsen, 2004) raised the issues which we attempt to illuminate and explain in this chapter. Both focussed on 'assessment criteria' (Woolf, 2004), that is, the different items or elements that will be assessed, and not 'grade criteria' which are the characteristics required to achieve a particular grade.

The first study was undertaken with first year undergraduate students in the Department of Education at the University of Oslo where portfolio assessment was introduced in 2001. Undergraduate students from three departments: Educational Research; Special Needs; and Teacher Education were interviewed between 2001 and 2003 (Wittek, 2003). Two clear findings emerged from the study. Students were generally unaware of criteria in all three programs, even when they were published and available. However, the students felt that there was a need for more transparency in the assessment process. One obvious implication of this finding is that posting or publishing criteria is insufficient if they are not actively used by the teacher as a resource for involving students (Rust, Price, & O'Donnovan, 2003; Sadler, 1983; Woolf, 2004). A great majority of the students stated clearly that they would like to have explicit criteria. They were convinced that good knowledge of assessment criteria would: make it easier to work on portfolio assignments; be of great help in their peer review activities; and make it easier to prepare for the final exam.

The second study draws on data from the evaluation of an innovative program of ICT[1] in teacher education (Engelsen, 2004) at Stord/Haugesund University College and from an interview study with six students and two teachers in two subjects. The interviews took place in September 2003; three months after the students, who were now Master's students, had finished their teacher education. The innovative program in which they had participated included digital portfolios introduced in order to foster student centred learning and the integration of theory and professional practice (Dysthe & Engelsen, 2004). It emerged from the interview study that these graduate students, in contrast to the undergraduate students in the first study, had strong reservations about explicit quality criteria and voiced fears that explicit criteria would limit their creativity and lead to more instrumental learning.

In this case, neither students nor teachers had felt a need for explicit criteria. Students claimed that a culture of involvement and negotiation between teachers and students and among students made explicit criteria superfluous. The students stressed the dialogic learning culture that had developed in the subjects and stated that criteria developed from close negotiation among the students and with the teachers. The students painted a picture of belonging to a community of practice where they knew the disciplinary expectations, where they had learnt how to negotiate, and were treated as partners by the teacher. In such a learning culture the negotiation of criteria makes sense (Elwood & Klenowski, 2002). Students and teachers agreed that explicit criteria could lead to an instrumentalisation of the learning process and limit creativity. Students clearly felt that their interests were better served in a culture of negotiation and collaboration where they struggled with uncertainties than by traditional criteria explicitly formulated in writing.

The interviews revealed that not only did students and teachers agree that ongoing discussions replaced the need for explicit formulation and explanation of criteria, but they actually thought that such explicit criteria could be harmful. Students talked about getting to know themselves, a process of maturity, both professionally and related to subject matter. What really seemed to be the underlying issue was taking control of how to do an assignment, of what counted as good quality, and ultimately control of their daily life as students, and of their own learning. Interestingly, they saw this happening only when the road was not set for them and there was a potential for chaos:

> And in the meeting point between chaos and cosmos, all the way seeking coherence...and when the road is not made for you, I personally have a tendency to take control myself. And in the discussions of the criteria, I think most of us were very active in trying to find our own direction—and developing criteria during the process made us involved in a totally different way (Ann, Teacher Education).

THEORETICAL FRAMEWORK DISCUSSION: COMMUNICATION AND PARTICIPATION

In this section we present our theoretical framework and draw on the empirical studies as examples of contextual differences in two settings. We discuss ways in which the student experience of criteria is related to their participation in communities of practice.

Dialogism

Underlying the notions of explicitness and transparency in assessment criteria is a monological view of language and communication resulting in a belief that the message can be directly transferred from the sender to the receiver. As Wertsch (1991) has pointed out, the communication model of monologism, often called 'the conduit metaphor' after Reddy (1979), is deeply entrenched in the Western way of thinking and it is still the dominant paradigm in linguistics, cognitive psychology, information technology, and communication (Linell, 1998; Markova & Foppa, 1990, 1991; Wold, 1992). However, dialogism represents an alternative analytical perspective and epistemology. Where monologism sees knowledge as a given, dialogism sees knowledge as emerging from the interaction of voices; and where monologism is concerned with transmission of knowledge, dialogism is concerned with transformation of understandings (Nystrand, 1997). From a Bakhtinian perspective, meaning is always constructed in the interaction between participants: '...understanding and response are dialectically merged and mutually condition each other; one is impossible without the other' (Bakhtin, 1981, p. 282). A dialogic view of language and communication does not negate the need for transparency and explicitness, but it reduces our expectations of what can be communicated. It gives a theoretical underpinning to explain why explicitly formulated criteria are only transparent for those who develop them or have appropriated them through practice, discussions and negotiations, just as the graduate students had experienced in their innovative program.

Wenger's communities of practice: Participation, reification and negotiation

While dialogism provides the basic framework, Wenger's theory of communities of practice gives us a deeper understanding of the educational cultures where criteria are used. 'Participation refers to a process of taking part and also to the relations with others that reflect this process' (Wenger, 1998, p. 55). Students in teacher education are simultaneously participants in the wider disciplinary or professional communities of practice and the more limited communities constituted by the particular class or course. While students in their first year can be seen as central participants and full members of their class communities, they are also peripheral members, striving to become enculturated in the professional communities of practice. Learning what counts as quality work is part of the process of becoming full professionals, and standards and criteria are invaluable tools in this process.[2] However, we need to remember that formal education is a transitory community of practice. What counts as quality is different for first year students, third year students, and for experienced professionals because they belong to different communities of practice. In our research we saw that the majority of first year students had problems identifying implicit assessment criteria. They needed to become involved in discussions in order to make explicit the implicit criteria.

We see criteria as 'reification' of what counts as quality. Reification is used by Wenger to denote 'the process of giving form to our experience by producing objects that congeal this experience into "thingness". In doing so we create points of focus around which the negotiation of meaning becomes organised' (Wenger, 1998, p. 58). The process of reification is central to every practice, whether expressed in material objects, symbols, stories, terms, or concepts that 'reify something of that practice in congealed form' (p. 59).

We must also bear in mind the close connection, even complementarity, between reification and participation that is so vividly illustrated by our graduate student informants. From their position, explicit criteria could be understood as reifications of the collective ideas about the quality of a particular kind of work within a community of practice. But, for new students, explicit criteria must acquire a status as objects before being practised. However, as our research with first year students revealed, it is only through the experiences of participation that the reifications become meaningful for students.

One of the constant dilemmas in teaching at all levels is to find a balance between requiring students to accept criteria and standards that are reified in other contexts and enabling students to develop their own. When students are given explicit criteria to work with, they work in a very different manner from when they are asked to develop their own criteria. Reification shapes our experience, and experience shapes reifications. The power of reification is also its danger. As the politician's slogan can become a substitute for a deep understanding of and commitment to what it stands for (Wenger, 1998, p. 61), so can students' conformity with preset standards become a substitute for struggling with the material. This was exactly the point made by the graduate students when they rejected explicitly formulated criteria and even thought they might be harmful.

On the other hand, reification of quality standards into a set of explicit criteria gives them a new concreteness, and as such is necessary and useful. 'It becomes something people can point to, refer to, strive for, appeal to, and use or misuse in arguments. Yet, as reification, it may seem disconnected, frozen into text that does not capture the richness of lived experienced and that can be misleading in may ways' (Wenger, 1998, p. 61). Wenger concludes that reifications can potentially gain a degree of autonomy from the occasion and purposes of education and thus become counterproductive. This may be the case when criteria are handed ready-made to the students without any grounding in the particular situation. It is therefore important to bear in mind that 'Reification as a constituent of meaning is always incomplete, ongoing, potentially enriching and potentially misleading' (Wenger, 1998, p. 62). Explicitly formulated criteria are just the tip of the iceberg of participation in practice.

A further central concept in Wenger's social theory of learning is 'negotiation'. Wenger uses this concept to illustrate how human beings create meaning through engagement within a particular community of practice. Students are constantly struggling to make sense of what they are doing, both when the assignments are teacher-directed and when activities are self-directed. Making sense of assessment criteria, whether implicit or explicit, is an integral part of understanding what to do and of actually doing it. Interpreting and acting are part of the same process when it comes to interpreting preset criteria and trying to fulfil them or when struggling to develop one's own criteria:

> The negotiation of meaning is a process that is shaped by multiple elements and that affects these elements. As a result, this negotiation constantly changes the situation to which it gives meaning and affects all participants. In this process, negotiating means both interpretation and action (Wenger, 1998, p. 54).

Bakhtin's 'authoritative' and 'inner persuasive word'

The process of understanding what others understand with the relevant standards and criteria and negotiating a space for creativity within accepted limits may be experienced by students as a power struggle. Bakhtin's concepts of 'the authoritative' and 'inner persuasive word' (Bakhtin, 1981, p. 342) are other ways of conceptualizing the conflict between preset criteria handed down with the authority of the experts ('demanding obedience') and the inner persuasiveness of criteria that are negotiated. While the 'authoritative word' is compelling only because of its authority, 'inner persuasive' words bind us because they are 'half-ours and half-someone else's' (Bakhtin, 1981, p.345). When students deal with assignments in academic settings, whether they are asked to write texts in traditional genres or do projects, it entails enculturation and appropriation of the words of others, as well as finding an identity for themselves in a new culture. The pertinent question is to what extent 'the word', in this case the criteria, can be transmitted. Bakhtin's problem with the authoritative word is that it does not invite dialogue or give room for doubt and resistance. The authoritative word always has social authority and power, as is the case with the word from the teacher and the assessor. The danger is that this word may remain alien and unproductive, as happens when students unquestioningly take the teacher's preset criteria as the 'word of god'. The teacher's word, indeed any authority's word according to Bakhtin, needs to be questioned, even resisted, in order to become productive and internally persuasive.

The teacher in higher education, the university professor, has traditionally occupied a place from where the authoritative word is spoken. The change in pedagogy in the direction of more collaboration and dialogue means that the teacher must insist on the position as dialogic partner in order to achieve the dual goal of student enculturation and independence. Enculturation is not a neat, one-way process: it implies reciprocity and co-production of meaning, as the graduate students so forcefully expressed after finishing their three-year teacher education program.

CRITERIA AS REIFICATIONS OF NEGOTIATED PRACTICE IN PORTFOLIO ASSESSMENT

The graduate students had experienced an innovative program at Stord/ Haugesund College including digital portfolios, intended to foster student-centred learning and the integration of theory and practice. From the interview study it appeared that this process had given them control over their portfolio assignments and gradually over their lives as students. Negotiation of meaning was for them a fundamental aspect of gaining control. Wenger underlines that reification and participation are interdependent. This means that if students participate in negotiations about criteria, but nothing is formulated or reified, something is lacking. On the other hand, if everything is reified, for instance written down in detail without negotiation and dialogue, it is difficult for students to find shared meaning. If criteria are explicitly formulated as reifications of continuous negotiation and participation, they become part of a meaningful learning process. Explicit criteria cannot be understood in isolation from the negotiation process and students' participation in different communities of practice.

Portfolios exemplify the close connection between process and product identified by Wenger (1998, p. 60). In portfolio work, the process will always be an integral part of the product and vice versa, so that portfolios reify both and enable full participation. This enables a more developed level of negotiation between teachers and students. The first level of negotiation is the interpretation and appropriation of 'authoritative' and explicitly formulated criteria that takes place through discussion amongst students and between students and teachers. Gibbs and Simpson (2003, p. 14) call this process the 'alignment of students' perceptions with teachers' intentions'. The goal is that the students accept and internalise commonly accepted criteria. The second level is when criteria are actually developed by students and teachers in ongoing discussions and negotiations around open ended assignments, such as portfolio tasks. These criteria are not static, but dynamic.

Portfolios in teacher education may contain a great variety of written genres, for instance: comprehensive projects; traditional academic essays; case based texts; and a range of short genres with varying degrees of formality such as reflective essays; as well as digital genres. The portfolios of the first year undergraduate teacher education students in Oslo consisted of a number of fairly short texts based on didactical cases and reflective essays. The graduate students who had participated in the innovative program at Stord/Haugesund University College worked in groups on a small number of relatively demanding and long-term project assignments. The nature of the tasks may affect engagement with assessment criteria. Project tasks are usually more complex than specific written assignments, and one of the purposes is to leave more choices open for the students to discuss and decide. Whilst it is possible to formulate some general criteria for what constitutes a good project, explicit instruction and teacher-determined criteria are counterproductive to the very purpose of such assignments. Criteria for what constitutes quality of such texts are therefore often reified through negotiation and joint development among teachers and students. In the case of the master's program, a major goal of learning was to be able to see the connection between theory and practice. This goal had not been reified or made explicit, but nevertheless served as an overarching criterion and assignments were long-term and complex ones.

Negotiations between students and the teachers about the content and form of the task were ongoing. Within this context we found students categorically stating that a formulation of criteria at the outset would have been counter-productive and limiting:

> Then it would have been the way it usually is: the teachers make their demands clear at the outset and we as students try to satisfy them as well as we can by doing exactly as the instructions and the criteria say. But this leads to a very passive learning situation (Ruth, Teacher Education).

SUMMARY AND PRACTICAL IMPLICATIONS

Students in the programs in our two studies expressed, in different ways, the importance to them of assessment criteria. This is an area where development work is needed. In this section we summarise some practical implications for higher education, and we draw on international studies which can provide guidance.

Explicit criteria and negotiation are complementary

Many assignments consist of genres where there is an existing high degree of consensus about quality criteria in the disciplinary or professional community, and it makes sense to formulate criteria explicitly. In our view it will always be necessary and useful to articulate quality criteria. This process of articulation will in itself serve as an important source of raising consciousness about what quality the students are striving to achieve, not only at an individual level, but also at a collective level. However, this in itself is not sufficient, and we need to pay attention to how the criteria are communicated, interpreted, understood and used by the students individually and collectively.

Our theoretically-grounded analysis of findings from two research studies has strengthened our belief that explicit criteria and negotiation are complementary aspects in the process of assessment. The criteria have to be explained and become meaningful to participants through an ongoing process of collaboration and negotiation or they have to be developed in a dynamic working process (Klenowski, 2003; Rust et al., 2003; Sadler, 1983; Wiliam, 2000a, 2000b). Criteria development should therefore be seen as an ongoing process of negotiation rather than as static reifications of beliefs about the quality of a particular product. How to do this effectively is crucially bound to the specific context, the group of people involved, and the interaction among them. A number of studies have shown possible approaches: various kinds of negotiations, including discussion, modelling, peer feedback, (Sluijsmans, 2002), criteria-based teacher feedback and exemplars (Orsmond, Merry, & Reiling, 2002).

Avoid instrumentalism by fostering a culture for collaboration

In the case of assessment methods such as portfolios, quality criteria are not as well-established as they are for traditional genres. Teachers should take care not to formulate portfolio criteria that are predictable or could be used as instrumental tools. There is no better way to avoid instrumentalism than to foster a culture of collaboration and negotiation in the higher education classroom. Sadler (1983, p.72) stresses the importance of 'evaluative experiences shared between novice and expert'. He suggests that criteria are critically important when there is only limited sharing of expectations between learner and teacher, typically earlier than rather later in a course of study (p. 71). The process of developing criteria is 'a progression towards more sophisticated criteria and higher standards on existing criteria'. This suggests that a well-developed climate for negotiation will reduce the need for specific explication.

Students should be involved in assessment

Our study confirms the findings of several other studies. It is necessary to involve students directly in the processes of assessment in order to make assessment a powerful tool for learning: 'Given that assessment practices may or may not precipitate powerful or transformative learning it seems important to appreciate the central involvement of students themselves in the assessment process' (MacLelland, 2001, p. 317). Rust et al. (2003) state that explicit criteria in themselves are not enough if the purpose is to use assessment to support the process of learning. An understanding of what the criteria mean within the specific community needs to be developed. The main conclusion of their research is that explicit criteria alone fail to establish a common standard. Staff and students agreed on the need for discussion to support the use of criteria. Students also identified exemplars and further explanation as useful in making the assessment criteria more understandable (Orsmond et al., 2002). The conclusion is that continued emphasis on explicit articulation of assessment criteria and standards is not sufficient to develop a shared understanding of 'useful knowledge' between staff and students. Socialisation processes are necessary for students to grasp the meaning of criteria and make their use productive for learning.

CONCLUSION

Assignments in higher education exist on a continuum between traditional genres with strict norms and problem or project based assignments. The degree of explicitness of criteria and how to develop them or negotiate their meaning and use need to be determined in each case. The aspect of *time* also has to be considered. Our interviews with graduate students and first year students illustrate that building a culture of collaboration takes time, and it also takes time to build the competence necessary for students to develop their own criteria.

Discussions of explicit criteria in higher education are often couched in language from a technicist and instrumental view of education. We have drawn upon our own research and that of others to challenge this view. By using socio-cultural theory, including the theories of Wenger and Bakhtin, we have been able to change the discourse and focus on the importance of participation in a particular community of practice as the way in which students can become involved in criteria as a way of improving learning.

NOTES

1. PLUTO – Program for Teacher Education, Technology and Change
2. According to (Maxwell, 1993, p. 293), the terms criteria and standard should be distinguished. He has defined criteria as '...the various characteristics or dimensions on which the quality of student performance is judged. Standards are the levels of excellence or quality applying along a developmental scale for each criterion'.

REFERENCES

Bakhtin, M. M. (Ed) (1981). *The dialogic imagination: Four essays by M. M. Bakhtin.* Austin: University of Texas Press.
Dysthe, O. & Engelsen, K. S. (2004). Portfolios and assessment in teacher education in Norway. A theory based discussion of different models in two sites. *Assessment and Evaluation in Higher Education, 29*(2), 239–258.
Elwood, J. & Klenowski, V. (2002). Creating communities of shared practice: The challenges of assessment use in learning and teaching. *Assessment and Evaluation in Higher Education, 27*(3), 244–251.
Engelsen, K. S. (2004). *IKT og den nye lærerutdanninga i et økologisk perspektiv* [ICT and the new teacher education in an ecological perspective]. Doctoral dissertation (Dr. Polit), Universitetet i Bergen, Bergen.
Gibbs, G. & Simpson, C. (2003). *Does your assessment support your students' learning?* Centre for Higher Education Practice, Open University.

Klenowski, V. (2003, 5–10 October). *Rethinking assessment in higher education.* Paper presented at 29th Annual IAEA Conference, Manchester.

Linell, P. (1998). *Approaching dialogue, talk, interaction and contexts in dialogical perspectives.* Amsterdam: John Benjamins.

MacLelland, E. (2001). Assessment for learning: The differing perceptions of tutors and students. *Assessment and Evaluation in Higher Education,* 28(4).

Markova, I. & Foppa, K. (Eds.) (1990). *The dynamics of dialogue.* Hertfordshire, UK: Harvester Wheatsheaf.

Markova, I. & Foppa, K. (Eds.) (1991). *Asymmetries in dialogue.* Hertfordshire, UK: Harvester Wheatsheaf.

Maxwell, G. (1993). Criteria and standards based assessment in applied statistical mathematics, reshaping assessment practices: Assessment in the mathematical sciences under challenges. *Proceedings of The First International Conference On Assessment in the Mathematical Sciences.*

Miller, P. J. (2003). The effect of scoring criteria specificity on peer- and self-assessment. *Assessment and Evaluation in Higher Education,* 28(4), 383–394.

Nystrand, M. (1997). *Opening dialogue: Understanding the dynamics of language and learning in the English classroom.* New York: Teachers College Press.

Orsmond, P., Merry, S., & Reiling, K. (2002). The use of exemplars and formative feedback when using student derived marking criteria in peer and self-assessment. *Assessment and Evaluation in Higher Education,* 27(4), 309–323.

Reddy, M. (1979). The conduit metaphor—A case of frame conflict in our language about language. In A. Ortony (Ed.) *Metaphor and Thought.* Cambridge: Cambridge University Press.

Rust, C., Price, M., & O'Donnovan, B. (2003). Improving students' learning by developing their understanding of assessment criteria and processes. *Assessment and Evaluation In Higher Education,* 28(2).

Sadler, D. R. (1983). Evaluation and the improvement of academic learning. *Journal of Higher Education,* 54(1), 60–79.

Sluijsmans, D. (2002). *Student Involvement in Assessment. The Training of Peer Assessment Skills.* PhD. dissertation, Open University, Netherlands.

Taras, M. (2002). The use of assessment for learning and learning from assessment. *Assessment and Evaluation in Higher Education,* 27(6), 501–510.

Topping, K. (2003). Self and peer assessment in school and university; Reliability, validity and utility. In M. Seegers, F. Dochy, & E. Cascallar (Eds.), *Optimising new modes of assessment: In search of qualities and standards.* London: Kluwer Academic Press.

Wenger, E. (1998). *Communities of practice. learning, meaning, and identity.* Cambridge: Cambridge University Press.

Wertsch, J. V. (1991). *Voices of the mind. A sociocultural approach to mediated action.* Cambridge, MA: Harvard University Press.

Wiliam, D. (2000a). *Integrating formative and summative functions of assessment.* Paper presented at Working Group 10 of the International Congress on Mathematics Education, Makhuari, Tokyo. http://www.kcl.ac.uk/education/papers/integrating.pdf (accessed August 2006).

Wiliam, D. (2000b). The meaning and consequences of educational assessment. *Critical Quarterly,* 42(1), 105–127.

Wittek, L. (2003). *Mapper som lærings- og vurderingsform, eksempler fra Universitetet i Oslo* [Portfolio as a method for learning and assessment]. Oslo: Unipub forlag.

Wold, A. H. (Ed.) (1992). *The dialogical alternative. Towards a theory of language and mind.* Oslo: Scandinavian University Press.

Woolf, L. (2004). Assessment criteria: Reflection on current practice. *Assessment and Evaluation in Higher Education,* 29(4), 480–493.

10 Real or imagined?
The shift from norm referencing to criterion referencing in higher education

Susan Orr

In this chapter I will explore and problematize the policies and practices of norm referencing and criterion referencing in higher education assessment. Writing from the position that assessment is a social practice, I will argue that norm referencing and criterion referencing are interconnected approaches and that this interconnection creates dilemmas at the level of policy and practice. Whilst this chapter has a UK focus and quotes from the author's UK based doctoral work, it draws on research from a range of non-UK contexts. The chapter concludes by briefly exploring the staff development implications arising from the discussion and findings.

ASSESSMENT AS A SOCIAL PRACTICE OR A TECHNICAL PROCESS?

In this chapter I am particularly concerned with the marking or grading aspects of the assessment process. Rowntree (1987) points out that the individual who assigns a mark to a student's work holds a set of ideas, beliefs, and constructs about assessment. As discussed in the introduction to this book, assessment and grading need to be viewed at the levels of individual action, institutional practice, and the wider societal context. This emphasis on assessment as a practice situated within the wider socio-cultural, political context defines a social practices view of assessment. Lecturers marking student work are working within institutions that have certain expectations and in turn these institutions are located within a society that has particular values and priorities. Adopting the perspective that assessment is socially constructed, Delandshere (2001) argues that assessment reproduces the values of the society in which it operates. Higgins (2000) underlines this point when he states that assessment is a social affair 'embedded within a particular social relationship involving power, emotion, control, authority and discourse' (p. 5). From this perspective, student work does not have a 'true' score in any absolutist sense. Instead, marks awarded will be contingent on a variety of factors (Rowntree, 1987).

This view of assessment is not mainstream in contemporary assessment research or practice. To the contrary, I would argue that there is a current emphasis on assessment as a technology and that this emphasis has drawn focus away from the politics inherent in the act of assessment (Allen, 1998; Filer, 2000; Delandshere, 2000). Allen (1998) claims that 'the social processes and political economy of grading in British higher education is a neglected subject' (p. 241). To understand the technicist perspectives that are dominant in assessment one needs to recognize that assessment research grew out of the field of psychometric testing and cognitive psychology, both of which are grounded in experimental science (Dunn et al., 2004). Filer (2000) argues that the modernist rationalism implicit within contemporary assessment literature is explained by these disciplinary origins. Working within this paradigm, assessment is viewed as an objective science and the focus is on the implementation of processes and procedures. Thus there is a range of formulaic assessment textbooks for lecturers that Dunn et al. (2004) refer to as the 'A to Z of assessment methods' texts (p. 79). Within these texts there is the implicit assumption that all student work has a 'true' score and the focus is on making sure that this is the actual mark awarded. To this end, Sadler (1987) aspires to develop assessment approaches that enable assessors to report on 'the *actual* achievements of students rather than simply how each student ranks against others' (p. 192, my emphasis).

A technicist approach to assessment marginalizes the role of meaning making in the act of assessment. Higgins (2000) has drawn on 'academic literacies' perspectives that question assumptions about the transparency of language and the idea that language (whether written or verbal) sends messages that are understood in uniform ways by sender and receiver. In the context of assessment, it has been found that learning outcomes and guidance can be understood in different ways by students and lecturers. Sambell and McDowell (1998) concluded that: 'Individuals are active in the reconstruction of the messages and meanings of assessment' (p. 391). In the section below I explore the 'messages and meanings of assessment' in relation to norm referencing and criterion referencing.

NORM REFERENCING

Norm referencing is an approach to assessment that has several meanings and uses attached to it. At its simplest, the term *norm referencing* means that students' work is ranked so that a student's mark is dependent on others in the cohort. However, the term *norm referencing* is also used when lecturers simply compare students' work to arrive at a mark. The expectation that marks should approximate to a normal distribution curve, that is, a small number of high marks, lots of middle range marks, and a few low marks and fails, is also associated with norm referencing. In addition, norm-referenced marking is often associated with a 'connoisseur' model of assessment (Sadler, 1987; Rust, 2002) whereby the art of the assessor is likened to the skills of a wine taster, judging on the basis of specialist, complex and internalized expertise.

Officially, norm referencing, as opposed to judging each student's work against explicit criteria, is largely discredited in UK higher education. It is no longer seen to meet the needs of education. Sadler (1987) and Knight (2001) describe it as old fashioned. In contemporary research, norm referencing is presented as an approach to assessment that was used when education was fundamentally elitist and selective; the argument is that norm referenced approaches do not make the 'rules of the game' explicit to the students nor does it adequately indicate to the wider society the nature of students' achievements and capabilities. Such concerns led to the development of criterion referencing (Sadler, 1987).

LEARNING OUTCOMES AND CRITERION REFERENCING

In this section I will explore research that sets out the theoretical and political case for criterion referencing and I will contrast this with the limited research that looks at lecturers' lived experiences of assessment as a social practice. I will argue that whilst much has been written about the benefits of criterion referencing, very little research has been carried out to see how the approach is used when lecturers grade student work. What research there is points to a position where lecturers use complex combinations of criterion referencing and norm referencing (Hawe, 2003). If this is the case, there are disjunctions between stated policy and the actuality of practice.

For the purposes of this work I will use the term *learning outcomes* to encompass attempts to explicate (in writing) the criteria or standards against which students will be marked. Learning outcomes that aim to 'specify assessment outcomes' (Freeman & Lewis, 1998 p. 18) are a dominant approach in education today. Schools and universities 'reflect themes of explicit centralized definitions of outcomes and criterion referencing' (Ecclestone & Swann, 1999, p. 377). A number of alternative or closely-related terms are used. For example, some researchers differentiate between learning objectives, standards based assessment and criteria descriptors (Wyatt-Smith, 1999; Sadler, 1987). The term *learning outcomes* is, however, sufficiently broad to encompass most of these more specific terms.

Criterion referencing (at least at policy level) is now popular across all sectors of education with the aim of replacing the apparent opacity of norm referencing (Wolf, 2000). It was also introduced as a result of increasing concerns about reliability and standards (O'Donovan et al., 2000). Criterion referencing is seen as a way of 'ensuring consistent standards between markers' (O'Donovan et al., 2000, p. 74). This approach is viewed as fair because it appears to promote equality and to support students' learning

(Ecclestone & Swann, 1999). Textbooks state (e.g. Dunn et al., 2004) that when lecturers are using criterion referencing they use the stated learning outcomes to mark students' work and they do not use normative approaches. Thus, 'clear standards of expected student performance have increasingly become recognized as the vital ingredient of effective assessment' (Dunn et al., 2004, p. 4). There is the implication that in the 'old days' students had to guess the assessment rules (Wyatt-Smith, 1999). In sharp contrast, the use of criterion referencing and learning outcomes make assessment 'transparent' because students are told what they have to do. As a result of the above, in today's higher education environment, there is an assumption that criterion referencing is the modern contemporary way to approach assessment and that this approach has largely replaced the use of 'elitist' norm referencing.

INSTITUTIONAL AND SOCIAL CONTEXTS OF ASSESSMENT IN UK HIGHER EDUCATION

The wider political context within which higher education assessment operates is complex and multi-faceted. I would argue that a criterion referenced approach is congruent with the UK Government's emphasis on benchmarks, league tables, performance indicators and the notion of open government. At policy level, the specification of learning outcomes and the use of criterion referencing is promulgated by the UK Quality Assurance Agency (QAA) in a range of documents (for example: QAAHE, 1997; QAA, 2000). The QAA approach to assessment reflects the need to make higher education highly accountable and transparent to its stakeholders. Dominant political and pedagogic contexts have led to the development of assessment approaches that aim to be explicit and highly accountable (Yorke et al., 2000).

Assessment approaches in UK higher education have also been strongly influenced by developments in vocational education and in the school sector (Wolf, 2000). Barnett (1999) discusses the effects of the new vocationalism in higher education in relation to the concept of competency. The emphasis on competency has led to an assessment approach in which assessors attempt to specify the 'competences' necessary for a given job and then assess people against these competences. Competences are premised on the notion that skills (and more recently, knowledge and understanding), can be broken down into constituent parts and assessed sequentially (Barnett, 1999). The competency model adopted in the UK has drawn on developments in the United States (Glaser, 1963) and today this model has been applied far beyond the technical training for plumbers and electricians for which it was developed (Wolf, 2000). This has been referred to as the 'skillification' of higher education (Hyland & Johnson, 1998). Criterion referencing and competency are interconnected approaches, one implying the presence of the other. If an assessor is able to specify attainment and standards against which students' work will be judged then there is no longer a need to compare students with each other; instead they can be assessed against the standards.

The influences of the school sector can be identified in relation to the higher education curricula developments. The development of the national curriculum in the UK school sector signalled a shift to criterion referencing (Gipps, 1995). Once the curriculum is tightly specified, the logical progression from this is to attempt to assess students against these tightly specified attainment targets. Thus the national curriculum, in part, led to the development of criterion referencing. The rigid specification of curricula in the school sector was influential in the development of the QAA Benchmark Statements in higher education. These Benchmark Statements set out expected learning across a number of undergraduate subject disciplines (QAA, 2004). Whilst the current Benchmark Statements are open ended when compared with the rigidity of the school sector national curriculum, they represent a first attempt at setting out broad curricula expectations (James, cited in Filer, 2000). It is significant that the QAA has stated that it expects students to be assessed in relation to Benchmark Statements (QAA, 2000).

ASSESSMENT PRACTICE IN THE CONTEMPORARY CONTEXT

Criterion referenced approaches based on learning outcomes have been sufficiently widely used in the UK for some of the practical problems to be revealed. Research suggests that when lecturers and students use learning outcomes, they understand them in very different ways (O'Donavan, 2000; Rust, 2002). In the vocational sector of education this has led to a 'spiral of specification' where guidance is written to clarify standards and in turn guidance is written to clarify the meaning of the guidance (Wolf, 2000). The spiral of ever more minute specifications can divert attention away from broader achievements (Gipps, 1995).

The apparent clarity of written guidance belies the complexity of the conscious and unconscious reference frames that lecturers draw on when making decisions about students' work. Hawe (2002, 2003) and Wyatt-Smith (1999) have researched the range of tacit references that lecturers utilize. Dunn et al.'s (2004) book appears to be contradictory in this respect, providing an illustration of the dilemmas that we face in assessment practice. In one chapter lecturers are exhorted to set clear learning outcomes and assess against them, whilst another chapter explores tacit practice in relation to assessment. The connoisseur model of norm referencing accommodates this more easily because there is an expectation that a wine taster will have skills/knowledge that she is unable to define or quantify. To illustrate this in an assessment context, Wyatt-Smith (1999) refers to the large networks of tacit associations that sit privately in the teacher's head and the 'interplay that occurs between defined assessment criteria and a range of other existentially generated considerations' (p. 220). Such tacit practice will militate against attempts to be transparent and cannot be put to one side as if it is not a problem within criterion referenced models.

This has been researched by Hawe (2003) who found that when lecturers in New Zealand were making judgments about participants on a teacher education course, they would put the written criteria to one side and utilize other criteria to judge students, particularly when their students would be at risk of failing if they were marked *only* against the written criteria. This practice was observed when Hawe attended a group moderation meeting. In common with the author's findings (Orr, 2003), Hawe found that lecturers' discussion about student work rarely related to the learning outcomes that were publicized. Instead, there were discussions about what constituted a 'good student'. Similarly, Ashcroft and Palacio (1996) carried out research that indicated that 'there are some criteria that are used to assess students that are not featured explicitly in course aims and objectives or in assessment or competence criteria' (p. 62). Hawe (2000, p. 103) suggest that these assessment practices 'appeared to reflect an overt rejection of assessment as a technocratic activity' (p. 103). Wyatt-Smith (1999) carried out research in Queensland. She found that, even in educational contexts where highly developed standards-based criterion referencing systems were adopted as policy, *in practice* teachers drew on a 'network of contending influences' (p. 220) that included reference to the students' cultural and personal circumstances. She points out that little was done to prepare teachers for the huge shift in approach that the criterion referencing policy necessitated and virtually no research was done to find out 'whether the stated criteria as supplied to students, mirror the actual criteria used by the teacher to award grades' (p.197). In this instance, the mismatch between the written learning outcomes and the actuality of assessment practice is stark. It could be argued that criterion referencing is little more than a repackaging that has not changed or challenged the assessment practices that preceded it. The research indicates that a policy shift to criterion referencing does not necessarily lead to a shift in assessment practices.

DILEMMAS

Although assessment literature states that norm referencing is outdated, this, in itself, does not signal that it is no longer in operation. Norm referencing has left a strong legacy. I would argue that this is clearly evidenced in the strong cultural expectation that marking distributions should follow a typical bell-shaped distribution curve that does not change from year to year. This long-established expectation is still a mainstream contemporary view. We assume that there will always be a very few firsts, rising numbers of 2A and 2B degrees, and very few failures (Oppenheim et al., 1967, cited in Elton, 1998, p. 35).

If universities are really operationalising purely criterion referenced approaches to assessment there should be no outcry if, in a particular year, more students than usual get first-class degrees. If students are marked against written standards and in some years more students achieve well against the standards, this should be unproblematic. Instead this can herald alarm about so-called 'dumbing down' and give rise to concerns that the standards themselves are being eroded. Hornby (2003) points out that if more first-class degrees are awarded than usual in a particular year, the university can be simultaneously accused of lowering standards or commended for improving teaching. These contradictions reveal the complexity of perceptions in relation to criteria and norm referencing.

Even in cases where student work is not formally ranked Wolf (2000) observed that lecturers have an apparently 'natural' preference for marking student work by comparing it to other students' work. In the school sector, Wyatt-Smith (1999) found that within a clearly articulated criterion referencing system, teachers' judgments included comparisons between pupils' work. One of her respondents 'confessed': 'Most teachers would never publicly admit that they compared what kids write. But I need to do it. I firm up what I am looking for. But we are not supposed to do that since the advent of criterion referenced based assessment' (p. 218).

The concept of criterion referencing rests on the notion that it is possible to write clear learning outcomes or standards against which students' work can be judged so that student to student comparisons are no longer needed. But this gives a veneer of exactness that Gipps (1995) refers to as 'pseudo precision' (p. 982). Barnett (1999) argues that learning outcomes are 'partial and debatable' (p. 73) and, whilst it may be relatively easy to set, say, swimming standards of achievement, setting standards for higher education level work is highly contestable (Freeman & Lewis, 1998; Gipps, 1994; O'Donovan et al., 2000). Rowntree (1987) and Freeman and Lewis (1998) argue that criterion referencing and norm referencing have been falsely dichotomized and that both approaches to assessment influence each other. Thus when learning outcomes are written for criteria referencing purposes they usually refer to what may be typically expected of students under norm referenced approaches.

As part of my doctoral studies I conducted a small assessment case study. I interviewed lecturers in two university art and design departments. In addition I sat in on moderation meetings where final marks are agreed amongst a group of markers for final year work. The aim of this research was to explore the ways that lecturers operationalize assessment in a live assessment context. What emerged from my findings was an emphasis on comparative and ipsative approaches. Ipsative assessment was evidenced when student's marks were viewed in relation to their individual previous attainment. Lecturers appeared to root their marking practice in a series of comparisons between the students in the cohort they were marking, or in comparison to previous years' students, or to marks given at other institutions. For example, when moderating one student's mark, a lecturer referred to a mark given to another student to make sure that the mark was fair in relation to this. She commented: 'What did we give X? I think Y should be of a similar order'. In a second instance a student's low mark was defended because she was: 'not in same league as some of the others'.

The lecturers employed ipsative approaches but implied that they knew it was 'naughty talk'. For example, when defending a mark awarded, one lecturer made the following comment:

> She's made tremendous leaps. I was influenced by the fact that she woke up and started to work. I know you shouldn't [be influenced by that].

This case study points to the complex combination of approaches that are adopted when student work is marked.

POLICY INTO PRACTICE

When assessment policy across all educational sectors shifted towards criterion referencing, there was much optimism about its strengths, which were contrasted with the weaknesses of norm referencing. An extreme denunciation of norm referencing is quoted in Wood (1987) who refers to two educational philosophers stating that 'norm referencing constituted a violation of students' civil rights' (p. 154). However, Wood cautioned academics against expecting too much from criterion referencing, explaining that, whilst there were massive policy shifts in the U.S. school sector in the 1980s, the legacy of norm referencing continued in that the marks were not allowed to vary too much from year to year, which implied that norm referencing approaches remained in use.

The policy shift from norm referencing to criterion referencing in UK higher education, was influenced by a number of factors, but there was an assumption that the policy shift would lead to a shift in assessment practice. Changes to assessment practices have been viewed as unproblematic by policy-makers (Hawe, 2002). However, a range of strategies can be adopted to avoid implementing new policies. In New Zealand, it is argued that teachers were 'passive resistors of the criterion referencing system' (McCallum et al., 1995, cited in Hawe, 2002, p. 102). A policy shift cannot simply be announced with an assumption that it will be implemented precisely as set out (Bell & Gilber, 1996, cited in Hawe, 2002). In devising policy shifts from norm referencing to criterion referencing, policy-makers should not ignore the strength of the existing culture of assessment (Hawe, 2000). Ecclestone and Swann (1999) go further when they state 'there is an enduring legacy of a norm referenced classification system' (p. 381) because, as Wood (1987) argues, the need to make comparisons between students' work seems to be deeply rooted and this will militate against the development of criterion referencing.

The distinctions between norm referencing and criterion referencing are complex and it might be more appropriate to admit that norm referencing is still operating in the academy (Rowntree, 1987). Arguably, the imprecision of language means that it is easier to benchmark performance through a series of comparisons with other students as opposed to assessing performance against written descriptors. Strathern (2000) argues that there is an assumption that the more that is written the more that is clear, but in the field of assessment 'such practices cannot be made fully transparent simply because there is no substitute for the kind of experiential and implicit knowledge crucial to expertise' (p. 313). In New Zealand, the dramatic shift to criterion referencing and a standards based assessment heralded a backlash against the original proponents of this approach. The view emerged that criterion referencing promised more than it could deliver (Hawe, 2002). In the United States and in Australia the competence advocates are gradually moving from their original positions (Popham, cited in Wolf, 2000) and in the UK Yorke argues that HE lecturers use hybrids of criterion referencing and norm referencing (Yorke, 2001).

So, how should lecturers situate their practice in relation to the complexities of criterion referencing and norm referencing? Working from Torrance's position that assessment is a 'dominant and all pervasive social practice' (cited in Broadfoot, 1996, p. xi) I will outline some practical strategies. Firstly, it is important to emphasize that a reflective approach is required. If lecturers adopt a reflective, evaluative approach where they consider their practice in relation to criterion referencing and norm referencing this will enable them to understand intuitive practices and unwritten rules. This process will be facilitated by offering groups of lecturers opportunities to discuss, in a supportive context, the approaches they actually adopt when marking student work. To structure this dialogue, lecturers could look at past papers and exemplars together, in the way that school sector exam markers are trained (Hornby, 2003; O'Donovan et al., 2000). Alternatively a program team member might be appointed to observe all group moderation meetings and to reflect back the themes and approaches adopted. In this way lecturers can explore the implicit and explicit rules and practices relating to the allocation and spread of marks from year to year. It is important that colleagues openly explore whether or not there is an institutional or personal expectation for marks to be normally distributed in the departments within which they work. If there is such an expectation, lecturers can then decide how to communicate this effectively to students and staff, or they can explore ways to challenge it. If lecturers are marking, in part by comparing students' work, they need to be able to discuss this without feeling that they are doing something wrong. These discussions would be designed 'to give tacit factors external formulation' (Sadler, 1987, p. 199). The overall aim is to align, as far as possible, policy and practice in relation to norm and criterion referencing.

I am not calling for a return to norm referencing but I would argue that it would be unwise to underestimate the durability of norm referencing approaches in education today. I would suggest that, in the words of Angoff: 'If you scratch a criterion referenced interpretation you will very likely find a norm referenced set of assumptions underneath' (Angoff, 1974, cited in Woods, 1987, p. 155).

REFERENCES

Allen, G. (1998). Risk and uncertainty in assessment: Exploring the contribution of economics to identifying and analysing the social dynamic in grading. *Assessment and Evaluation in Higher Education, 23*(3), 241–258.

Ashcroft, K. & D. Palacio (Eds.) (1996). *Researching into assessment and evaluation in colleges and universities. The practical research series.* London: Kogan Page.

Barnett, R. (1999). *The limits of competence.* Buckingham: Open University Press.

Broadfoot, P. (1996). *Education, assessment and society: A sociological analysis.* Buckingham: Open University Press.

Delandshere, G. (2001). Implicit theories, unexamined assumptions and the status quo of educational assessment. *Assessment in Education, 8*(2), 113–132.

Dunn, L., C. Morgan, O'Reilly, M., & Parry S. (2004). *The student assessment handbook.* London, RoutledgeFalmer.

Ecclestone, K. & J. Swann (1999). Litigation and learning: Tensions in improving university lecturers' assessment practice. *Assessment in Education, 6*(3), 377–389.

Elton, L. (1998). Are UK degree standards going up, down or sideways? *Studies in Higher Education, 23*(1), 35–42.

Filer, A. (2000). *Assessment: Social practice and social product.* London: RoutledgeFalmer.

Freeman, R. & R. Lewis (1998). *Planning and implementing assessment.* London: Kogan Page.

Gipps, C. (1995). *Beyond testing: Towards a theory of educational assessment.* London: Falmer Press.

Glaser, R. (1963). Instructional technology and the measurement of learning outcomes. *American Psychologist, 18*, 519–521.

Hawe, E. (2002). Assessment in a pre-service teacher education programme: The rhetoric and the practice of standards-based assessment. *Asia-Pacific Journal of Teacher Education, 30*(1), 94–106.

Hawe, E. (2003). 'It's pretty difficult to fail': The reluctance of lecturers to award a failing grade. *Assessment and Evaluation in Higher Education, 28*(4), 371–382.

Higgins, R. A. (2000). '59 % Excellent!': Making sense of assessment feedback, http://www.ilt.ac.uk/archives/itac2000-resources/Higgins/default.htm. 2001.

Hornby, W. (2003). Assessing using grade-related criteria: A single currency for universities. *Assessment and Evaluation in Higher Education, 28*(4), 435–453.

Hyland, T. & S. Johnson (1998). Of cabbages and key skills: Exploding the mythology of core transferable skills in post-school education. *Journal of Further and Higher Education, 22*(2), 163–171.

Knight, P. (2001). *A briefing on key concepts.* York: Learning and Teaching Support Network.

O'Donovan, B., M. Price et al. (2000). The student experience of criterion-referenced assessment (through the introduction of a common criteria assessment grid). *Innovations in Education and Teaching International, 38*(1), 74–85.

Orr, S. (2003). *Talking to other tutors has been the mainstay of getting to grips with assessment.* Unpublished Doctoral work.

Quality Assurance Agency (QAA) (2000). *Code of practice for the assurance of academic quality and standards in higher education: Assessment of students.* Bristol: Quality Assurance Agency.

Quality Assurance Agency (QAA) (2004). *Subject benchmark statements.* (accessed 14/04/04). http://www.qaa.ac.uk/academicinfrastructure/benchmark/default.asp

Quality Assurance Agency Higher Education (QAAHE) (1997). *Subject review handbook, October 1998–2000.* Bristol: QAA.

Rowntree, D. (1987). *Assessing students: How shall we know them?* London: Kogan Page.

Rust, C. (2002). The impact of assessment on student learning: How can the research literature practically help to inform the development of departmental assessment strategies and learner centred assessment practices. *Active Learning in Higher Education, 3*(2).

Sadler, R. (1987). Specifying and promulgating achievement standards. *Oxford Review of Education, 13*(2), 191–209.

Sambell, K. & L. McDowell (1998). The construction of the hidden curriculum: Messages and meanings in the assessment of student learning. *Assessment and Evaluation in Higher Education, 23*(4), 391–401.

Strathern, M. (2000). The tyranny of transparency. British Educational Research Journal, 26(3), 309–321.

Wolf, A. (2000). *Competence-based assessment.* Buckingham: Open University Press.

Wood, R. (1987). *Measurement and assessment in education and psychology.* London: Falmer Press.

Wyatt-Smith, C. (1999). *Reading for meaning: How teachers ascribe meaning and value to student writing. Assessment* in Education, 6(2), 195–221.

Yorke, M. (2001). *Assessment: A guide for senior managers.* York: Learning and Teaching Support Network.

Yorke, M., Bridges, P., & Woolf, H. (2000). Mark distributions and marking practices in UK higher education. *Active Learning in Higher Education, 1*(1), 7–27.

11 Teacher or assessor?
Balancing the tensions between formative and summative assessment in science teaching

Olga Gioka

INTRODUCTION

This chapter is about the dilemmas faced by teachers when they teach and assess science coursework in upper secondary school in England. Current thinking about assessment places a high value on coursework activities since, in contrast with end-point examinations, they can provide considerable scope for formative assessment and the enhancement of student learning. However, teachers' practice of formative assessment will be strongly influenced by the context in which they work. The chapter reports some of the findings of a research study (Gioka, 2004) exploring the ways in which teachers use formative assessment practices as they help their students improve science coursework reports and how they manage this alongside their role in summative assessment. Teachers play an important role as assessors in the national examination system where teacher grades for science coursework contribute to students' overall final grades. By examining the case of teaching and assessment of coursework, I explore how teachers cope with their role as both instructors and assessors of coursework

FORMATIVE ASSESSMENT

In this study, I use the term of *formative assessment* or *assessment for learning* as: '...encompassing all those activities undertaken by teachers, and/or by their students, which provide information to be used as feedback to modify the teaching and learning activities in which they are engaged' (Black & Wiliam, 1998, p. 7). There is well-documented research evidence that formative assessment can produce significant gains in students' learning when designed to provide them with qualitative feedback and guidance on what they can do to improve. This conclusion is supported by several reviews of the research literature including those by Natriello (1987), Crooks (1988), Black and Wiliam (1998), and Allal and Mottier Lopez (2005).

Formative assessment has also been examined from the viewpoint of socio-cultural theories of teaching and learning. Referring to the Vygotskian concept of social mediation of learning, Allal and Pelgrims Ducrey (2000) argued that interactive formative assessment is aimed at providing 'scaffolding' of learning in the students' 'zone of proximal development'. Within the socio-cultural theory of learning, assessment is seen as a social process (Broadfoot & Black, 2004) giving attention to the quality of teacher–student interaction. Assessment is an interactive, dynamic, and collaborative process between the teacher and students, as well as between and among students. This means that the teacher should not only be interested in what students can do on their own (i.e. summative assessment), but what students can achieve in collaboration with the teacher within the 'zone of proximal development'. One function of assessment would be then, to help to identify this 'zone' for each particular student and to support progress within it. Consequently, formative assessment rather than being an external and formal activity, such as external exams, is embedded within the social and cultural life of the classroom. Emphasis on formative assessment as an interaction has important practical consequences for sharing and understanding learning goals and assessment criteria, for providing good quality feedback (oral and written), and for providing time for self- and peer-assessment.

The main theoretical analysis quoted by those writing about formative assessment is that of Sadler (1989). He argues that the implementation of formative assessment practices requires a view of quality according to which teachers and students make judgments. Students should be able to develop skills of evaluating the quality of their own work, especially during the process of its production. Sadler gave feedback a crucial role in learning; he identified ways in which feedback should be used by teachers to unpack the view of excellence, which is part of teachers' 'craft knowledge' so that students are able to acquire the standards for themselves. Teaching has to facilitate the transition from teacher-supplied feedback to the development of self-monitoring and meta-cognitive skills in the learner. Sadler argued that formative assessment should equip learners with the essential tools for managing their own learning; that is, with a clear view of the learning goals, and with some understanding of their present state of learning, so that they can understand the nature and the extent of the gap that has to be crossed. To achieve that crossing, students must possess the means to do so. As Sadler (1987) put it:

> The indispensable conditions for improvement are that the *student* comes to hold a *concept of quality roughly* similar to that held by the teacher, is able to monitor continuously the quality of what is being produced *during the act of production itself*, and has a repertoire of alternative moves or strategies from which to draw at any given point. (p. 121, emphasis in original)

Sadler's point was that, for formative assessment to be truly effective, it requires the provision of high quality feedback. More recently, Sadler put it as follows:

By quality of feedback, we now realise we have to understand not just the technical structure of the feedback (such as its accuracy, comprehensiveness and appropriateness) but also its accessibility to the learner (as a communication), its catalytic and coaching value, and its ability to inspire confidence and hope. (Sadler, 1998, p. 84)

There is international evidence that there are tensions between assessment for learning and assessment for summative purposes which, if not reconciled, can have a negative impact on learning and teaching (Harlen & Deakin Crick, 2002). However, the difference between formative and summative assessment lies in the way in which evidence is interpreted and used and not in the nature or mode of collection of that data (Wiliam &Black, 1996; Wiliam, 2003). Whilst formative assessment must be pursued for its main purpose of feedback into the learning process, it can also produce information which can be drawn upon for summative purposes (Black, 1998). In fact, Black and his team suggested the use of summative tests for formative purposes (Black & Wiliam, 2003; Black et al., 2003, 2004). External assessments can be used formatively when curriculum revisions are made on the basis of assessment results. Along the same lines, Shavelson and his colleagues argued in favour of an alignment between formative and summative assessment (Shavelson et al., 2002; Shavelson, 2003). These perspectives on balancing formative and summative purposes are highly relevant to this study.

SCIENCE IN THE UPPER SECONDARY SCHOOL: THE RESEARCH STUDY

In the English secondary school system, teacher assessment of coursework represents 20% of the total mark in the national exams (GCSE, the General Certificate Secondary Exams, and A-level, University entrance exams). The grade that students obtain for science coursework contributes to the final grade for the subject. However, science coursework is assessed by the teachers themselves rather than by external examiners. This makes the role of the science teacher challenging. On the one hand, the teacher has to teach and support the learning process. On the other hand, she has to assess, examine, and award a grade to each of her own students. This chapter has two foci. The first is to discuss the extent to which the participant teachers communicated the expected quality and the related criteria to students during teaching and assessment. Attention then shifts to the second focus which is on the ways in which these teachers perceived their role in both teaching and assessing coursework and the dilemmas they may experience.

A year-long study with nine secondary science teachers in four schools in the greater London area was designed. The participant teachers were observed over the course of their ordinary teaching of science lessons and they were interviewed twice. On completion of the observation period, in the second interview, teachers were presented with samples of students' coursework reports. These were photocopies of real samples of GCSE coursework, of low and average attainment and served as the basis for discussion during the interviews. The purpose was to get teachers to talk about how they address students' weaknesses and difficulties in coursework and the feedback they give to students. Also, copies of students' coursework reports were collected to look at teachers' marking and the written feedback that teachers gave. All the teachers' and schools' names are pseudonyms. Further details of the research design have been given in Gioka (2004).

The importance of the exam

In observing the participant teachers, it was evident that their main aim was the preparation of students to obtain a high mark in GCSE and A-level exams. During teaching, the teachers very often referred to the exam board criteria and highlighted the importance for students of fulfilling the exam board criteria in order to obtain a high grade. They tended to give high priority to topics or questions most likely to be asked in the exam papers. Thus, work identified as likely to be tested had a higher status than work not so identified. All teachers created a supportive environment to provide the necessary preparation for students to succeed in their exams. In interviews they emphasized the pressure to cover the syllabus and prepare students, in a limited length of time, for the national exams. Mr. Hall's statement was very typical:

> The way I teach, to be honest with you...I am playing the game, I am trying to help them get the best mark possible. Personally, I think, coursework is a bit of game.... It's very much exam-driven really.

Teachers stressed that they make the quality standards and the exam board criteria as clear and explicit as possible to students. They guide students by continually referring to the exam board criteria and emphasizing 'secrets' of success. They also constantly explain to them what they need to do and encourage them to improve their work in relation to the criteria.

Coursework assessment—formative or summative?

Both classroom observations and teacher interviews show that many teachers consider coursework as a 'final product'. They see coursework as an end in itself to which they assign a grade. In other words, they do not see coursework as a piece of work under development and along the route of progression and improvement. This approach is mainly due to the fact that coursework 'counts' in the final grade for GCSE and A-levels and thus, teachers take for granted that they are not allowed to help, intervene, or suggest ways for improvement. Only two teachers, Mr. Hall and Mr. Scott, talked about the possibility of improving draft reports as an aspect of the policy of their science departments.

One can see here how the external summative exams can dominate and distort the teaching and assessment of science coursework. After assessing a coursework report, teachers carry on with a different coursework topic. Each topic area is treated as an isolated and separate event. Teachers rarely refer to topics previously taught. Thus, for most of the teachers in the study, teaching and assessment are two separate events. Assessment seems to be separated from further planning and teaching. Overall, the requirements for the exams and the whole exam preparation seemed to restrict teachers' instruction and, to a great extent, students' learning opportunities. In other words, it is a case of 'teaching to the test'. It is also worth noting that all the participant teachers with the exception of one, Mr. King, said that opportunities for self- and peer-assessment of coursework did not exist. They justified this on the basis that a coursework report should be marked only by the teacher as it is for summative assessment purposes: the teacher is required to report students' grades.

Separating teaching/learning and assessment

Seven of the nine participant teachers distinguished between 'usual' science teaching and coursework teaching. They also distinguished between marking 'usual' science work and coursework marking. This distinction was made on the basis that the grade they assign 'counts' in the total grade in external exams. For example, in Rosehill School, a sixth form college, two teachers, Mr. Moss and Mr. Scott, said that they are not 'allowed' to talk and give much help with coursework since the grades 'count'. Rather, the teachers talk to students and provide help only during the teaching in advance of coursework activities. For example, students are required to carry out experiments, in silence, under 'exam conditions'. Similarly, teachers said that they were not 'allowed' to tell students how to improve a particular piece of coursework:

> I help them but I cannot for ever be giving them feedback [...] because that would affect the way I am marking their coursework, then, if I give them excessive amount of help...it is not fair!

Mr. Michael in St. Margaret's School said that he is not allowed to give much help to students with how to improve their coursework:

If I did get back reports from my students, which were poor...I cannot really advise them much. I am not supposed to tell them what to do. In essence, I would expect them to actually be able to write good reports. Obviously, if they have problems I would try and help them but at the end of the day I cannot for ever be giving them feedback in terms of how to write a report, because that would affect the way I am marking their coursework, then, if I give them excessive amount of help...it is not fair!.

In this context of science coursework, the tension between advice from the teacher and exam requirements has been clearly revealed.

Embedding coursework in formative assessment practices

Two participant teachers, Mr. King and Mr. Smith, employed formative assessment practices in relation to assessed coursework. They were committed to sharing clear criteria for judgment of attainment with students and to providing feedback. Both teachers had a clear view of the required coursework quality and this enabled them to provide informative oral and written feedback and to 'scaffold' and model the learning process in terms of the cognitive demands involved. For example, Mr. King would provide qualitative feedback by setting a target for personal improvement for each individual student. An example from an observed lesson is:

It was very difficult to find clear evidence of your achievement. I feel this is because you did not plan your writing or check it after completing it. By writing it 'off the top of your head' you did not fully deal with one point before moving on to the next. This can be avoided by having a writing plan or flow chart to follow so that you can check off points as you complete them. In the next piece of work I would like to discuss your writing plan with you before you start the main account.

At the individual level, Mr. King and Mr. Smith directed their students and their thinking towards the learning goals and the assessment criteria by providing guidance about what needed to be improved and how it could be done. At the whole class level, they were also explicit since they used modelling strategies to show students the quality of work expected of them. In addition, Mr. King was the only teacher in the research study who gave students opportunities for self- and peer-assessment. Students could 'see' the quality of work for themselves, what they had to do to improve, and they reflected on their own learning and progress. They started to become active participants. In talking about the strategies he uses in his teaching, Mr. King said that he initially teaches in a very directive way, as he wants to model the quality of the laboratory report. After a certain time, he gives more responsibility to students themselves:

And then, I will continue along those lines in the future where the intention will be to withdraw the amount of input given to the students (quote from the first interview).

And for coursework writing:

> Before they start their extensive writing, I say: 'Do your own planning. Planning goes before you start writing'. I aim to be explicit and show them the required levels of work. I also want them to see the improvement and progress for themselves. I take items from my store and give them to look at their work from the previous year and say what else they need to show this year. Then, I say: 'You can use this checklist. It must contain this point, this point', sort of, planning check, for them to see...(quote from the second interview).

In making the learning process transparent to students, Mr. King was committed to showing students their own progress in coursework over time, and thus helping them monitor their own work and develop meta-cognitive skills.

Differences between teachers in formative assessment practice

Evidence from this study has shown that there are two groups of teachers. One group (seven teachers) took for granted that their role was only to assess students' performance during the actual carrying out of the experiment and then mark students' coursework reports. Their help as educators should be limited. By adopting the examiner's role, they avoided supporting the learning process. One can see here how assessed coursework tasks like these can significantly interfere with normal classroom relations: talk, help, and feedback are very limited. Teachers refused to answer students' questions and distinguished between 'normal' teaching and coursework teaching. What is more worrying is that these seven teachers believed that the assessment regulations required them not to give students any help, even though the exam board regulations did not explicitly state this. Hence they did not make attempts to resolve the problem of the 'conflict' between the two roles. The exam board rules, as they thought, required teachers and students to behave differently from the way they would in normal lessons. This simply made teachers feel that what they were doing was good educational practice 'You've got to be a lot less helpful than you are usually prepared to be' (second interview). Consequently, by putting the exam regulations and, particularly, the criterion of 'fairness' first, they allowed their students to miss out on important learning experiences.

For a second group (two teachers: Mr. King and Mr. Smith), as clearly demonstrated in classroom observations and articulated in the interviews, assessment for learning and summative assessment *did* go together to support learning. That is, the same piece of students' work, here a coursework report, was made to serve formative and summative assessment purposes. Furthermore, for Mr. King, opportunities for self- and peer-assessment of coursework helped students to internalize and share assessment criteria and the expected quality of coursework.

WAYS FORWARD

Evidence from this study suggests that teaching and assessment of coursework need to re-focus on learning. Teaching is about helping students to improve. Furthermore, teaching by employing formative assessment practices is about good interactions, mainly by providing good quality feedback and opportunities for self- and peer-assessment. The balance between 'being fair' and providing the kind of feedback that leads students to improve should be a focus for considered attention and an issue of professional judgment for teachers. However, my research shows that this was often not the case.

One reason for this may be related to teachers' individual professional competence. It can be argued that making judgments about students' achievement and, subsequently, about how to support students to improve is an issue requiring professional judgment that has to be informed by teachers' subject knowledge and 'pedagogical content' knowledge (Shulman, 1986). Teachers' pedagogical content knowledge must be sufficiently developed so that they can be flexible in responding to students' understanding and emerging learning needs. This responsiveness makes teachers' decision making very demanding: 'To pitch feedback at the right level to stimulate and help is a delicate skill' (Black and Harrison, 2000, p. 38). Therefore, we need to train teachers so that they are confident and secure in their subject and pedagogical content knowledge. We need teachers competent and confident in their own professional judgments. A clear view of good quality coursework is one fundamental component of teachers' pedagogical content knowledge. It is also important that the quality of the expected attainment and the criteria for judging quality are communicated and shared with the learner so that the learning process is clear and transparent. Consequently, marking has to be based upon teacher's professional judgment in order to feed forward into students' current and future learning. That is, the formative function of feedback is not to measure, grade or level but to inform, support and develop learning.

A tension is clear between syllabus coverage and the need for the implementation of formative assessment practices in order to improve attainment. Mr. King was well aware of having to manage this tension:

> So, there is the awkward decision about: 'Do I devote more lesson time to covering a point that the vast majority of the class has not had opportunities to learn or move on to the next topic?'

Often teachers let students undertake the coursework, assess their work, and then do something else or move on to another module topic. Many teachers confine teaching to what is in the exams. They succumb to the pressure of achieving high marks in external exams and they sacrifice other educational considerations. Students may indeed achieve high marks but teachers do not question their own approaches and methods nor reflect on how students might be able to improve. Rather than developing a deeper understanding of science coursework, students learn to provide the desired products. One important reason why teaching is exam-led is that teachers must try to guarantee that their schools are maintaining good exam standards. In this way, assessment, at the school level, for the purposes of accountability and for the certification of student attainment, dominates teaching and learning. However, extensive research evidence has pointed out that assessment *for* learning can make an important contribution to raising achievement and school standards.

I would suggest that the tension between the two roles of the teacher can be resolved in the first instance by changes in departmental and school policies. This is important because it is unrealistic to expect or require teachers, in isolation, to develop formative initiatives alongside the summative testing aspects of their work. Policy needs to grow in ways that support teachers in employing formative assessment practices in the classroom. More widely, Black (2003) argues that the potential of classroom assessment to raise standards will never be fully realized unless the regimes of assessment for the purposes of accountability and certification of pupils are radically reformed. The current assessment regime favours public accountability. Partnership among policy-makers, teachers and researchers is needed in order to support teachers' professional judgment and place more importance and value on teachers' assessment. In the particular case of science coursework, we need a model of assessment that trusts and relies heavily on classroom-based teacher assessment. Firstly, an increase in the weighting of internal assessment and less emphasis on external exams is needed. Ideally, national exams would be gradually replaced by school-based teacher assessment.

However, it will be difficult for teachers to fulfil their challenging role unless they receive sufficient help and support. Teachers need support to cope with tensions between formative and summative assessment duties and their double role as instructors and assessors. With regard to the role of the teacher in teaching coursework, we might follow Black's (1990) suggestion that we have to give more weight to teachers' assessment of pupils' routine work in lessons. In his own words: '...it is ironic [that] the GCSE and its predecessors seem to command public and political confidence where newer approaches do not, and amazing that external SATs[1] are seen to command trust and support while teacher assessment has to fight for comfortable recognition' (p. 26). Black argued that teacher assessment demonstrates greater reliability than any other external test can achieve. Along the same lines, a recent publication by the National Research Council on Testing and Assessment in the United States reported: 'The balance of mandates and resources should be shifted from an emphasis on external forms of assessment to an increased emphasis on classroom formative assessment designed to assist learning' (Pellegrino et al., 2001, p. 310). If one considers the very nature of practical work in science, it can be argued that only teacher assessment can secure the validity of the examination. Achievement in experimental science cannot be effectively assessed by large-scale, external assessment. To assess students' writing skills and how coherently students present ideas in the lab report, one has to give more importance and value to the teacher assessment.

Based on the current discussion and a reading of the wider literature, I would suggest that further research must be conducted on the alignment between formative and summative assessment to throw more light onto the following questions:

- What support do teachers need to cope with the dual role as instructors and assessors of their own students' performance? What kinds of professional development and pre- and in-service training will be needed to help teachers fulfil this challenging role?
- How can we develop both formative and summative assessments in such a way that they support each other and enrich rather than distort good classroom learning?
- How can we, at the systems and policy level, bridge the gap between large-scale and classroom assessments, to create a system to support learning? (National Research Council, 2003).

ACKNOWLEDGMENTS

Thanks to the schools and teachers who participated in the study and gave freely of their time to meet and talk with me. I am grateful for this generous assistance. A special thanks to the editors for their patience and support and to the two anonymous reviewers.

NOTE

1. SATs are national Standard Assessment Tasks used to test students at key stages of their schooling.

REFERENCES

Allal, L. & Mottier Lopez, L. (2005). Formative assessment of learning: A review of publications in French. In J. Looney (Ed.), *Formative assessment. Improving learning in secondary classrooms*, 241–261. Paris: OCDE.

Allal, L. & Pelgrims Ducrey, G. (2000). Assessment of—or in—the zone of proximal development. *Learning and Instruction, 10*(2), 137–152.

Black, P. (1990). APU Science—The past and the future. *School Science Review,* 72(258), 13–28.

Black, P. (1998). *Testing: Friend or foe? Theory and practice of assessment and testing.* London: Falmer Press.

Black, P. (2003). The nature and value of formative assessment for learning. *Improving Schools, 6*(3), 7–22.

Black, P. & Harrison, C. (2000). Formative assessment. In M. Monk & J. Osborn (Eds.), *Good practice in science teaching. What research has to say,* 25–40. Buckingham: Open University Press.

Black, P., Harrison, C., Lee, C., Marshall, B., & Wiliam, D. (2003). *Assessment for learning: Putting it into practice.* Maidenhead: Open University Press.

Black, P., Harrison, C., Lee, C., Marshall, B., & Wiliam, D. (2004). Working inside the black box: Assessment for learning in the classroom. *Phi Delta Kappan,* September, 9–21.

Black, P. & Wiliam, D. (1998). Assessment and classroom learning. *Assessment in Education, 5*(1), 7–75.

Black, P. & Wiliam, D. (2003). 'In praise of educational research': Formative assessment. *British Educational Research Journal, 29*(5), 623–637.

Broadfoot, P. & Black, P. (2004). Redefining assessment? The first ten years of assessment in education. *Assessment in Education, 11*(1), 7–27.

Crooks, T. J. (1988). The impact of classroom evaluation practices on students. *Review of Educational Research, 58*(4), 438–481.

Gioka, O. (2004). *Formative assessment in teaching graphing skills in investigation lessons: A study of teachers' goals, strategies, assessment criteria and feedback.* Unpublished PhD thesis, London South Bank University.

Harlen, W. & Deakin Crick, R. (2002). *A systematic review of the impact of summative assessment and tests on students' motivation for learning.* Research Evidence in Education Library. London: EPPI-Centre Social Research Unit, Institute of Education.

National Research Council (2003). *Assessment in support of instruction and learning. Bridging the gap between large-scale and classroom assessment. Workshop Report.* Washington, D.C.: National Academy Press.

Natriello, G. (1987). The impact of evaluation processes on students. *Educational Psychologist, 22,* 155–175.

Pellegrino, J., Chudowsky, N., & Glaser, R. (2001). *Knowing what students know. The science and design of educational assessment.* Washington, D.C.: National Research Council/National Academy Press.

Sadler, D. (1989). Formative assessment and the design of instructional systems. *Instructional Science, 18,* 119–144.

Sadler, D. R. (1998). Formative assessment: Revisiting the territory. *Assessment in Education, 5*(1), 77–84.

Shavelson, R. J. (2003). *On the integration of formative assessment in teaching and learning with implications for teacher education.* For the Stanford Education Assessment Laboratory and the University of Hawaii Curriculum Research and Development Group. http:// www.stanford.edu/dept/SUSE/ SEAL [Accessed 29 June 2004,].

Shavelson, R. J., Black, P. J., Wiliam, D., & Coffey, J. (2002). *On linking formative and summative functions in the design of large-scale systems.* http:// www. stanford.edu/dept/SUSE/SEAL [Accessed 29 June 2004,].

Shulman, L. S. (1986). Those who understand: Knowledge growth in teaching. *Educational Researcher, 15*(2), 4–14.

Wiliam, D. (2003). Validity: All you need in assessment. *School Science Review,* *85*(311), 79–81.
Wiliam, D. & Black, D. (1996). Meanings and consequences: A basis for distinguishing formative and summative functions of assessment? *British Educational Research Journal, 22*(5), 537–548.

12 Changing assessment practices in Norwegian higher education
From where to where?

Per Lauvås

INTRODUCTION

Assessment in higher education was for many years an issue of little concern in Norway. Traditional examinations maintained their high status and prestige as the hallmark of quality. New legislation has recently changed the priorities and assessment has become a prime concern.

A national policy with modularized courses and close monitoring of student performance and progress is being introduced into a system that has been driven by final examinations. New assessments in addition to the final examinations and replacements for some examinations have to be implemented. The Ministry of Education has not been prescriptive but the intentions are clear:

> The Ministry finds that regular evaluations giving the students frequent feedback on the outcome of the learning process should be an integral part of the teaching process.... Evaluations during the study period can be organized in a number of ways such as homework, intermediate examinations, portfolio assessment and more. (St.meld. nr. 27, 2000–2001: 31)

This case study will highlight commonalities as well as peculiarities of one national system, and point to some key questions that have to be addressed today in many countries.

FROM WHERE? THE CONTEXT OF ASSESSMENT IN NORWEGIAN HIGHER EDUCATION

The external examiners: Rights and equity

The tradition of using external examiners can be traced back to the late 18th century. External examiners are mandatory for all examination elements. In case of any dispute between internal and external examiners, the latter have the final word. Until recently, the requirement to employ external examiners, enforced by law, has had a strong impact on all aspects of assessment. The system was based on the belief that it would maintain high academic standards and secure some basic rights for students by ensuring impartial assessment. Objectivity was emphasized, for example, by ensuring student anonymity. Students also had extensive rights to file complaints and to have such complaints handled rigorously. Standardisation was another key aspect. In examinations, students undertake the same tasks with the same time limit, the same aids, and so on. However, the system also meant that it was difficult to introduce new assessment methods. When project work was introduced after 1968, some examination methods were adapted to meet new demands, but it has not been easy to change, mainly because of the strong conviction that our traditional examinations were hallmarks of quality. Available options are highly restricted when external examiners have to be involved in all elements of summative assessment. Consequently, the higher educational system has, to a large degree, been driven by final examinations.

Modularisation of higher education: Assessment and attainment

At one time a standard examination unit occupied at least a semester, often a year or even more. The units have decreased in length over the years, and modularisation is part of recent higher education reforms. Partly this was deemed necessary for motivational purposes. In a system propelled by the final examination, problems with low levels of study activity had become prominent. Although highly motivated students worked steadily and diligently on their own throughout the semester, many students, it was believed, did not and therefore more frequent examinations associated with each module were thought necessary to ensure that the students would study longer and harder.

Whilst students may appear to be achieving more with the regular checks and requirements of module examinations, this is not necessarily the case when we scratch beneath the surface. Similar systems of continuous assessment have been in place for many years in secondary education, testing students frequently on small units of learning. The results that ought to be evident from this increased learning activity are not always as we would expect. For example, knowledge in mathematics among students entering higher education from school has been tested at regular intervals and there is now substantial documentation of a steady decline rather than an increase in attainment. Only just over half of beginning students in 2003 and 2004 produced the correct response to the following problem:

$$2.8 * \tfrac{3}{4} =$$

The latest report concluded that:

The level of mathematical knowledge and skills among entering students embarking upon the most mathematics-demanding studies is now approaching a critical level. (Rasch-Halvorsen & Johnsbråten, 2004, p. 46)

Reliability of assessment

Despite an apparently rigorous and high quality system based upon external examiners, there is evidence that, in some subject areas, the student's examination result depends as much on the judgments made by assessors as on the quality of the examination answers. The most frequently used marking scale, until recently, in Norway had 1.0 as the best mark and 4.0 as the pass mark with decimals in between; that is, a scale with 32 steps. In psychology, Raaheim (2000) obtained marks from seven independent assessors. Although the inter-rater reliability was acceptable as shown in Table 12.1, in seven cases out of 50, differences of 10 or more steps on the scale were found between two or more assessors.

The same student papers were then given to four 'super-assessors', carefully selected from the most experienced professors in the country. They were informed about all the marks suggested by the previous assessors and asked to offer their best opinion. Even among these assessors, large differences could be observed. Some individual students could have received quite different marks from different configurations of assessors as shown in Figure 12.2.

In the most extreme cases, a student could receive a mark between 1.8 and Fail when individual assessors were compared; from 2.7 to Fail amongst individual expert assessors; and between 2.8 and Fail when the marks awarded by pairs of assessors were compared.

TABLE 12.1 Inter-rater reliability, psychology (Raaheim, 2000)

	Inter-rater correlations and the final examination result						
	Ass. 1	Ass. 2	Ass. 3	Ass. 4	Ass. 5	Ass. 6	Ass. 7
Ass. 1	1.00						
Ass. 2	.778	1.00					
Ass. 3	.739	.649	1.00				
Ass. 4	.801	.827	.705	1.00			
Ass. 5	.832	.793	.721	.783	1.00		
Ass. 6	.910	.747	.700	.805	.789	1.00	
Ass. 7	.702	.742	.555	.789	.650	.774	1.00
Final	.905	.733	.880	.812	.822	.852	.665

Table 12.2 Range of marks between individual assessors, psychology (Raaheim, 2000)

	Marks given by individual assessors						
	Stud. 4	*Stud. 19*	*Stud. 26*	*Stud. 31*	*Stud. 35*	*Stud. 37*	*Stud. 48*
Ass. 1	2,8	3,0	2,8	fail	3,0	fail	2,6
Ass. 2	2,5	2,5	2,6	2,9	fail	3,4	1,8
Ass. 3	2,9	fail	fail	fail	3,6	fail	2,9
Ass. 4	2,8	2,8	2,7	3,2	2,9	2,8	2,0
Ass. 5	3,3	3,6	2,9	fail	fail	fail	2,9
Ass. 6	3,2	2,9	2,4	fail	3,0	3,6	2,9
Ass. 7	3,9	2,9	2,4	2,7	3,2	2,4	2,0
Final	2,8	fail	3,5	fail	3,3	fail	2,7

This study was conducted in the context of a high-stakes examination where marks are used to select the students to be admitted into the study program to become a psychologist. Such differences originating from the selection of assessors are difficult to defend to students, especially those who are not admitted. In the selection process, the cut-off point is specified to three digits. With an average mark of 2.07 a student could be admitted to the program, but not with 2.08.

Standards and validity

The traditional examination system has been regarded as upholding standards. We would therefore expect to see a high level of validity with the examinations testing the desired levels and quality of knowledge and understanding. In a Danish research study, Jakobsen and colleagues (1999) invited departments to take part in a study to test understanding by way of non-traditional assessment procedures and compare the results with the outcomes of ordinary examinations. The teachers who took part in the study were in full control of the process. They agreed on both the areas to be tested and the method of testing. An example from the non-traditional test, an item designed to test understanding of flow, is given in Figure 12.1.

In the examination the students were required to solve computational problems by applying the Bernoulli equation. In the test of understanding, they had to solve the problem above; that is, choose between three alternatives and explain in an interview why the selected alternative was considered the right one. The tabulation of marks from the two tests presents a disturbing picture; almost half of the students who passed the examination failed the test in understanding.

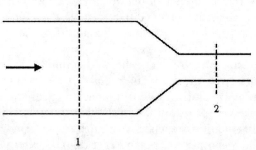

A horizontal pipe has a contraction as indicated in the figure. The flow from section 1 to section 2 is without friction. The pressure at the two sections is referred to as p_1 and p_2, respectively.

Indicate what should be expected (and substantiate the choice):

A: $p_1 > p_2$ B: $p_1 = p_2$ C: $p_1 = p_2$

Figure 12.1 Test item from a test of understanding (Jakobsen et al. 1999, p. 28)

The report made a distinction between understanding and calculation competence:

> In many cases students have received a high mark at the examination on the basis of calculations related to concepts and relationships of which they have a quite shallow understanding. In several cases,

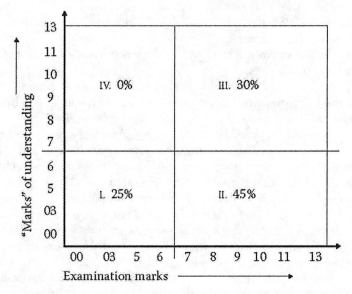

Figure 12.2 Understanding and examination results (Jakobsen et al. 1999, p. 34).

students were not capable of making an account of the physical significance of the elements included in a formula they applied in calculating
examination problems. (Jakobsen et al. 1999, p. 28)

Jakobsen's results may relate to the predictability of examinations; that
is, predictability from the students' point of view. Students seem to have
developed impressive skills in securing maximum predictability that enables them to prepare for examinations. When some specific manipulations
of the Bernoulli equation are what are needed to perform well in the examination, then the preparation is much easier than the alternatives. The problems given at the examination can be solved by analogy and do not really
require understanding. What else should the students do with an over-
crowded syllabus, as is often the case, other than to put pressure on their
teachers for high predictability? The higher the predictability, the easier it
is to prepare for the examination, but the shallower the understanding and
the quicker most of it is forgotten.

Assessment and motivation

The greater numbers of students entering higher education today is a fairly
recent development. It has highlighted some of the problems discussed
above which may have gone unnoticed in the former elitist system. Young
students are more heterogeneous than before and, for whatever reason, it
appears that many are not motivated to study hard. This perception has
been a factor in recent decisions about changes in assessment.

Poorly motivated students could be characterized as minimalists or
instrumentalists (Snyder, 1971; Ditcher & Hunter, 2000) with relatively
low ambitions, contrasted with the traditional image of the university student utterly and intrinsically motivated, happy to sit with his or her books
for long days and weeks.

However we find considerable variation and hidden potential amongst
these minimalist students, but this potential is not best developed by assessment systems that are based on pressure and fear of failure. These students
may be victims of previous educational provision and certainly do not need
more of what produced their minimalist strategy in the first place. It does
not normally work to try to 'save' a minimalist by force, by preaching, or
by appeals. Motivation is most often stimulated by becoming involved in
intriguing problems in a stimulating, often competitive environment, by
facing challenges instead of chores. Instead of more conventional examinations and tests, one way forward is to make examinations as 'authentic'
as possible; that is, to assess students' competencies in realistic settings,
not too far away from the situations where knowledge is applied. Unfortunately, it is well documented that the tendency inside educational institutions is such that exact, abstract knowledge not directly related to any

context of application is most often assessed, often in sharp contrast to what is valid outside the academy.

MAKING THE TRANSITION—TO WHERE?

In the recent changes to assessment we have attempted to diversify forms of summative assessment, rather than relying solely on conventional examinations. We have tried to increase the amount of formative assessment which research and experience shows is essential for learning. However, we have also introduced more continuous, that is, summative assessment. In too many cases, the final examinations have been kept and more assessment has been added (homework, intermediate tests, portfolio assessment). This approach is outlined in scenario 1 below. We are not always sure of how to maintain the ideals of equity and student rights alongside promoting learning and authenticity in assessment. In some way, we need to find a better balance and my second scenario could suggest ways towards this.

Scenario 1: Continuous assessment to replace, or complement, final examinations

Assessment may become a way of disciplining students and forcing them study from day one. We make students work by assigning them tasks to do. In continuous assessment there is no way the students can escape from the firm grip of the teacher. If the student does not comply with the requirements, he or she will not be allowed to continue. For example, a course may require a minimum number of tasks that have to be completed at specific deadlines and submitted to and accepted by the teacher. If the target is not met, the students are not allowed to sit the final examination. External examiners can be involved at all stages. Some of what is implemented in Norwegian higher education today as 'portfolio assessment', where students are given assignments to do, and the student's work is subjected to summative assessment all along, is also a kind of continuous assessment. Students will often put pressure on the teachers to have artefacts that are produced during the teaching and learning process accepted or even marked as soon they are 'finished'.

The continuous assessment alternative is obviously an attractive one, although it is demanding on teachers' and examiners' time. Continuous assessment is easily enforced. Students are familiar with it from secondary school and have developed adequate coping strategies. If it is not considered to be sufficiently controlled and perhaps prone to cheating, a final examination on top resolves the problem. We also maintain legitimacy by retaining examinations alongside other assessed tasks. Academic examinations retain high status, prestige, and support. As Broadfoot has put it, examinations are institutions:

No other assessment technique so far devised has so perfectly combined the two principal legitimating ideologies of industrial societies: the liberal democratic principle of fair competition and the belief in scientific progress. (1996, p. 33)

We may consider this continuous assessment/exam scenario in terms of the main functions of assessment identified by Gibbs (1998):

- Capturing student attention and effort.
- Generating appropriate learning activity.
- Providing feedback to the student.
- Allocating marks—to distinguish between students or to distinguish between classifications.
- Accountability—to demonstrate to outsiders that standards are satisfactory.

Continuous assessment is mostly intended to strengthen the first function—to make students work. It might also address the second function as well, depending upon the tasks assigned. But there is a great risk, however, that the learning activity that students find to be the best coping strategy when facing continuous summative assessment is the one we do not want to encourage, namely memorisation and regurgitation. A problem also lies with the third function. It is a rudimentary form of feedback to get a mark back or a piece of work accepted. In the short term, continuous assessment may seem to work well in higher education, since it provides power to the teacher throughout the teaching–learning process. It makes it possible to get students through, often with good marks. However, in the longer term, the picture could prove to be one of steady decline in quality of learning and attainment.

Scenario 2: Separate formative and summative assessment

It is tempting to combine formative and summative assessment under the umbrella of continuous assessment. But continuous assessment can squeeze formative assessment out of the teaching–learning interaction by adding even more intensive summative assessment than in a pure final examination system. Students' motivation to do more than cope may be lost and their legal rights will be greatly weakened. Summative assessment takes over and formative assessment is not supported. It is evident that formative assessment must be sheltered and fostered, yet this is difficult to do in practice.

There is a potential problem with student perceptions. When students face summative assessment, they know the rules of the game. When they are introduced to formative assessment, the message is not so straightforward and easily understood. Students may accept that they are being assessed in order to inform them about their present achievements and suggest how to improve. But if students doubt the purposes of formative assessment and believe that they are going to be judged, they are likely to face the assessment as if it is summative and fake as good as possible.

Students need to be convinced that assessment can be formative. They need to experience assessment as an essential part of their learning processes. They should experience the active support of formative assessment while they are learning and its usefulness in preparing for summative assessment. They should not feel that it is necessary to try to conceal their errors and weaknesses but instead get adequate assistance to identify them and correct them. In order to learn, errors are as significant as the correct answers. That is one of the advantages of genuine portfolio assessment.

In portfolio assessment students should produce and collect artefacts during the process of study. These will normally be objects of formative assessment so that the learning process is supported by feedback and so that quality can be improved. At a certain point in time, students are stopped from producing more artefacts. They may improve artefacts in the portfolio and finalize their products. They may also be given some choice over the selection of artefacts to be included. The production, building up, revision and improvement of the portfolio is supported by formative assessment. There is a 'summative free zone' that lasts until the portfolio is submitted or, in the case of electronic portfolios, 'the CD is burnt' as one teacher put it. And after that, the student is well prepared to enter the zone of summative assessment. In principle, the summative assessment of the portfolio can be handled in the traditional way with the same number of examiners, applying the same marking scale, with the same legal rights for student.

THE POWER OF FORMATIVE ASSESSMENT: A CASE STUDY

To illustrate one pathway towards our second scenario, a case study of mathematics in teacher education is described here. Mathematics is a problem, worldwide it seems. It is a subject that is in critical need of better teaching. A recent meta-study based on research from the last 15 years on the teaching of mathematics (Hart, 1999) concludes:

> The most compelling reason to do research on postsecondary mathematics teaching is because what we are doing in mathematics classrooms now is not working for the vast majority of students.

Colleagues teaching mathematics in the teacher education department experienced very bad examination results in 2002 and decided to make some changes to enhance formative assessment. It should be kept in mind that this group of students, in the very beginning of their teacher training, had a poor background in mathematics, and, perhaps even more significant, often strong negative feelings: 'It's simply something I do not understand'; 'This is simply out of reach for me—I will certainly fail, no matter what I do'. Yet the consequences of failing the mathematics course in the teacher training program are grim; failing mathematics means that teacher training cannot be completed.

The most significant change made to the program was introducing peer assessment (Maugesten & Lauvås, 2004). One (out of six) of the weekly teaching hours was dedicated to students correcting each other's problem sheets. The students were told that they were not required to arrive at the correct answer. What was required from them was that they, in writing, documented serious attempts to solve the problem. They had to put in writing what they had done, how they had been thinking, and what the stumbling block might be. If the written statement was accepted as a serious attempt, then the learner gained the right to have the correct solution explained to her or him. Students who did not bring along any solutions were given an hour off. It certainly did not turn out to be just a pleasant break. Students did not want to exclude themselves from a learning community that was deeply involved in conducting formative assessment, because they could see that a real opportunity to learn was lost. The results from this change were encouraging. The teachers decided to have the same type of final examination as before with the same external examiners to prevent any doubts being voiced about the maintenance of academic standards. The comparisons were stark:

2002: 54% failed, 2/3 of those who passed, received the lowest passing mark.[1]

2003: 15% failed, 1/5 of those who passed, received the lowest passing mark.

What became evident was the power of the propelling device, namely the formative assessment. Students who had given up before getting to the starting line, had to work on the mathematics problems. They were engaging in the type of learning activity most widely recognized as optimal in this subject and they received prompt feedback. They were able to document that they had mastered the week's problems or that they had undertaken serious work without mastery. Both alternatives were perfectly acceptable. The only thing they were not allowed to do was to do nothing. Almost all of the minimalists and the reluctant maths students were turned into serious learners who experienced progress that they did not anticipate. Students were required to learn, not by cramming over a brief period of time, but by engaging in steady, regular learning activity. They went through a learning process with access to formative assessment and were given the opportunity of preparing for the final examination without interference of summative assessment along the way. And the teachers did not have to pay the high price of having to correct piles of problem solutions!

CONCLUSIONS

Ten years from now, we will know what took over after the traditional final examinations ceased to completely dominate summative assessment. At the moment we have choices to make. We could increase the volume of summative assessment even more. If the final examinations are kept much the same with several additions such as tests, mid-term examinations, problems to be solved and included in a portfolio, to mention a few of the possibilities, there will hardly be any room for formative assessment at all. If formative assessment is practically ruled out of higher education, what then? Will teaching to the tests be the only way out?

My main concern is not to make the case to abolish examinations in the form of final tests nor to indicate that the traditional academic examinations are so outstanding that they should be protected from the zeal of eager reformists who would like destroy them. My main concern is to see that formative assessment is given a crucial role to play, as the 'engine' of the teaching–learning process and then design the summative assessment which does not work against this. The volume of summative assessment must be kept to a reasonable level. 'Summative free zones' must be established in which the students can learn, in part by making mistakes and learning from them instead of only concentrating on producing the correct answers.

NOTE

1. The recent reform of higher education in Norway also contained the implementation of a new marking scale. From the 32 steps of the most widely used scale, the scale used in the European Credit Transfer Scheme (ECT) with 5 pass marks (A–E) was adopted. Consequently, 2/3 of the students received an E in 2002.

REFERENCES

Black, P. (1998). *Testing: Friend or foe? Theory and practice of assessment and testing.* Master Class in Education Series. London: Falmer Press

Black, P. & Wiliam, D. (1998). Inside the black box: Raising standards through classroom assessment. *Phi Delta Kappa, 80*(2), 139–148.

Broadfoot, P. M. (1996). *Education, assessment and society.* Buckingham: Open University Press.

Ditcher, A. & Hunter, S. (2000). *The instrumentalist student: An increasing problem?* Educational Research & Advisory Unit, University of Canterbury, Christchurch, New Zealand.

Gibbs, G. (1998). *Improving teaching, learning and assessment.* http://www.chelt.ac.uk/gdn/conf/gibbs.htm.

Hart, L. C. (1999). The status of research on postsecondary mathematics education. *Journal of Excellence in College Teaching, 10*(2), 3–26.

168   *Per Lauvås*

Jakobsen, A., Rump, C., Clemmensen, T., & May, M. (1999). *Kvalitetsudvikling-sprosjektet "Faglig Sammenhæng." Hovedrapport.* CDM's skriftserie nr. 1, DTU.

Lauvås, P., Havnes, A., & Raaheim, A. (2000). Why this inertia in the development of better assessment methods? *Quality in Higher Education,* 6(1), 91–100.

Lauvås, P. & Jakobsen, A. (2002). *Exit eksamen – eller? Former for summativ evaluering i høgre utdanning.* Oslo: Cappelen Akademisk Forlag.

Maugesten, M. & Lauvås, P. (2004). *Bedre læring av matematikk ved enkle midler?* Rapport 2004: 6, Høgskolen i Østfold (http://fulltekst.bibsys.no/hiof/rapport/2004/hefte6–04.pdf).

Raaheim, A. (2000). En studie av inter-bedømmer reliabilitet ved eksamen på psykologi grunnfag (PS 101). *Tidsskrift for den norske psykologforening,* 37, 203–213.

Rasch-Halvorsen, A. & Jonsbråten, H. (2004). *Norsk Matematikkråds undersøkelse blant nye studenter høsten 2003.* Høgskolen i Telemark avd. EFL, Notodden.

Sadler, D. R. (1989). Formative assessment and the design of instructional systems. *Instructional Science, 18,* 119–144.

Snyder, B. (1971). *The hidden curriculum.* Cambridge, MA: MIT Press.

St.meld. nr. 27 (2000–2001). Gjør din plikt—Krev din rett. Kvalitetsreform av høyere utdanning.

Wiliam, D. (2000). *Integrating formative and summative functions of assessment.* Paper presented at Working Group 10, The International Congress on Mathematics Education, Makuhari, Tokyo.

13 Performance assessment in nursing education

Exploring different perspectives

Marieke H. S. B. Smits, Dominique M. A. Sluijsmans, and Wim M. G. Jochems

INTRODUCTION

This chapter presents research into performance assessment in nursing education. Our aim is to contribute to the effective implementation of performance assessment through a research study of the perceptions of the different stakeholders involved, chiefly, students, teachers, and professional practitioners. We specifically address varying perceptions of the utility and the consequential validity of the performance assessment and ways in which performance assessment be improved.

Performance assessment is an important component within the array of alternative or innovative assessment methods and strategies. The goal is to assess students in relation to realistic and relevant tasks. Performance assessments require students to apply what they know and can do in real-life situations and demonstrate competent professional behaviour (Gonczi, 1994). This approach fits the context of nursing education very well. The nursing profession is characterized by complex performances in which students must demonstrate combinations of several skills, such as coping with high responsibility, critical thinking in stressful situations, and conducting clinical procedures.

Performance assessments may be based on multiple products or processes; for example, written assignments, simulations, and work-samples. Perhaps most powerfully, they can be assessments where students are observed while they are performing realistic, relevant tasks. Although this approach presents some challenges, it enables students' levels of proficiency to be judged against predetermined standards of competent behaviour required in the world of practice, whilst they remain in an educational setting. This is particularly appropriate in initial professional education, especially in the early stages. In addition to evaluating students' performance, such assessments can be used to provide formative assessment, diagnosing the level of performance and supporting students with constructive, individualized, and ongoing feedback. Research evidence shows that these assessments *for* learning instead of only assessments *of* learning improve learning (Birenbaum, 2003) and enhance students' achievement (Black & Wiliam, 1998).

Research underlines that the outcomes and consequences of *students' and teachers' perceptions* can be an important guide to improving teaching and assessment practices in higher education (Sambell, McDowell, & Brown, 1997). Prior research on perceptions shows that alternative assessments, in comparison with more traditional methods, motivate students to engage in their learning and to approach it in different ways (Sambell & McDowell, 1998). Furthermore, teachers' perceptions of assessment influence their work as teachers. Those who focus on the role of assessment in professional development perceive a need for carefully planned, sustained, holistic development and wish to design relevant learning tasks (Aitken, 2000). Students' perceptions can indicate the extent to which performance assessments lead to high quality learning, active student participation, and offer feedback opportunities and meaningful tasks.

In perceptions research, *utility* and *consequential validity* are important issues. *Utility* implies that performance assessments focus on students' proficiency in performing complex tasks that have relevance in the professional working field. In relation to utility, the key question is whether students really experience the assessment and its tasks as meaningful and engaging, as is argued in literature (Hibbard & Michael, 1996). *Consequential validity* concerns the impacts of assessment on learning and teaching. This means that performance assessments should deliver evidence of positive effects on the curriculum, such as subsequent teaching and learning activities (Messick, 1994). The consequences of performance assessments in professional education are significant and for this reason it is important that evidence is gathered of the positive and negative effects of assessment on teaching and learning processes and outcomes (Messick, 1994).

TURNING PERFORMANCE ASSESSMENT INTO PRACTICE

In recent years, the professional nursing field in the Netherlands has signalled that students are not well equipped when they encounter real life situations in their work placements. In an attempt to improve the situation, a performance assessment program based around the core competency of 'nursing caretaker' has been established.

During the first seven months of training, in advance of the performance assessment, students followed five lecture courses, and undertook educational working group activities with peers, as well as assignments, consultations with simulated patients, and practical exercises in skills such as measuring blood pressure and giving an injection. All participants, including the simulated patients, received instruction about the purpose and the organisation of the performance assessment and their roles within it. The tasks were based on all the skills and knowledge that students should have acquired through the program. During the performance assessment, students demonstrated their professional behaviour in two performance tasks (glass boxes) and three assignments (black boxes) under time constraints. Glass-boxes were transparent, observable tasks in which students demonstrated their professional behaviour during consultations with patients. A checklist was used to enable teacher and peer assessors to observe and interpret students' behaviour and score their performance. Students had already worked with this checklist during previous course assignments. Black boxes were non-transparent, non-observable tasks resulting in written reports, assessed by teacher-assessors.

During the five-day performance assessment period, performance tasks and assignments were arranged in the order that would be encountered in the daily work activities of a professional in the nursing field. For practical reasons student groups had to be divided for some of the tasks. The arrangement of tasks was as follows:

Day 1: Anamnesis/problem, anamnesis/diagnosis

Glass box: intake consultation with a simulated patient (Group A=quarter of students)

Glass box: problem consultation with a simulated patient (Group B=quarter of students): Students had to read a written case before the consultation session

Task as peer-assessor (Group C=other half of students)

Black box: Written report on a diagnosis (All students)

Day 2: Nursing plan

Black box: Written nursing plan with intended interventions and actions (All students)

Glass box: Consultation with a simulated patient on this nursing plan (Group C)

Task as peer-assessor (Group A and B)

Day 3: Intervention plan

Black box: Written intervention plan with quality criteria prepared by the students themselves (All students)

Days 4 and 5: Conducting interventions

Glass box: Use of intervention plans in action with patients (All students)

Students were not only assessed during the performance assessment but they also had the role of peer-assessor during the glass box tasks. They had to evaluate the performance of their peers by filling in the scoring check-lists and by giving feedback on their peers' performance in the glass boxes. Teachers also filled in the scoring checklists and gave feedback at the end of the student's task performance. This meant that students received brief oral feedback from both of their assessors at the end of each glass box task. Teacher assessors also had to judge the assignments in the black boxes, such as the nursing and intervention plans, and they gave timely written feedback to students on these. Teachers also gave an overall judgement to the students at the end of the five-day performance assessment. Nursing professionals observed the demonstration of students' performance on the glass box tasks and did not formally assess the students.

   As part of the research study, at the end of the performance assessment, all participants were asked to fill out questionnaires. The students were also required to write their conclusions on the performance assessment in their portfolio in Blackboard (an electronic learning environment).

Research method

Participants

The case study included 50 first-year nursing students, 10 teachers from a Dutch Health Care Faculty, and 10 nursing professionals. The teachers gave lectures during the courses, coached students in education working groups, and gave comments and judgements on electronically-submitted student assignments. During the performance assessment their role was to assess students, to give feedback to them, and to determine whether they passed the performance assessment. Students had the role of peer-assessor and were required to score and to give feedback to their peers. Professionals from the nursing field occasionally gave lectures and brought their know-how from various nursing fields to the different courses. They were observers during the performance assessment.

Materials

To explore the experiences of students, teachers and professionals regarding the performance assessment, three questionnaires were designed: a *student questionnaire*, a *teacher questionnaire,* and a *nursing professional questionnaire.* In each of the questionnaires two clusters were central: firstly, the utility of performance assessment, in which the issues of acceptability and meaningfulness were addressed, and secondly, the consequences of performance assessment for learning and teaching. Means and standard deviations were calculated for all variables of the three questionnaires. Open questions were analyzed by categorizing the answers and by calculating the frequencies.

In the student questionnaire, the cluster 'utility' consisted of three variables:

- Clarity of the goal of performance assessment
- Being prepared for the performance assessment
- Meaningfulness of performance assessment

The cluster 'consequences' for teaching and learning consisted of five variables:

- Acquiring professional competency through performance assessment
- Influence of feedback on student learning
- Influence on the learning process as a whole
- Assessors' agreement about scoring
- Need for assessor training

The student questionnaire consisted of 62 items scored on a five-point Likert scale, varying from 'I totally disagree' to 'I totally agree'. The students could answer two open items giving comments and also suggestions for improvements. Because of very low reliability coefficients, the items of four variables, 25 items in total, were removed from the questionnaire. After a reliability analysis of the variables, 37 items remained. The clusters, variables, number of items, reliability coefficients and example items of the eight variables are presented in Table 13.1.

In the teacher questionnaire, the cluster 'utility' consisted of three variables:

- Clarity of the goal of performance assessment
- The content of the performance tasks
- The meaningfulness of performance assessment

The cluster 'consequences' on teaching and learning consisted of two variables:

- Skills in giving feedback
- Assessors' agreement on scoring.

The questionnaire consisted of 59 items, also using a five-point Likert scale. The same two open questions about improvement could be answered. Because of very low reliability coefficients, the items of three variables were removed from the questionnaire, 38 items in total. After a reliability analysis 21 items remained. The clusters, variables, number of items, reliability coefficients and example items of the five variables are presented in Table 13.2.

Table 13.1 Clusters, number of items, reliability coefficients, and example items of the student questionnaire

Variable	#	α	Example items
Cluster: Utility			
Clarity of the goal of the performance assessment	4	.63	The goal of the performance assessment is clear thanks to instructions and introductory lectures
Being prepared for performance assessment	3	.66	I did not know what to expect from the performance assessment
Meaningfulness of performance assessment	4	.65	Through the 'glass boxes' I am more aware of my strengths and weaknesses in my role as beginning nursing caretaker.
Cluster: Consequences			
Acquiring professional competency by performance assessment	11	.76	I am competent in carrying on a professional conversation with a patient
Influence on student learning of feedback received	3	.81	The feedback helped me to realise which skills I need to practice more
Influence of performance assessment on the learning process as a whole	5	.77	I have learned much about myself during this performance assessment
Assessors' agreement about scoring	3	.70	Often I disagree with my peer assessors
Need for assessor training	4	.75	I recommend practice in advance with scoring of students' performances

Table 13.2 Clusters, number of items, reliability coefficients, and example items of the teacher questionnaire

Variable	#	α	Example items
Cluster: Utility			
Clarity of the goal of the performance assessment	3	.77	The goal of the performance assessment is to identify if the student is ready for a traineeship
Content of the performance tasks	7	.67	The cases represent day-to-day nursing practice
Meaningfulness of the performance assessment	3	.91	This performance assessment is valuable for the curriculum
Cluster: Consequences			
The skill of giving feedback	5	.74	I am skilled in discussing the scoring list with the candidate
Assessors' agreement about scoring	3	.66	I often disagree with other assessors

In the nursing professional questionnaire, the cluster 'utility' consisted of four variables:

- The clarity of the goal of the performance assessment
- The content of performance tasks
- The meaningfulness of performance assessment
- Satisfaction with the organisation of the performance assessment.

The cluster 'consequences' on teaching and learning consisted of four variables:

- Giving feedback
- Students as peer assessors
- The need for assessor training
- Assessors' agreement on scoring

The questionnaire consisted of 42 items, using a five point Likert scale and the same two open items about improvement could be answered. Because of very low reliability coefficients, the items of two variables were removed from the questionnaire, 12 items in total. After an analysis of the reliability 30 items remained. The clusters, variables, number of items,

Table 13.3 Clusters, number of items, reliability coefficients, and example items of the nursing professional questionnaire

Variable	#	α	Example items
Cluster: Utility			
Clarity of the goal of the performance assessment	4	.64	The goal of the performance assessment is to identify if the student is ready for a traineeship
Content of the performance tasks	6	.59	The cases represent day-to-day nursing practice
Meaningfulness of the performance assessment	3	.76	This performance assessment is valuable for the curriculum
Satisfaction about the organisation of the performance assessment	3	.87	The performance assessment is well-organised
Cluster: Consequences			
Giving feedback	4	.72	Teachers give constructive feedback to candidates
Students as peer-assessor	4	.73	Students can function well as peer-assessor
The need for assessor training	3	.76	I think that assessor training is necessary
Assessors' agreement about scoring	3	.73	It is important that assessors score in the same way

reliability coefficients and example items of the eight variables are presented in Table 13.3.

As an additional means of gathering data on the performance assessment, two oral evaluation sessions were organized with teachers (N =10) and one session with the nursing professionals (N =5). The main questions during these sessions concerned their satisfaction, their critical comments, and their suggestions for improvement. Involving students in the evaluation sessions was not possible.

Questionnaire results

Utility of performance assessment

Students' perceptions

Table 13.4 presents the means and standard deviations of the variables that were measured with the student questionnaire.

In general the goal of performance assessment was relatively clear for students (M=3.34, SD=0.81). Results on the performance tasks provided information about the significance of the tasks for learning their role of beginning nursing caretaker (M=3.59, SD=0.73). Students were not very satisfied with the training for the performance assessment (M=2.71, SD=0.93).

Teachers' perceptions

Table 13.5 presents the means and standard deviations of the variables of the teacher questionnaire.

Table 13.4 Means and standard deviations of the student questionnaire

Variable	Mean	SD
Cluster: Utility		
Clarity of the goal of the performance assessment	3.34	0.81
Instruction preceding performance assessment	2.71	0.93
Meaningfulness of performance assessment	3.59	0.73
Cluster: Consequences		
Acquiring professional competency by performance assessment	3.79	0.48
Influence on student learning of feedback received	4.28	0.69
Influence on the learning process as a whole	3.66	0.73
Opinion on the need for assessor training	2.58	0.86
Opinion on assessors' agreement	1.85	0.79

Table 13.5 Means and standard deviations of the teacher questionnaire

Variable	Mean	SD
Cluster: Utility		
Clarity of the goal of the performance assessment	3.86	0.88
Content of the performance tasks	3.77	0.56
Meaningfulness of the performance assessment	4.43	0.67
Cluster: Consequences		
Skill of giving feedback	3.36	0.75
Assessors' agreement about scoring	4.04	0.81

Teachers perceived the performance assessment as meaningful (M=.43, SD=0.67).

The goal of the performance assessment was also clear to them (M=3.86, SD=0.88). In general, they agreed with the content of the performance tasks (M=3.77, SD=0.56). The findings gathered in the oral discussion evaluation sessions showed that teachers agreed that this performance assessment contributed positively to the curriculum of nursing education. In their view, the subject matter of the cases was representative of daily nursing practice. However, teachers also mentioned that they were not familiar with job content, which is crucial for the professional caretakers' approach, within all of the different nursing working fields.

Professionals' perceptions

Table 13.6 presents the means and standard deviations of the variables, measured by the professional questionnaire.

Table 13.6 Means and standard deviations on the nursing professional questionnaire

Variable	Mean	SD
Cluster: Utility		
Clarity of the goal of the performance assessment	4.41	0.54
Content of the performance tasks	3.55	0.60
Meaningfulness of the performance assessment	4.41	0.57
Satisfaction about the organisation of the performance assessment	2.90	0.90
Cluster: Consequences		
Giving feedback	3.43	0.83
Opinion about students as peer assessors	3.52	0.75
Need for assessor training	4.53	0.52
Assessors' agreement about scoring	3.33	0.91

In the questionnaire the professionals also confirmed the importance of the performance assessment for nursing education (M=4.41, SD=0.57). The professionals were convinced of the representativeness of the content of the performance tasks (M=3.55, SD=0.66). The goal of the performance assessment, presented as: 'preparing students to acquire skills as a beginning nursing professional' was clear to them (M=4.41, SD=0.54). They were not as satisfied about the organisation of the performance assessment (M=2.90, SD=0.90). During the oral evaluation session, the professionals were very enthusiastic about the realistic value of the cases and the role-play of the simulated patients.

Consequences of performance assessment

Students' perceptions

The students reported (see Table 13.4) a positive learning impact on the acquisition of competencies from the performance assessment (M=3.79, SD=0.48). They stressed the learning effect of feedback (M=4.28, SD=0.69). Positive consequences for their learning process as a whole were confirmed (M=3.66, SD=0.73). The low score on the variable 'assessors' agreement about scoring' (=teacher and peer assessor) (M=1.85, SD=0.79) indicated students' concerns on this aspect.

Teachers' perceptions

The teachers recognized (see Table 13.5) that agreement between assessors was important (M=4.04, SD=0.81). They also recognized that frequent practice is necessary to acquire the skill of giving feedback (M=3.36, SD=0.75).

Professionals' perceptions

The professionals (see Table 13.6) agreed that giving feedback is important (M=3.43, SD=0.83). They also agreed that students can learn a lot by acting as peer-assessors (M=3.52, SD=0.75). Assessors need training (M=4.53, SD=0.52) and they should be trying to reach consensus about scoring (M=3.33, SD=0.91).

Comments and suggestions

The field reports from the evaluation sessions with teachers and professionals and the open questions in the questionnaires yielded critical comments and suggestions for improvement.

Student comments

It is interesting to note that 12 of the 15 students that completed the open questions experienced the performance assessment as stressful and chaotic. Seven students experienced severe time pressure on the different performances tasks. Nine students indicated that the performance assessment could be better organized. Ten students reported that it took too long to receive feedback on their written assignments. Their suggestions for improvement were mainly focused on a better training for the assignments and about the use of the scoring checklist.

Teacher comments

Teachers' comments were that the time schedule was too tight and that cases should contain less information (four of five teachers). Five teachers suggested more consultation between assessors to get consistency in judgement.

Professionals' comments

Professionals suggested reconsidering the teachers' competencies. They considered that teachers needed more support in their coaching skills and feedback skills.

Balancing different perspectives: Implications and dilemmas

Our findings clearly indicate that all participants agreed about the utility of the performance assessment for nursing education. All participants thought that clear information about the goal and meaningfulness of the performance assessment was important. Professionals were especially positive about one aspect, namely 'preparing students to acquire skills as a beginning nursing professional'. This aspect seems consistent with the students' belief that this performance assessment provided them with information about their strengths and weaknesses in their caretaker role. This positive student response corresponds to earlier research findings (Sambell et al.1997) that students experience assessment as positive and fair, when it encourages them to apply knowledge to realistic contexts. This research has confirmed that the goals perceived by students consistently matched the purposes of the designers of this performance assessment.

Teachers valued the *content quality and content coverage* of the performance tasks. These perceptions match two components of validity evidence as recommended by Linn, Baker, and Dunbar (1991). Teachers agreed that the breadth of the professional nursing field is covered better by this kind of performance assessment task than by the former more traditional assessment. This seems to be a step forward in improving students' professional performance as nursing caretakers and corresponds with research of Tillema, Kessels, and Meyers (2000) who argue that success in enhancing students' performance is a significant value in performance assessment. Based on these findings, we conclude that all stakeholders have a positive perception of the *utility* of this performance assessment.

The participants also viewed positively the *consequences for learning and teaching*. In other words, the educational impact of this assessment (Van der Vleuten & Schuwirth, 2005) has been perceived positively. In their research, Sambell et al. (1997) also confirm high levels of consequential validity: students' beliefs are positive with respect to the effects of alternative assessment on their learning. The *focus on feedback* as a consequence was especially striking. Students emphasized the learning impacts of feedback. This is in line with several studies in the assessment field (Black & Wiliam, 1998; Topping, 2003) that also argue that assessments could lead to significant learning gains.

Alongside the positive perceptions of utility and consequential validity, two significant shortcomings of performance assessment were also raised. The first of these concerns teachers' lack of content knowledge of the different jobs within the professional nursing field, which could hinder the connection of professional practice with teaching based on lifelike, realistic performance tasks. Secondly, all participants recommended improving the organisation of the five-day performance assessment. This is in line with guidance from Mehrens et al. (1998, p. 20): 'Make certain that the student is not surprised, and hence confused, by the performance assessments' format'.

Our suggestions for improvement of this performance assessment are first that nursing professionals, teachers, and the students should consult each other more often. As part of this they should discuss professional topics in the field and the meaning of criteria for performance. The experience of the practising professionals would thus complement the expertise of the teachers. Attention should be especially focused on the skills of judging performance and of giving feedback. We recommend that students should be trained in peer assessor skills, because this has a positive effect on their learning results (Sluijsmans, 2002). This seems to be needed although students' questionnaire responses did not confirm that. From their perspective, it was important for assessors to agree about their scoring. A possible explanation is that being an assessor was a new role for students, which they would prefer to avoid. In particular, giving feedback to a peer who is a friend presents difficulties for them. They may also have not thought about the implications and consequences of this new role. Performance assessments also require feedback skills from teachers who should have the opportunity to acquire skills in rating and giving feedback. Kolk (2001) argues that each assessor should be trained thoroughly.

We recommend developing feedback and assessor training for teachers and students as an investment in performance assessment that could be highly effective. Guidelines for the content of such training could be based on research of Percival et al. (1994). According to Percival et al. (1994) assessor training programs should aim to assist participants to: (1) enhance the understanding of the competencies, processes, and issues related to their implementation; (2) become sensitized to competency-based assessment in the workplace; (3) develop skills in the use of competencies and (4) identify cues for the demonstration of competencies in a variety of practice settings. This training will be one of the main challenges for students, teachers, and professionals to balance the different perspectives and to reach more of a consensus. We have revealed the perceptions of different educational stakeholders on a new and important approach assessment. Performance assessment is perceived as a valuable innovation within the curriculum of nursing education. Implementing this assessment in nursing education is worthwhile and stimulates stakeholders to think about their new roles. All stakeholders are challenged to overcome the dilemmas and to find a balance amongst a variety of complex elements crucial to the success of performance assessment.

REFERENCES

Aitken, R. (2000). Teacher perceptions of the use and value of formative assessment in secondary English programmes. *Professional Development, 3,* 15–20.

Birenbaum, M. (2003). New insights into learning and teaching and their implications for assessment. In M. Segers, F. Dochy, & E. Cascallar (Eds.), *Optimising new modes of assessment: in search of qualities and standards,* 13–37. Dordrecht, the Netherlands: Kluwer Academic.

Black, P. & William, D. (1998). Inside the black box: Raising standards through classroom assessment. *Phi Delta Kappan, 80*(2), 139–148.

Gonczi, A. (1994). Competency based assessment in the professions in Australia. *Assessment in Education, 1,* 27–44.

Hibbard, K. M. & Michael, K. (1996). *A teacher's guide to performance-based learning and assessment.* Alexandria, VA: Association for Supervision and Curriculum Development.

Kolk, N. J. (2001). *Assessment centers, understanding and improving construct-related validity.* Amsterdam: Vrije Universiteit Amsterdam.

Linn, R. L., Baker, E., & Dunbar, S. B. (1991). Complex, performance-based assessment: Expectations and validation criteria. *Educational Researcher, 16,* 1–21.

Mehrens, W. A., Popham, W. J., & Ryan, J. M. (1998). How to prepare students for performance assessments. *Educational Measurement: Issues and Practice, 17,* 18–22.

Messick, S. (1994). The interplay of evidence and consequences in the validation of performance assessments. *Educational Researcher, 2,* 13–23.

Percival, E., Anderson, M., & Lawson, D. (1994). Assessing beginning level competencies: The first step in continuing education. *Journal of Continuing Education in Nursing, 25,* 139–142.

Sambell, K., McDowell, L., & Brown, S. (1997). But is it fair? An exploratory study of student perceptions of the consequential validity of assessment. *Studies in Educational Evaluation, 23,* 349–371.

Sambell, K. & McDowell, L. (1998). The construction of the hidden curriculum: Messages and meanings in the assessment of student learning. *Assessment and Evaluation in Higher Education, 23,* 391–402.

Sluijsmans, D. M. A., Brand-Gruwel, S., & van Merriënboer, J. J. G. (2002). Peer assessment training in teacher education: Effects on performance and perceptions. *Assessment and Evaluation in Higher Education, 27,* 443–454.

Tillema, H. H., Kessels, J. W. M., & Meijers, F. (2000). Competencies as building blocks for integrating assessment with instruction in vocational education: A case from the Netherlands. *Assessment and Evaluation in Higher education, 25,* 3, 265–277.

Topping, K. (2003). Self and peer assessment in school and university: Reliability, validity and utility. In M. Segers, F. Dochy, & E. Cascallar (Eds.), *Optimising new modes of assessment: In search of qualities and standards, 55–89.* Dordrecht, the Netherlands: Kluwer Academic.

Vleuten van der, C. P. M., & Schuwirth, L. W. T. (2005). Assessing professional competence: From methods to programs. *Medical Education, 39,* 309–317.

14 The challenge of assessing portfolios
In search of criteria

Kari Smith and Harm Tillema

RAISING STANDARDS IN PORTFOLIO APPRAISAL

Raising standards in the appraisal of portfolios is an issue of considerable importance (Shephard, 2000). A teaching portfolio for documentation
of professional competence is increasingly required as a regular condition
for certification (in pre-service teaching education as well as for advanced
teaching certificates). There is, however, less research on the assessors'
appraisal of portfolios and the judgmental processes involved, especially
with reference to explicit use of criteria and standards of quality (Burns,
1999; Smith & Tillema, 2001). There are questions about the criteria that
are applied, and the extent of agreement about the utilization of these criteria (Heilbronn et al., 2002).

The focus of the present study is the quality of portfolio appraisal in
actual assessment practices. The practice of appraisal and grading of portfolios and the actual criteria used are characterized by a wide a variety of
approaches (Winsor et al., 1999). In most cases portfolios are appraised
against some institutionally-based benchmark to judge quality or there is
even an assessor-based appraisal according to certain self-selected standards. Earlier studies (Wade & Yarbrough, 1996) show some initial reluctance on the part of teacher educators to maintain strict criteria in order
not to disrupt the process of competence development in their students.
They clearly recognize a dilemma between their positions as assessor and
mentor. Furthermore, our studies (Smith & Tillema, 1998, 2003) show
a current lack of explicitness in determining quality of portfolios due to
heavy reliance on context and circumstance in portfolio construction.

Despite this lack of agreement and explicitness regarding appraisal,
portfolios have been found to be a useful learning and professional development tool (Smith & Tillema, 2003; Shulman, 1998); and teachers' portfolios may document professional competence and certify accomplishments
(Campell et al., 1997; Tucker et al., 2002; Delandshere & Arens, 2001,
2003; Zuzowsky & Libman, 2002). The lack of clarity regarding appraisal
stems, in our view, precisely from the ambitious assumption that the same
portfolio can be used for learning (professional development) purposes and

summative assessment purposes (Snyder et al., 1998; Zeichner & Wray, 2000). This causes a conflict of interest and perspective for both the portfolio compiler who is required to be aware of external assessment criteria and standards when compiling the portfolio, and for the teacher educator as assessor who plays the dual role of being the supporter of a professional development process as well as the judge of the final portfolio product. This conflict may well affect the choice and use in practice of selected criteria in the appraisal of a portfolio. It is therefore, in our opinion, of major importance to examine the process of using appraisal criteria in greater depth to discover how criteria are determined, interpreted and applied in concrete evaluations of individual portfolios.

Given that portfolios need to document or provide evidence of the attainment of standards, criteria are used to direct the content required in a portfolio which then needs to be appraised against these criteria to determine its quality or worth. Marked differences and even disagreement are to be found as to what constitutes core content to be rated in the portfolio (Yinger & Hendricks Lee, 1998). We conducted an inventory of available Internet sites on teaching portfolios which indicated an enormous variety of content of criteria. Agreement on core issues to be rated in a professional portfolio would serve the interest of the valid appraisal of accomplishments both from an interventional and an accountability perspective (Cochran Smith & Fries, 2002). Moreover, agreed criteria would serve as prospective guidelines for teacher educators and their students when working with the portfolio, since they provide a focus for assessment.

The present study explores criteria used in the appraisal of portfolios by studying how the quality of a portfolio is established in the actual practices of teacher educators and by offering a typology of these different utilizations of criteria. Based on the likelihood of different types of criteria being used for evaluating the quality of portfolios we warn against an overly reductionist checkbox approach to appraisal. However, we also caution against a too holistic 'connoisseur' view on portfolio grading. We propose, as an alternative approach to portfolio appraisal, the process of auditing, as it allows and accounts for diversity of goals and contents, an essential principle for using portfolios in teacher education.

THE STUDY

The focus of this study is on criteria used for portfolio assessment of teaching practice in pre-service teacher education. The study consisted of three steps. Firstly, we explored conceptions with respect to criteria use in portfolio appraisal in teacher education programs, one in Israel and one in the Netherlands. We asked 35 teacher educators who act as regular assessors of their students' teaching portfolios to respond to a questionnaire gauging their perceptions.[1] Secondly, we conducted an Internet query on criteria lists used for portfolios appraisal. This inventory, in turn, was used to arrive at a typology of criteria use. This was used to develop a tool for determining the variety and scope of actual criteria use by assessors in teacher education.

Findings

Open inventory phase

Teacher educators as assessors of portfolios responded to the questionnaire items (data in Table 14.1) under three categories: the purpose of criteria, the process of utilizing criteria, and issues in measuring criteria levels.

Table 14.1 indicates that our participants' importance score was highest for criteria use related to the portfolio as a tool for self-development (4.37) and the lowest scores were for evaluation of a portfolio (2.74) and clarity in rating (2.51). More specifically, we found no large variation in scores under the purpose category, meaning all selected purposes are somehow

Table 14.1 Inventory of portfolio criteria use (5-point likert scale on importance)

		Mean
Purpose		3.84
	Supporting development	4.14
	Promoting learning	4.11
	Giving feedback	3.49
	Establishing actual level	3.83
	Documenting achievement	3.63
Process		3.39
	Self-development.	4.37
	Prior knowledge	3.37
	Reflection	3.71
	Evaluation	2.74
	Performance	3.11
	change of belief	3.00
	Certification	3.40
Quality of measurement		3.36
	Reliable measurement	3.11
	Valid measurement	3.57
	Clear criteria	2.51
	Authentic measurement	4.03
	Quality of evidence	3.60

relevant in appraisal. However, in the other two categories larger variation was found. The main issue of concern under the process of criteria use is determination of self-development or student growth (4.37). Under the category of measuring quality the most important issue is establishing student attainments in an authentic way (i.e., avoiding a check box approach) with a score of 4.03.

These labels signify the main issues and concerns in the assessors' perceptions of utilizing criteria while appraising individual portfolios. The findings indicate there may be a major dilemma present between, on the one hand, establishing performance levels for certification in a reliable way and, on the other hand, using the portfolio to support further development and learning of their students.

In search of criteria use on the Internet

As the assessors responding to our questionnaire indicated, there is no accepted approach or set of common and shared guidelines on how to evaluate a portfolio. Subsequently an Internet search was carried out under the terms: *portfolio evaluation, portfolio criteria*, and *portfolio standards*, to explore lists of criteria in use at institutes offering portfolios to their students. We collected and selected different sets of combined as well as separate criteria against which the portfolio is being judged or evaluated. Predominantly, our analysis showed that the portfolio is considered as a collection of performance outcomes and appraised by assessors (qualified or not) who rate the evidence presented on each criterion separately (i.e., in isolation). In its ultimate form, appraisal is performed as a checkbox procedure. A judgmental evaluation of the portfolio product is most typical, that is, after the portfolio has been handed in for grading its final presentation, not its progress or building of evidence, is scrutinized. This judgmental evaluation utilizes a wide variety of criteria such as: breadth of collected material, orderliness of presentation, or coverage of the topics that were stated in advance.

A typical list of criteria extracted from our Internet search is the following:

- Completeness of presentation
- Progress being made
- Clearness of evidence, transparency
- Coherence of evidence
- Level of explanation, reflection
- Opportunity to provide feedback
- Well- preparedness of material
- Relationship to standards set
- Variety in presentation and material
- Required entries included

Table 14.2 A typical example of a set of portfolio criteria

Your report will be evaluated on the basis of the following criteria:
The extent to which you have identified items (i.e., products or portions of products) that are appropriate indicators of specific competencies.
The quality of your description of how items in your portfolio (and/or your efforts in creating them) serve to demonstrate specific competencies.
The overall quality of your competency analysis report, in terms of organization, professional appearance, and writing style.
The overall quality of your print-based portfolio, in terms of organization and professional appearance.

Numerous examples can be found of sets of criteria for a judgmental evaluation of portfolios. A typical example would be: (taken from Instructional Systems Masters Comprehensive Examination—Florida State University).

What is most typical in using judgmental evaluative criteria is that they refer to the final portfolio product only and not to the attainment of objectives related to accomplished competences or performance. Criteria in use for this self-referencing can be found on the Internet, for example:

- Use of evidence is varied and well up-to-date
- The evidence can be easily validated
- The material is well organized

(for instance: http://www.ecu.edu.au/lsd/pd/uso/tlp.html)

This self-referencing even can be taken a step further when criteria refer only to the portfolio construction process. Examples found under the Internet address http://www.tlc.murdoch.edu.au/eddev/grants/awards/tables.html are:

- Does reflect workload
- Does reflect normal duties
- Uses disciplinary knowledge
- Justifies teaching

This judgmental self-referencing is especially to be found for electronic portfolios (for instance http://eportfolio.psu.edu.select/criteria.shtml) leading to criteria such as:

- Connects all evidence into an integrated whole
- Images are optimized for the web
- Appearance is clear and consistent

Towards a typology of criteria use

The practice of appraising and grading of the portfolio product seems to take on different forms and is conducted using a number of methods. Our

Table 14.3 Typology of different ways of criteria use

Criteria as judging evidence
• Common sense benchmarks
• Normative prescriptions for attained minimum levels
Criteria as rules of accountability
• Quality assurance (external reference)
• Account of approval (internal reference)
Criteria as critical appraisal
• Auditing the way purposes are reached
• Quality improvement (dimensions for development)

inventory of Internet sites showed a coloured palette offering diverse ways of establishing the quality of a portfolio. Ratings of both product and process, of content and procedure, of knowledge, action, and reflection were found, and these could be developmental or selective, integrative or piecemeal.

These different strands in the utilization of criteria to judge the quality of a portfolio can be distilled into distinct types, which make it easier to clarify different approaches to appraisal (see also Table 14.3 for an overview).

CRITERIA AS JUDGING EVIDENCE

In this case, the portfolio is viewed as a product, as a collection of materials presented to be rated and evaluated as such. The material presented is taken at face value without much consideration of its origination, the process of collection, or the purpose for which the portfolio was constructed. The rating of a portfolio is primarily a matter of connoisseurship (i.e. use of hidden, assessor dependent criteria).

Two variants can be distinguished with respect to criteria use:

Common sense benchmarks

The criteria applied in the overall rating of a portfolio are based on common sense notions of what seems to indicate the quality of the product, for example: Have sufficient materials been collected, how well is the collection presented, are enough entries filled with material?

For instance on the site under the following address, http://unr/edu/homepage/nbaird/eng11cbe/cberubric.htm, one of the evaluation criteria is:

The portfolio consistently informs, surprises, and delights the reader. Another site, http://www.bridgewater.edu/departments/pdp/pdp_evaluation.html, presents a portfolio evaluation form with 32 rubrics scored by faculty members who give points on a variety of issues such as:

- Student's personal voice
- Discussion of life goals
- Resumé and cover letter

Normative prescriptions

We can also find directive descriptions for minimum levels of attainment which present a second, more grounded level of criteria use. Here, benchmarks are specified with some norm or arbitrary standard; that is, competencies that need to be considered in the portfolio, or a specification of evidence for each entry. These normative criteria specify what is minimally to be included in the portfolio, sometimes at a detailed level, by specifying criteria areas, indicators, and rating scales.

Examples of the above are:

- Showing reflection by indicating 'quality of your description of *how* items in your portfolio (and/or your efforts in creating them) serve to demonstrate specific competencies'.
- Giving reflective comments, by indicating short-term goals, and interpreting one's own learning (i.e., by describing audience and purpose and so forth).

These criteria are rated as: lacking, satisfactory, or exemplary. (Taken from http://unr/edu/homepage/nbaird/eng11cbe/cberubric.htm, http://eportfolio.psu.edu/select/criteria.html)

CRITERIA AS RULES OF ACCOUNTABILITY

In this case, the portfolio is rated as a product against regulatory standards being set. Ultimately, criteria refer to performance assessment goals for which the portfolio has to provide evidence of attainment. These standards are specified beforehand, referring to the requirements of a program or a curriculum. Criteria are used to identify compliance with the admission levels set for professional certification (either for entry or retention in the profession).

Quality Assurance (external reference).

The criteria are specified with reference to external standards set by a certifying or selecting board or agency. They refer to content domains or performance levels relating to a professional level of functioning. For example under the address: www.tlc.murdoch.edu.au/eddev/grants/awards/tables.html we found specified required items of evidence, their detailed description, and validity criteria in different domains of teaching such as:

Demonstration of how teaching strategies improved student learning by:

- Developed student understanding of concepts,
- Justifying teaching,
- Developed learning plans,
- Communication with students,

Account of Approval (internal reference).

The selected criteria are inherent in a specified program or curriculum and refer to the specific attainment levels belonging to that program (i.e., in case of a learning course). They are used for grading achievements in that program. This often means that the criteria can be more specific and highly tailored to the purposes of the assessors. The intention is to make a judgement about passing or failing a course.

On the website http://www.ecu.edu.au/LDS/pd/uso/tlp.html we found that the site presents a specific and detailed framework of items which are relevant to demonstrate accomplishments:

- The extent to which set or advertised criteria are addressed
- The degree of understanding of common aims and principles
- The extent to which evidence can be validated

Criteria as Critical Appraisal

In this case, not only the portfolio product in itself is placed under scrutiny but also its contextual background, its origination, and its construction. The portfolio is regarded as an outcome of a process that serves to meet specified purposes. The construction of the portfolio within a specific setting, including the institutional constraints as well as the outcomes achieved, is scrutinized relative to the process of collection that has taken place. The portfolio is appraised in the light of the context in which it has been compiled. Again, two typical approaches to quality appraisal can be identified:

Auditing the way purposes are attained

Criteria are negotiated and constructed with regard to the purposes acknowledged and accepted by those involved in the appraisal process: both assessors and assessees. The constraints under which the portfolio was constructed are taken into account. This often leads to meta-criteria for auditing the portfolio construction; that is, having trust in the outcomes presented, credibility of evidence, groundedness of the materials, and unity of the product. These criteria are preferably negotiated before rather than after the collection process.

Quality improvement (dimensions for development)

Building on the previous strand, criteria now act as common and shared dimensions intended to incrementally improve the quality of the portfolio product; that is, the performance of its collector. Shared dimensions are extracted from the literature or professional debate on competence and could include, for instance, richness of content, compliance to standards, performance evidence, and growth in professional development.

Perspective and proposal

When we look at these last types of criteria used, it becomes clear that the appraisal of a portfolio is not only a matter of rating an artefact but is better viewed as evaluating a practice. It is a manner of assessment that has been established at a particular institution. Judgement of an individual portfolio product is always embedded in a specific practice (i.e., procedures that operate in context). Therefore, portfolio appraisal needs to fit these assessment practices, and this will structure, codify, regulate, and circumscribe individual cases of appraisal.

We could view this appraisal process in context as a form of *auditing*. Auditing (a term stemming from the world of financial accounting and budget control) scrutinising, monitoring what an investment contributed to outcomes, or in more sympathetic terms: What is being laid out in the portfolio, does it really show and give evidence of the attainment of goals that were set?

Auditing is basically a process of study and inquiry. Its main focus would be on evaluating the portfolio product relative to the way in which it was constructed (i.e., can the person who collected the portfolio defend or warrant its outcome?). The assessor is not so much a criteria box checker but more an enquirer, even detective, and investigator.

In evaluating assessment practices, an audit may serve as an instrument for determining the quality of procedures and instruments relative to their purpose (Herriot, 1989). An audit primarily indicates what improvements and modifications of an assessment procedure are needed (i.e., the portfolio) and may legitimize outcomes of portfolio use. Furthermore, an audit can scrutinize existing portfolio practices, as well as ascertain prospects for certification and licensing (Darling-Hammond & Snyder, 2000). In this respect, an audit combines an accountability perspective with an improvement perspective (Smith & Tillema, 1998).

Auditing the quality of assessment practices

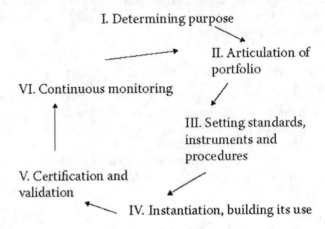

I. Determining purpose

II. Articulation of portfolio

VI. Continuous monitoring

III. Setting standards, instruments and procedures

V. Certification and validation

IV. Instantiation, building its use

Figure 14.1

An audit viewed as a specifically designed evaluation process does not consist merely of a measurement procedure, but is better being regarded as an encompassing and context sensitive process enquiring into the intentions, goals and perspectives, as well as the construction process, and the outcomes of assessment practices such as the portfolio. More specifically, the following steps constitute an audit process (Tillema, 2003) (see Figure 14.1).

1. Determining purpose: For the quality control of portfolio use, an audit must be closely aligned with the context and purpose for which the portfolio was constructed in order to ascertain its relevance. A key question in the audit would be: What does the portfolio as a product aim to accomplish for its users (collector, assessors)?
2. Articulation: The precise delineation of what a portfolio must contain implies both specification of scope and objectives as well as determining the specifics of the collection process itself e.g., being mandatory or voluntary, having open or closed entries, developmental or selective (Smith & Tillema, 2001). A key question in the audit would be: How does the portfolio construction process accomplish the goals and outcomes being set?
3. Setting of standards, instruments, and procedures: A precise description is needed for all stakeholders indicating what precisely is entailed in the portfolio construction and evaluation process, in order to warrant a lucid and transparent activity for both collector and evaluator. Therefore, taking into account the purpose and outcomes of a portfolio (that is, both previous aspects), an audit needs to determine the quality standards for executing and appraising the outcomes. The

central question here is: What standards will be used to determine and ascertain quality of the portfolio as a product and as a process?

4. Instantiation or the actual delivery and use of portfolio as a unitary process: The actual deployment of a portfolio as a practice (at an institute) needs to be carefully scrutinized to determine its fitness for purpose which is in fact a real auditing perspective. An in-depth look at the collection process, its procedures, and practices is required to establish the portfolio as an assessment tool *in use*. A key question would be: How does the portfolio practice evolve within its context and how is it actually deployed?

5. Certification and validation: Not only the conceptual underpinning of the portfolio practices is under scrutiny, but the consequential nature of a portfolio practice, whether for selection or development, needs to be recognized. Therefore, not only legitimization of procedures and instruments is required, but the portfolio practice needs to be publicly audited in order to avoid situations in which candidates may dispute the outcomes of appraisal. The central question and concern is: What is the knowledge base on which the portfolio as an assessment practice rests? This can be translated as: What has been revealed with regard to procedures and instruments used?

6. Continuous monitoring: As a practice the overall portfolio in use needs to be carefully checked in individual cases. Conducting the steps 1 to 5 in the audit may indicate how a portfolio practice operates at an institutional level. It then needs subsequently to be applied and maintained at an individual level, that is, for each specific portfolio which is being collected. Choices made concerning the assessment activity/product eventually require compliance with external standards set by the profession or certification boards. A key question in the audit would therefore be: Can the quality of the portfolio assessment practice be maintained, accredited/certified?

The purpose of such an audit process would be to determine the quality of a portfolio assessment practice as a whole, including its context, purpose, actual deployment in individual cases, and outcomes.

These questions relating to the quality criteria can be put into action through diverse means: observation of practices, questionnaires, and interviews of assessors and assessees, unobtrusive measurements such as consulting guidelines, regulations and written documents. All of these can highlight substantial and relevant information on the key questions. This makes an audit of a portfolio more like an investigative review than a judgmental evaluation. The ultimate aim is reaching a soundly-based decision about the attainment of goals set for the portfolio. We believe an audit, thus conceived, can easily transform or evolve into a consultation for improvement or development of portfolio goals (i.e., the highest level of criteria use as explained above).

An appraisal approach based on the concept of auditing can be beneficial to teacher education at an institutional as well as at the individual teacher/student level. The institution, when engaging in a discussion on how to implement a portfolio as a learning and appraisal tool in the program, can structure the discussion according to the questions raised in the above six steps. The aim of the discussion is that the staff involved agree on the main structure of portfolio use and its appraisal, and are therefore able to convey transparency to all stakeholders, and foremost to the students. The discussion process itself is likely to initiate a professional development process for the staff as a whole and moreover, for the individual teacher educator. Another main benefit of the auditing process outlined is the support it gives to careful scrutiny and inquiry of actual practices in portfolio collection and grading. In this way continuous monitoring and improvement of the utilization of portfolios in an institution is made possible.

On the individual level there are benefits as well. When teacher educators have clarified the use of portfolios at an institutional level, they are better prepared to be clear in conveying messages during face-to-face meetings with individual students (which is part of the auditing process) and assist the students in setting their personal goals with the portfolio. This makes the process of collection and appraisal more transparent and open to scrutiny. The audit process is individual, and at the same time it aligns with standards required by the institution and beyond.

NOTE

1. The empirical data belonging to this first part of the study are more extensively reported in Smith and Tillema (in press).

REFERENCES

Burns, C. W. (1999). Teaching portfolio and the evaluation of teaching in higher education: Confident claims, questionable research support. *Studies in Educational Evaluation, 25*, 131–142.

Campell, D. M., Cignetti, P. B., Melenyzer, B. J., Nettles, D. H., & Wyman, R. M. (1997). *How to develop a professional portfolio—A manual for teachers.* Needham Heights, MA: Allyn & Bacon.

Cochran-Smith, M. & Fries, M. K. (2002). The discourse of reform in teacher education: extending the dialogue. *Educational Researcher, 31*(6), 26–28.

Darling-Hammond, L. (2000). Teacher quality and student achievement: A review of state policy evidence. *Education Policy Analysis Archives, 8*(1), (http://www.epaa.edu)

Darling-Hammond, L. & Snyder, J. (2000). Authentic assessment of teaching in context. *Teaching and Teacher Education, 16*, 523–545.

Delandshere, G. & Arens, S. A. (2001). Representations of teaching and standard-based reform: Are we closing the debate about teacher education? *Teaching and Teacher Education, 17*, 547–566.

Delandshere, G. & Arens, S. A. (2003). Examining the quality of the evidence in preservice teacher portfolios. *Journal of Teacher Education, 54*(1), 57–73.

Heilbronn, R., Jones, C., Bubb, S., & Totterdell, M. (2002). School based induction tutors, a challenging role. *School leadership and Management, 22*(4), 34–45.

Herriot, P. (1989). *Assessment and selection in organizations: Methods and practice for recruitment and appraisal.* Chichester, UK: John Wiley.

Shephard. L. (2000). The role of assessment in a learning culture. *Educational Researcher, 29*(7), 4–15.

Shulman, L. S. (1998). Teacher portfolios: A theoretical activity. In N. Lyons (Ed.), *With portfolio in hand: Validating the new teacher professionalism.* New York: Teachers College Press, 23–37.

Smith, K. & Tillema, H. (1998). Evaluating portfolio use as a learning tool for professionals. *Scandinavian Journal of Educational Research, 41*(2), 193–205.

Smith, K. & Tillema, H. (2001). Long-term influences of portfolios on professional development. *Scandinavian Journal of Educational Research, 45*(2), 183–203.

Smith, K. & Tillema, H. (2003). Clarifying different types of portfolio use. *Assessment & Evaluation in Higher Education, 26*(6), 625–648.

Smith, K. & Tillema, H. H. (in press). Portfolio assessment, in search of criteria. *Teaching & Teacher Education.*

Snyder, J., Lippincott, A., & Bower, D. (1998). The inherent tensions in the multiple uses of portfolios in teacher education. *Teacher Education Quarterly, 25*(1), 45–60.

Tillema, H. H. (2003). Auditing assessment practices: Establishing quality criteria in the appraisal of competencies in organisations. *International Journal of Human Resource Development and Management, 3*(4), 359–369.

Tucker, P. D., Stronge, J. H., & Gareis, C. R. (2002). *Handbook on teacher portfolios for evaluation and professional development.* New York: Eye on Education.

Wade, R. C. & Yarbrough, D. B. (1996). Portfolios: A tool for reflective thinking in teacher education. *Teaching and Teacher Education, 12*(1), 63–79.

Winsor, P., Butt, R. L., & Reeves, H. (1999). Portraying professional development in pre-service teacher education. *Teachers & Teaching, 5*(1), 59–33.

Yinger, R. & Hendrikcs-Lee, M. (1998). Professional development standards as a new context for professional development in the US. *Teachers and Teaching, 4*(2), 273–299.

Zeichner, K. & Wray, S. (2000). The teaching portfolio in US teacher education programs: What we know and what we need to know. *Teaching and Teacher Education, 17*, 613–621.

Zuzowsky, R. & Libman, Z. (2002). *Standards of teaching performance and teacher tests; Where do they lead us?* Paper presented at ATEE conference Warsaw, August.

15 A workplace perspective on school assessment[1]

Steinar Kvale

When introducing new modes of assessment in school in order to enhance learning, it is worthwhile to take into account modes of assessment that facilitate learning in apprenticeship training. What today may be announced as significant innovations in assessment for learning in school—such as feedback, formative assessment, peer assessment, and self-assessment—have been key parts of apprentice training in European crafts since medieval times. The introduction of new modes of assessment in schools, in line with principles of modern learning psychology, tends to run into a series of dilemmas, which will be highlighted here by addressing assessment for learning within the institutional practices of the workplace and the educational system. The societal functions of assessment for selection, for disciplining, and for learning, differ markedly within apprenticeships and schools. The dominant roles of selection and disciplining in school assessments provide major obstacles to the implementation of new modes of assessment to facilitate student learning.

LEARNING THROUGH ASSESSMENT OF PRACTICE

In this section some key forms of assessment in apprenticeship training will be outlined. They are taken from a research project on learning in the Danish dual system of vocational training, where the students alternate between the workplace and vocational school (Nielsen & Kvale, 2003). On the basis of field observations, interviews and questionnaires to vocational students, and inspired by situated learning theory (Lave & Wenger, 1991), we have depicted the workplace as a landscape of learning, emphasising learning in communities of practice, learning as a quest for identity, learning through practice, and the emphasis in this chapter, learning through assessment (Nielsen & Kvale, 1997, 2005). We also draw upon Becker's (1972) comparison of apprenticeship learning and school learning.

Assessment in apprenticeship training is commonly associated with the ceremonial and strict summative assessment of the apprentice's final test piece that will enable him or her to become a journeyman. In the present

Table 15.1 **Assessment in apprenticeship training**

Forms of workplace assessment	*Concepts from assessment literature*
Assessment in relation to goals	Goal transparency and self-assessment
Assessment in relation to models	Goal transparency and self-assessment
Assessment through use	Performance assessment and authentic assessment
Assessment by users	Authentic assessment
Assessment by colleagues	Peer assessment
'Straight talk'	
Assessment without words	
Assessment responsibility	Self-assessment
Assessment through increased responsibility	Reinforcement by access to more complex tasks

chapter the focus is on the multiple forms of on-the-job assessment, which may be so integrated in the daily work activities that they are barely noticed. In Table 15.1 some key forms of assessment in apprenticeship training, to be described below, are depicted in the left column, and in the right column corresponding concepts from the assessment literature are indicated.

Assessment in relation to clear goals

The goals of workplace learning tend to be rather transparent, allowing for a significant amount of self-assessment. With clear learning goals the apprentices may themselves assess how their products relate to the quality standards of their trade. With this high level of goal transparency in the workplace, during their training period the apprentices become gradually capable of assessing their professional skills. Subsequently, self-assessment becomes dominant in their working life.

Assessment in relation to models

Journeymen and masters embody in their work the standards and values of the craft that the apprentices identify with and aspire to join. In the daily work in the craft shop, the comparison between the quality of the master's work and that of the apprentice may be so obvious that assessment from others is superfluous. The performances of the novice apprentice are in this sense self-scoring and self-interpretative.

Assessment through use

The quality of the work of the apprentices is assessed by the use of their products. A use-assessment involves a judgement of the products in terms of their usefulness—does the joiner apprentice's table stand steady or does it rock? Are the tiles even? Does the apprentice's bread rise? These types of assessments are made instantly as an integrated part of the work process. In workplace assessment 'the proof of the pudding is in the eating'.

Assessment by users

The assessment of the apprentice's work may also come as a user-assessment from customers—are the baker apprentice's cookies sold during the day? The customers' purchases of the apprentice's cakes are here an indicator of the quality of his or her products. The amount and kind of leftovers at a restaurant provides feedback to the apprentice cook of the quality of his or her puddings.

Assessment by colleagues

The work of a novice apprentice is frequently checked with respect to the quality standards of the trade. Professional assessments are part of the social structure in a workplace, where the apprentice often spends substantial parts of his or her training with a journeyman, who constantly keeps an eye on the quality of the apprentice's production. Whereas the master may often be absent from the workshop floor, the daily assessments will come from the journeyman and also from the older apprentices.

'Straight talk'

Direct and rough talk is common at many workplaces, with rather clear assessments, where the message cannot be mistaken. A scolding by the master may leave a lasting impression. If the baker's apprentice forgets to add sugar to the dough, the reproach from the master or journeyman will soon come, or, still worse, there will be a complaint from a customer.

Assessment without words

Explicit verbal assessments are rare in the workplace. Assessment of a piece of work tends to be expressed in a few words, mumbled asides, and grumbles, and in an occasional rebuke. Assessments in body language are frequent—nods, frowns or smiles. Tacit assessment, as an absence of direct verbal assessment, may also be an important assessment; the following statement covers the opinion of quite a few apprentices: 'The master did not say anything, so it must be OK'.

Assessment responsibility

The apprentice is, to a large extent, responsible for the assessment of his or her work. Learning and assessment are very much left to the initiative of the apprentices: 'The learner here makes his own curriculum' (Becker, 1972, p. 96). By placing the process of assessment in the midst of the work setting, it becomes possible for the learners to test their performances at any time they feel ready, and to repeat the testing until a satisfactory quality has been attained. The good apprentices seek occasions for learning and being tested in their daily practice. They themselves test whether they have mastered a new task and ask more experienced colleagues to test them by giving them more demanding tasks.

Assessment through increased responsibility

A significant type of apprenticeship assessment may take place with hardly any verbal comments on the tasks performed, namely by assigning the apprentice to tasks that demand greater responsibility. Wilbrandt (2003) has depicted workplace assessment as a ladder of tasks with increasing responsibility. Recognition for a job well done is indicated when moving the apprentice to more difficult and significant parts of the work process. In particular, a request to perform a repair job alone outside the workshop reinforces the apprentice's identity as a craftsperson.

We may conclude that apprentices learn their trade through continuous on-the-job evaluations in an assessment-dense workplace with multiple overlapping "back up" assessments such as feedback from the products, colleagues, users, and through advancement to more demanding work tasks. We further note that such formative performance assessments are not confined to apprenticeships in the manual crafts, but are found more broadly, in particular in elite training, such as in the apprenticeships of Nobel laureates in the natural sciences (Kvale, 1997) and in musical apprenticeships (Nielsen, 1999).

PRACTICE ASSESSMENT FROM THE
PERSPECTIVE OF LEARNING PSYCHOLOGY

The forms of assessment in apprenticeship training are in line with key principles for efficient learning derived from modern psychology of learning. These address chiefly the role of feedback, goal transparency, intrinsic motivation, and also key aspects of programmed learning.

Feedback

Within learning psychology it is a well-established phenomenon that feedback furthers learning: 'the simple principle that knowledge of results facilitates learning is one of the few generalisations clearly supported by the research on college teaching' (McKeachie, 1962, p. 349). The more immediate and precise the feedback is, the stronger the facilitation of learning. In apprenticeship training the learners receive more or less immediate feedback on their performances, such as whether the product can be used, or by comments from colleagues on the quality of the performance.

Goal transparency

The more visible a goal of learning is, the better opportunities for learning. An educational researcher, Bloom (1971), has even postulated that if the learning goals in school are made sufficiently transparent, and the learners are given sufficient time to work towards the goals, 90% of the pupils will be able to fulfil the learning goals in school. In a craft shop, the work processes and products of the master and the journeymen tend to be directly visible. They act as models, giving ample opportunity for the apprentices to evaluate their own performances in relation to the quality standards of their trade.

Intrinsic motivation for learning

Within the psychology of learning an intrinsic learning motivation has long been recognized as superior to extrinsic forms of motivation, such as learning for grades or money: 'Whenever possible, it is advantageous to use goals that are intrinsically related to the learning task' (Hilgard et al., 1975, p. 261). The assessments throughout an apprenticeship refer to goals that are intrinsic to mastering the trade. Apprenticeship training involves an authentic assessment. The performances which are assessed are appropriate, meaningful and significant tasks of the able craftsman or craftswoman of a trade.

Programmed learning

Knowledge of results of performances, or feedback, is important in reinforcing learning. It is rather striking how the three principles Skinner (1978) outlines for programmed instruction are in line with learning and assessment in apprenticeships:

1. The student moves at his own pace.
2. The student 'should respond, and his responses should be immediately evaluated so that successful responses will be reinforced'.
3. The student should move through the material in such a way that what he has just learned helps him to take the next step. Signs of increasing power are important reinforcers. Reinforcement will be maximized if he masters each stage before moving on (1978, p. 156–157).

The apprentice learns at his own pace, receives more or less immediate reinforcement on his performances, and the access to more complex stages is contingent on mastery of simpler stages. There is a task ladder of increased responsibility (Wilbrandt, 2003).

DILEMMAS OF WORKPLACE ASSESSMENT

This short overview documents key forms of apprenticeship assessments, which have existed in Europe since medieval times and which we can still observe today in workplace settings in vocational training. They are firmly in line with general principles from modern learning psychology for fostering learning. There may, however, be important institutional barriers to the formative use of assessment in work-based learning. The rough culture at some workplaces, with occasional abuse and hazing, in particular of novice apprentices, may be for some too intimidating to promote learning. The apprentices may be exploited as cheap labour, assigned to the same peripheral and repetitive tasks, with little opportunity to observe the work of more experienced colleagues and few occasions for the apprentices to test their competences in a broad variety of the skills of the craft. The craft associations and guilds do not only serve the purpose of securing the standards of a craft, but also serve to protect the members' vested interests by restrictive criteria for admission to a craft (Black, 1984).

Today, traditional apprenticeship training is threatened from two directions. With a rationalisation of production in many workplaces, involving strong specialisation and time pressure, reinforced by piece-rate work, there may be little time and opportunity to perform a wide variety of the trade's tasks and little time for the journeymen to give ample feedback on apprentices' performances. There is also an increasing absorption of vocational training into the 'mainstream' educational system, with reduction in the workplace period and introduction of external formal grading of the apprentices' technical and social on-the-job performances (Tanggaard, 2005). We may, though, still conclude that within appropriate institutional settings, apprenticeship forms of assessment may be a strong force in promoting effective learning.

SCHOOL ASSESSMENT FROM A WORKPLACE PERSPECTIVE

When compared with the abundance of assessment resources in workplace apprenticeships, the traditional school setting appears to be a feedback-impoverished learning environment. Current assessment reformers have been struck by the minor role that facilitation of learning plays in the assessment practices of institutions of higher education (Falchikov and Boud, chapter 7). Becker (1972) remarked that while students want to know whether they have learned something as they proceed through the curriculum, the school often fails to tell them whether their understanding is correct and their skills adequate. In Denmark today university students frequently complain that they rarely receive any feedback, beyond a grade, on their learning performance, and if they do, the feedback may arrive a long time after their performance and be too vague to be useful.

The use of assessment to promote learning in school may today even be presented as 'new insights into learning and teaching' (Birenbaum, 2003). The use of assessment as a tool for learning is regarded as a fundamental change in views on assessment, where:

> Aligning assessment, learning and instruction can be seen as one of the most important issues in educational innovation in recent years. Certainly, this goes down to the initiatives at classroom level, such as planned feedback, implementation of peer-assessment and increased responsibility of students (Dochy et al., 2004, p. 4).

However, we may note in passing that recognition of assessment as a tool for learning is not new within educational settings. A report to the Oxford commissioners of examination reform in 1852 stated that 'Examinations...might be made most important adjuncts in promoting habits of...self-instruction, voluntary labour, and self-examination' (quoted from Cox, 1967). What has changed is our understanding of how effective learning can be promoted. In this context it may be helpful to discuss whether some of the abundant assessment resources of the workplace landscape of learning assessment can be transferred to schools. Could the transfer of some workplace practices inspire learning environments where learning and assessment are integrated?

The following discussion will be somewhat speculative. Our study of vocational learning in Denmark investigated learning in the workplace and not in the vocational school settings. Research on assessments as a means of promoting learning in school practice has been limited in comparison with the extensive psychometric studies of the reliability of school assessments for certification and selection purposes, and the multiple psychological studies of test anxiety. Some field studies and interview investigations of school assessment have shown disciplining and competition as the *students'* predominant perspective on school assessment (e.g. Becker et al., 1968; Kvale, 1980). Becker et al. report that of their 1,100 field observations, 93% indicated that the grade point average was the students' key learning goal at an American college.

The new modes of assessment for learning in schools are in several instances close to traditional forms of apprenticeship assessment as pictured in Table 15.1. Regarding *visible learning goals*, educational reforms emphasize transparent curricular goals to facilitate learning. Resnick and Klopfer (1989) have attempted to transfer forms of apprenticeship learning to the classroom, such as the teacher being a model and making visible the tasks to be learned. When it comes to *models for learning* it is, however, difficult for one teacher in a large classroom to match the multiple models—master, journeyman, and older apprentices—of the small workshop and the personal relations with a few apprentices.

As regards assessment by *practical use* and *by users* of the products and services of the apprentices, schools have attempted to mirror this through authentic evaluation with, for example, portfolio assessments. While approximating real life settings, there is also the possibility that such authentic evaluations remain 'as if' replications in schools of activities which, in apprenticeships, have real consequences for the workplace. When conducted in contexts of grading, the exchange value of the authentic school assessment practices in terms of grades may dominate the use value of the activities for learning.

Concerning *assessment by colleagues,* school assessment remains the domain of the teacher, without colleagues at different levels of competence to provide feedback. The other pupils in class at the same age level are formally at an equal stage of competence. In general, competition among pupils, enhanced by a grading of pupils relative to each other, does not further a helpful contribution to assessment of the learning of other pupils.

Assessment without words and as *straight talk* is also found in the classroom, though probably with more emphasis on verbalisation in the classroom, and today there is likely to be more soft talk than straight talk. Vocational pupils notice the differences between gentle and often vague feedback from the schoolteachers and the direct, personal, and sometimes rough feedback from the master in the workplace. Furthermore, they tend to prefer the straight talk at the workplace (Tanggaard & Elmholdt, 2003).

Assessment responsibility of the apprentices and *assessment through increased responsibility* are important in the workplace. The first is difficult to transfer to the classroom, where the dominating assessment by grades remains the responsibility of the teacher, assisted by externally provided tests. The second, assessment by assigning demanding tasks of real importance to the production process, is difficult to administer in a school setting separated from work.

We conclude that while some assessment forms may be transferred from the workplace to the classroom, important forms of assessments to facilitate learning are difficult to transfer to educational institutions.

DIFFERENCES BETWEEN WORKPLACE AND SCHOOL AS LEARNING ARENAS

Apprenticeships and schools involve rather different institutional practices. The root meaning of school as 'free of work' may caution any attempts at direct transfer to school of assessment practices from apprenticeships, where learning takes place as a side effect of participating in work activities. In the workplace, practical knowing is transmitted; in school theoretical knowledge is more often conveyed. In the former, learning by doing prevails, while in the latter learning by verbalisation dominates. The ratio of students to a teacher in school is also much higher than in apprenticeships, where there is a limit of about six apprentices to a master. This allows for a closer personal interaction and individual supervision.

Before turning to some of the institutional differences between the workplace and school, we may consider student preferences for the two learning arenas. It is striking how strongly students in vocational training prefer learning their trade in the workplace to learning in school. This is found in spite of the often rough tone at many workplaces, with occasional hazing and abuse. Student preferences remain strong in the face of current critiques of employer exploitation of apprentices as cheap labour, and the fact that masters and journeymen seldom have any educational training. In a questionnaire to Danish vocational students, a marked majority preferred learning their craft at work rather than in vocational school (Nielsen, 2003). In a corresponding Norwegian investigation of over 1600 apprentices more than 90% preferred learning in the workplace (Mjelde, 2003). In work-based learning the apprentices learn, and are assessed on, their performance of real tasks of the craft they aspire to master. This provides for authentic learning and assessment, fostering an intrinsic motivation for learning, which may be one reason why students prefer the workplace as learning arena.

Although there are differences between crafts and differences between educational systems, levels, and subjects, here we shall tentatively address general societal roles of assessment in apprenticeships and school. Traditional school assessments serve three key functions: certification and selection; control and discipline; and facilitation of learning (Kvale, 1972, 1977, 1996). Selection and disciplining of students through grading have dominated school assessment. The decisive teacher grades contain little specific information on how to improve learning, while providing precise information of the standing of the pupils in relation to each other. A teacher who neglected the certifying and grading aspects of school assessments would quickly receive an official reprimand, whereas passing over the learning potentials of assessment has hardly any consequences. The disciplining function of grading may be illustrated by Becker et al.'s (1968) observations of the pervasive dominance of the students' grade point perspective in virtually every aspect of college life.

Reformers of school assessment who advocate more authentic modes of assessment for learning run into a series of dilemmas in the face of the institutionally entrenched functions of school assessments, that is, selecting and disciplining. Attempts to enhance the role of assessment; as feedback on learning may run counter to psychometric test criteria for selection. Thus the grading of the individualized portfolios which can foster intrinsic motivation will tend to be less reliable than the computer grading of standardized tests.

In apprenticeship training, selection is undertaken at the entry into an apprenticeship contract, often with a reciprocal trial period. The summative certification for entry into the trade takes place at the end of the apprenticeship with the apprentices' test piece. Powerful discipline and control are strongly embedded in the hierarchical workplace structure. Assessment in apprenticeship may primarily serve to improve learning because it is largely freed of selection and disciplining functions during the training period. Furthermore, there is a collective interest in effective learning since the quality and quantity of the production of a craft shop depends upon apprentices mastering the quality standards of the craft.

In contrast, disciplining of students is a dominating feature of school assessments. We may note that the Jesuits, who introduced assessments by grades on a scale from 1 to 6 in European schools, advocated competition for grades as a means to enforce diligence and discipline. In their school curriculum from 1599 they emphasized competition for grades as a strong means of promoting diligence from their pupils, where the disciplining of the students 'will be, better than through blows, obtained through the hope of honour and the fear of shame' (Amulatio, 1887, § 39). The relatively mild disciplining effects of the competition for grades was so efficient that the Jesuits four centuries ago could refrain from using the dominating disciplinary means of the schools of their time—corporal punishment.

Taking into account some of the multiple societal functions of assessment in schools and apprenticeships, we may conclude that school grades serve a democratic bureaucratic selection procedure, with approximately equal conditions for all, and as a relatively mild means to enforce diligence and discipline. In conventional school assessment, selection and disciplining of students play a major role, and the promotion of learning a minor role. In apprenticeships, assessment primarily serves as a support for learning to fulfil the quality standards of a trade. Schools do not appear as optimally efficient institutions for promoting learning. In particular, the use of assessment falls short when judged against the principles of modern learning psychology. When we see a trend in vocational and professional training today, with schooling taking over much of workplace training, we should also consider the potential consequences as an impairment of learning to master a trade and vocation.

CONCLUSION: SCHOOL ASSESSMENT IN A KNOWLEDGE-BASED ECONOMY

The present chapter has documented that within appropriate institutional settings, such as traditional workplace apprenticeship, it is entirely feasible to apply assessment to promote learning in line with the principles of modern learning psychology. In the educational system, the selection and disciplining functions of assessment have, however, prevailed over the learning potentials of assessment. With a move towards a knowledge-based economy in a late modern or postmodern society, requiring a learning culture of lifelong and life wide learning, efficient learning becomes important. The dilemmas of the learning versus the dominant selection and disciplining functions of school assessment thus come to the fore.

In the current educational system, new modes of assessments to promote learning are at odds with the increased importance of high-stakes assessment for selection, strengthened by the new accountability demands on education. Both of these tend to favour assessment by standardized tests. In contrast, the increased importance of learning in a knowledge society supports a stronger role for the formative learning potentials of assessment. In conclusion, educational innovations in assessment to promote school learning are not mainly a question of new and old assessment techniques, but are enmeshed in the political dilemmas concerning the societal functions that school assessment and education shall serve.

NOTE

1. I want to thank Klaus Nielsen for cooperation in working out the concept of a learning landscape model and for helpful suggestions during the preparation of this chapter.

REFERENCES

Amulatio—Ratio studiorum et institutiones scholasticae societatis Jesu. (1887). Berlin: Hoffman.

Becker, H. S. (1972). The school is a lousy place to learn anything in. *American Behavioral Scientist, 16*, 85–105.

Becker, H, Geer, B., & Hughes, F. (1968). *Making the grade.* New York: Wiley.

Birenbaum (2003). New insights into learning and teaching. In M. Segers, F. Dochy, & E. Cascallar (Eds.), *Optimising new modes of assessment: In search of qualities and standards.* Dordrecht: Kluwer Academic Publishers.

Black, A. (1984). *Guilds and civil society in European political thought from the twelfth century to the present.* Ithaca, NY: Cornell University Press.

Bloom, H. S. (1971). *Alle Schüler schaffen es. betrifft: Erziehung,* 1970/11, 15–27.

Cox, R. (1967). Examinations and higher education: A survey of the literature. *Universities Quarterly, 21*, 352–358.

Douchy, F., Gijbels, D., & Van de Watering, G. (2004). Assessment engineering: Aligning assessment, learning and instruction. Paper presented at the EARLI/ SIG Assessment conference, University of Bergen, Norway.

Hilgard, E. R, Atkinson, R. C., & Atkinson, R. L. (1975). *Introduction to psychology.* New York: Harcourt, Brace, Jovanovich.

Kvale, S. (1972). *Prüfung und Herrschaft—Hochschulprüfungen zwischen Ritual und Rationalisierung.* Weinheim: Beltz.

Kvale, S. (1977). Examinations: From ritual through bureaucracy to technology. *Social Praxis, 3*, 187–206.

Kvale, S. (1980). *Spillet om karakterer i gymnasiet—Elevinterviews om bivirkninger af adgangsbegænsning.* København: Munksgaard.

Kvale, S. (1996). Assessment as construction of knowledge. In R. Hayhoe & J. Pan (Eds.), *East-west dialogue knowledge and higher education.* New York: Sharpe, 117–140.

Kvale, S. (1997). Research apprenticeship. *Nordisk Pedagogik—Nordic Journal of Educational Research, 17,* 186–194.

Lave, J. & Wenger, E. (1991). *Situated learning—Learning as legitimate peripheral participation.* Cambridge: Cambridge University Press.

McKeachie, W. J. (1962). Procedures and techniques of teaching: A survey of experimental studies. In N. Stanford (Ed.), *The American college.* New York: Wiley.

Mjelde, L. (2003). Hvad skal jeg med teori, når jeg skal være trykker. In K. Nielsen & S. Kvale (Eds.), *Praktikkens læringslandskab.* København: Akademisk Forlag.

Nielsen, K. (1999). Musical apprenticeship. Learning at the Academy of Music as socially situated. *Psykologisk Skriftserie, 24,* (2). Århus: Psykologisk Institut, Aarhus Universitet.

Nielsen, K. (2003). Når eleverne selv skal sige det. In K. Nielsen & S. Kvale (Eds.), *Praktikkens Læringslandskab.* København: Akademisk Forlag.

Nielsen, K. & Kvale, S. (2003). *Praktikkens læringslandskab.* København: Akademisk Forlag.

Nielsen, K. & Kvale, S. (2006). Learning in the workplace. In E. Antocanacopolou et al. (Eds.), *Learning, working and living: Mapping the terrain of working life learning.* London: Palgrave Macmillan.

Resnick, L. B. & Klopfer, L. E. (1989). Toward the thinking curriculum: An overview. In L. B. Resnick & L. E. Klopfer (Eds.). *Toward the thinking curriculum: Current cognitive research.* Association for Supervision and Curriculum Development, 1–18.

Skinner, B. F. (1978). *Reflections on behaviorism and society.* Englewood Cliffs, NJ: Prentice-Hall.

Tanggaard, L. (2005). Evaluering som regulering af læring. *Tidsskrift for Arbejdsliv, 6*(4), 57–75.

Tanggaard, L. & Elmholdt, C. (2003). Det er ikke snyd at abe efter—Forsøg med ekspert- og sidemands oplæring på en malerskole. In K. Nielsen & S. Kvale (Eds.), *Praktikkens læringslandskab.* København: Akademisk Forlag.

Wilbrandt, J. (2003). Lærlinge i bevægelse—mellem skole og virksomhed og fra lærling til svend. In K. Nielsen & S. Kvale (Eds.), *Praktikkens læringslandskab.* København: Akademisk Forlag.

Part IV

Assessment, learners, and teachers

The chapters in part IV address the perspectives of individuals who are at the front line of assessment as teachers or learners. This section is about their understandings and the ways of working that they have developed as they participate in learning, teaching, and assessment. We address the ways in which teachers and learners perceive and respond to institutional and societal imperatives, make sense for themselves, and negotiate their own assessment practices.

When we begin to consider individual actors, it is clear that variation between individuals is substantial. Tan shows how teachers vary considerably in their views of student self-assessment and in the ways they implement it in their courses. McDowell describes a range of ways in which students respond to the feedback they receive from their lecturers. In general we notice how individuals are aware of different aspects of the learning environment in which they operate, see different problems and respond differently to the dilemmas in assessment practice that they identify. Although within educational institutions there are accepted practices and normal ways of doing things, assessment is substantially experienced by teachers and learners as something that they do individually and, often, in private. Think of the student writing an exam answer or an assignment, the teacher marking the student work, or giving feedback and guidance to an individual student on an assessed portfolio. The experience of being 'on your own' with assessment limits its potential for learning; that is, if we view learning as construction of knowledge in a social context or participation in a community of practice. Discussion in these chapters perhaps emphasizes the need for the well-recognized shift in assessment culture towards collaboration on assessment and dialogue about assessment, but also shows the difficulties in really shifting the balance from individual to collective activity.

The dilemma of balancing formative and summative purposes in assessment has arisen throughout this book in almost every chapter. It appears again here. Orrell's work reveals the whole process of marking as one of balancing competing tensions. The university lecturers she studied as they marked student assignments tried to maintain something of a teaching role by offering guidance to students, but largely viewed their work in terms of summative assessment. They were strongly influenced by the perceived need to consider stakeholders *other* than students, to whom they had to justify the marks awarded. Broadfoot indicates practical ways in which the interests of learners can be placed at the centre of assessment, largely through integrating formative assessment with teaching and learning practice in the school classroom and adopting 'assessment for learning' approaches. From the learner point of view, McDowell shows how university students in the same course varied in their views of the summative or formative purposes of course work assignments. For some, their written assignments and the feedback they received on them were most significant as formative exercises, part of a process of learning, whilst for others the purpose was seen as almost entirely summative, with the grade representing the end-point.

Broadfoot highlights the wide-ranging impacts of assessment on individuals, in this case school students. Assessment is not just about measuring knowledge or skills (summative) or about correcting and directing learning (formative). Assessment has powerful effects on learners' emotions, attitudes and beliefs, although it has often, perhaps traditionally, been viewed as operating largely in the cognitive domain. She introduces the concept of 'learning power', which can be fostered by appropriate assessment. Learning power means taking an active approach to learning; trying to 'make sense'; using a variety of ideas and approaches; and being able to reflect on learning and act on one's reflections. Importantly it also means having positive views about one's own capacity to learn and a degree of confidence and resilience which enables one to work through the challenges and setbacks that genuine learning inevitably presents. There are similar themes in McDowell's study of university students. For some, feedback and grades on assignments were a threat to their self-esteem and they lacked confidence and resilience as learners, despite in many cases receiving good grades.

This leads us into considerations of whether assessment in its newer forms is really fostering and evaluating genuine and meaningful learning or is promoting a kind of parallel activity; that is, performance of the assessment task which may or may not be related to good learning. This is the kind of criticism which has often been levelled at conventional testing. Certainly the practice of engaging students in self-assessment, which was envisaged by lectures that Tan studied, did not always meet the criteria for 'genuine' self-assessment as determined by proponents of the new assessment culture and by academic developers. Appropriate self-assessment is associated with the empowerment of students, involving them in decisions about what is to be assessed, how it is to be assessed and how well they have performed. However, there was a balance to be struck between such empowerment and the need to adhere to the knowledge content and standards of the subject or course. Not everything is negotiable and some lecturers came down heavily on the side of using self-assessment to promote student conformity or to ensure that prescribed course goals were met. We consistently face the dilemma of whether genuine learning and genuine education are being promoted or a special kind of assessment performance is being enacted by teachers and students. Orrell found that teachers grading student work did not necessarily focus in their judgements on higher-level or critical thinking displayed by students even though they espoused the importance of such capabilities. Some students, McDowell discovered, used feedback to enable them to hone their assessment performances, showing that they could produce the right kind of academic work, relegating making sense and gaining understanding to a secondary place, or even avoiding it altogether.

The chapters in this section also discuss the dilemma noted elsewhere in the book concerning how well assessment can be understood and practised through the use of explicit requirements, standards, and so on, or to what extent understanding is developed through participation in assessment as teacher or student. McDowell found that some students did make use of published assessment criteria and explicit feedback given to them by lecturers, even though this was not always in the ways intended. Orrell shows that teachers did not make overt reference to explicit guidance, such as assessment criteria, when they made judgements about students' assignments. On balance they drew more upon their tacit expectations and beliefs about what was 'good work' for students at that level of study. She suggested that a much greater level of explicitness and use of published criteria should be mandated. This might be helpful in shifting the level of assessment thinking on the part of lecturers from the tacit to the public and their work as assessors from the private and personal to the collective, creating a communal practice in assessment. Broadfoot recommends that learners should be assisted to think and learn about learning. That includes *assessment literacy*; that is, thinking and learning about *assessment,* and applies to teachers as well as to students. Without such assessment literacy, on both sides, assessment cannot be problematized and effectively managed. This is something which is essential for new approaches to assessment where both teachers and students play active roles. Assessment thinking and practice which is simply taken for granted is difficult to critique. The idea of critique may not even arise because taken-for-granted assessment tends to be viewed as a merely 'technical' activity stripped of its moral, ethical, epistemological, and ontological dimensions.

Assessment of learning in educational institutions is ultimately about power and authority. It is clear that some of the teachers interviewed by Tan retained all of the authority to themselves, either as individual experts or perhaps as representative of the authority of the university, even when they implemented student self-assessment. Broadfoot's work on learning power is about making learners more powerful, but this may present dilemmas for teachers who are expected by institutions and society to be the ones with power and authority. As McDowell reports, university students who are offered feedback which is, ostensibly at least, designed to assist them to take control of their learning, see things differently: some see only the word of judgmental authority; yet others see a template for conformity. Teachers and students struggle to balance the dilemmas of assessment in an educational context which both parties would like to have a value beyond that context, to be 'future-driven' as Tan suggests. The key dilemma is what aspects of assessment practice in educational settings can promote and evaluate genuine and significant learning which is long-lasting, relevant, and important in the wider context. The development of learning power, capacities for lifelong learning, and autonomy in learning are the key elements.

16 Assessment for learners
Assessment literacy and the development of learning power

Patricia Broadfoot

INTRODUCTION

Assessment is not working, or at least it is not working as it should. In our attempt to generate forms of assessment capable of addressing all the purposes for which we use assessment, we have produced a Frankenstein that preys on the educational process, reducing large parts of teaching and learning to mindless mechanistic processes whilst sapping the transformative power of education. This may seem an overstatement of the current position. However, there is considerable evidence upon which we *can* condemn much of today's educational activity as mechanistic processes. Moreover, available evidence makes it clear that assessment has a key role in sustaining the current situation. We have evidence of the actual damage that our current obsession with summative assessment is doing to individual learners. Such damage concerns not only the impact on individuals as learners; it also embraces the effects that assessment can have on individuals more generally—on their emotions, their self-esteem, and their aspirations. There are well-documented ways in which teachers, schools, and colleges can implement assessment in more constructive ways. In attempting to do so, they have to manage the dilemmas in systems where societal needs for accountability and explicit standards, and the vested interests in ostensibly meritocractic educational systems, are in some conflict with supporting the needs of learners and their educational attainments.

One way forward calls for a fundamental reconception of what the core focus of the educational process should be. If, as the introduction to this section of the book argues, 'the development of learning power, capacities for lifelong learning and autonomy in learning are the key elements' in promoting learning which is 'long-lasting, relevant and important', then it is these qualities that we need to focus on. This perspective brings together societal needs in a knowledge economy, for productive, well-informed and innovative citizens and the educational needs to support the growth and attainments of individual learners. This perspective introduces the vital role for assessment in supporting not only the pursuit of particular learning objectives but also the generic capacity to learn. We need to develop assessment procedures that are capable of addressing all the factors that contribute to learning and so can be used to help build up the both an individual's enthusiasm for learning and their capacity to do so. As the pursuit of scientific measures of ability and achievement has gradually begun to give way to a recognition of development and learning as primarily social processes, a similar transformation needs to take place towards a recognition that learning involves heart and soul as well as head and mind; that emotions and relationships exert a fundamental influence on an individual's willingness and ability to learn in any given setting.

THE ASSESSMENT DISEASE

In the UK, there is a good deal of evidence to suggest that educational standards are rising. The league tables of schools based on examination performance suggest that government efforts to raise standards are paying dividends. However, there is a price to be paid for better exam performance and the current obsession with 'getting the scores up'. Do improved examination results really reflect better learning or are they simply the political tools of accountability? Newspaper headlines would suggest that all is not well.

Firstly there is the enormous cost of examinations in financial and resource terms. A report from the *Guardian* newspaper asserts that:

> The annual cost of exams and tests has risen to more than £200 million since [the current Government] came to power—a 50 % rise.... Secondary age children are out of lessons for at least 46 weeks during their seven years of secondary education because of the test system and spend something like 150 hours sitting exams.... English school pupils suffer the worst and take up to 105 tests and exams during their years at school (Berliner, 2003)

This time and money could clearly be spent in more educationally productive ways. Perhaps more important is the cost in human lives and happiness. In another *Guardian* newspaper report, Donald Hiscock reports that:

> every exam season brings fresh concerns. This summer for instance has seen a zooming rise in the number of teenagers popping antidepressants and other pills to see them through. (15 June 2004)

For some, the pressures of exams have even more tragic consequences as another newspaper report documents:

The family, friends and teachers of Tina Dziki, a bright 15-year-old south London student, are grief-stricken after she died last week as a result of taking an overdose. She left a suicide note that described a number of troubles including anxiety about two GCSE exams she was due to take a year early. (Guardian, June 2004)

Although most examination candidates are not driven to these extreme measures, there is considerable evidence that 'high-stakes', summative examinations encourage an instrumental, 'trading for grades' mentality that is profoundly inimical to genuine educational engagement. Gibbs (2006), for example, quotes the following university students:

I just don't bother doing the homework now. I approach the courses so I can get an A in the easiest manner, and it's amazing how little work you have to do if you really don't like the course.

I am positive there is an examination game. You don't learn certain facts for instance, you don't take the whole course. You go and look at the examination papers and you say 'looks as though there have been four questions on a certain theme last year, this year the professor said the examination would be much the same as before' so you excise a good bit of the course immediately. (p. 24)

These examples illustrate the now well-documented effect of excessive summative testing. The study of a wide range of research evidence by Harlen and Deakin-Crick (2003) identified these effects as:

- Teachers adopt transmission teaching.
- 'High stakes' tests drive classroom activity.
- Practising tests reinforces the low self-esteem of lower achievers.
- 'High stakes' tests tend to lower the self-esteem of lower-achieving students.
- Students react negatively to a 'performance ethos'. The amount of effort expended by students is affected by their anticipated achievement.
- Students adjust their future effort in response to the feedback they receive.
- Students become increasingly extrinsically motivated and grade obsessed.
- Girls and lower achievers are worst affected.

This powerful critique of the negative effects of high stakes examinations has been further validated by a study by Madaus (1988) who found that high stakes, high standards tests do not have a markedly positive effect on teaching and learning in the classroom, and that they do not motivate the unmotivated. Furthermore, contrary to popular belief, so called 'authentic' forms of high stakes assessment are not a more equitable way to assess the progress of students who differ in race, culture, native language, or gender. Rather, these high stakes testing programs have been shown to increase high school dropout rates, particularly among minority student populations.

This international evidence concerning the damaging effects of the examination rich diet that is served up to students in virtually every country in the world today should surely be giving us cause for concern. In particular, the evidence concerning the damaging effects of excessive summative assessment should be the focus of increasing concern among education professionals. We find ourselves ensnared in a global examination pandemic in which the pursuit of standards through what can be cheaply and defensibly measured is driving out genuine engagement in learning. This is an issue that urgently needs to be addressed since it has serious implications both for what students are learning today and whether they will become the lifelong learners of tomorrow. The lack of attention being given to this problem is partly because governments persist in their enthusiasm for 'paper and pencil tests' and show no sign of seeing political advantage in abandoning the prevailing contemporary discourse of standards and accountability. And, as this book as a whole makes clear, because assessment practice is necessarily outward-facing, it is profoundly affected by the external social and political context. This is a context that makes it difficult for practitioners and institutions to change their practices.

However, the fact that until recently, educational professionals have largely not sought to demand and implement change in assessment practice is as reprehensible as it is surprising. It cannot be that we do not care; thus it must be that educationists do not yet link the disaffection, the anxiety and the de-motivation that they encounter to the students' assessment diet. In short, it is arguably the lack of 'assessment literacy' among education professionals, with teachers of all kinds not having a well-developed understanding of assessment practices and issues, that has led to this problem not receiving the attention it urgently needs. Such a situation is all the more regrettable now that there is considerable research evidence available concerning the elements of more constructive approaches to assessment.

THE ASSESSMENT DISEASE: TREATING THE SYMPTOMS

As the introduction to this book has described, recent years have seen a surge of interest in what has become known as 'assessment for learning'. Early work on formative assessment, which may be defined as assessment that is designed to impact on the learning process, rather than measure its outcomes, has given way to a more comprehensive understanding of how assessment can enhance learning. In particular, the comprehensive research review by Black and William (1998) provided clear research evidence that assessment for learning 'is the single most powerful tool we have for both raising standards and empowering life-long learners' (Assessment Reform Group, 1999). It is clear that assessment enhances learning if it is designed to encourage intrinsic, rather than extrinsic motivation and if it builds the learners' confidence and gives them a sense of ownership and control.

At the heart of these findings is the key role that *motivation* plays in promoting learning. Indeed, it would not be going too far to argue that the key to learning is not ability or resources, good teaching or a well-designed curriculum, important as all of these are; it is motivation. Without motivation, students are not engaged, and if they are not engaged, then they are unlikely to learn. Indeed, the contrast between the kind of classroom described by Chiczenmihail et al. (1993), in which most students are either anxious or bored, and the typical informal learning context where an individual has sought out the opportunity to learn something they wish to pursue, perhaps a sport or a hobby, is marked. Learning to drive provides a good example in this respect. An individual who has hired a driving instructor is likely to be motivated by the desire to learn to drive and to pass the test; hence they have both intrinsic and extrinsic motivation. However, the individual will become rapidly demotivated if the instructor behaves in such a way as to erode the confidence and the enjoyment of their pupil. The outcome is likely to be the student abandoning the activity despite their initial motivation, or seeking another teacher.

Instructors who operate in the marketplace are likely to rapidly develop the skills of sustaining the confidence, motivation, and enjoyment of their pupils. This is less so in formal educational settings, where a host of other constraints affects the quality of the engagement between teacher and student. Yet the research evidence provides some simple messages which, if implemented, could transform even these formal educational settings. It suggests, for example, that students' motivation will increase if teachers offer them guidance about the next steps, if teachers avoid personal judgements on students, if teachers clarify what success looks lik, and if they substitute comments for marks and grades. It is particularly important to note that although students do appear to be motivated by marks and grades, the kind of extrinsic motivation so produced is not conducive to deep learning. Moreover, there is evidence (Weeden et al., 2002) that a large majority of students in the UK do not understand the meaning of the marks and grades they receive, especially in terms of how to improve their work. The available research evidence provides the clear message that learning is likely to increase if teachers provide feedback in sufficient detail and with sufficient timeliness for students to act on it. It is also important that assessment should communicate clear and challenging expectations to students. Indeed, feedback appears to have more impact on learning than anything else. These elements are incorporated by Perkins (2006) in his model of 'whole game learning' in which the joy and satisfaction that children find in learning to play a game and to improve their performance at it is contrasted with the de-contextualized, arbitrary, individualized and fragmented learning experience they typically receive in formal education

The Assessment Reform Group has distilled the now very substantial body of evidence attesting to the points made above into a set of 10 principles which inform assessment for learning, which they define as 'the process of seeking and interpreting evidence for use by learners and their teachers to decide where the learners are in their learning, where they need to go, and how best to get there'.

The ten principles are as follows. 'Assessment for learning':

- Is part of effective planning;
- Focuses on how students learn;
- Is central to classroom practice;
- Is a key professional skill;
- Is sensitive and constructive;
- Fosters motivation;
- Promotes understanding of learning goals and criteria by students;
- Helps learners know how to improve;
- Develops the capacity for self-assessment;
- Recognizes all educational achievement.

The lessons from the research on assessment for learning are clear and powerful. They suggest that educators of all kinds have available a powerful armoury of tools which they can use to help their students engage more effectively with learning opportunities, tools which until recently have been almost completely neglected.

THE ASSESSMENT DISEASE: FINDING A CURE?

In themselves the tools and resources discussed above do not go to the heart of the problem. They may be thought of as treating the symptoms of the assessment disease rather than leading towards a cure. The development of much higher levels of assessment literacy amongst educational professionals, so that they can and do use the tools available, is both urgent and vitally important. However, their efforts are likely to remain relatively marginal in their impact until we address the language of learning itself. There needs to be a shift in the focus of educational endeavour from *what is to be taught*, to *who is learning* and the mixture of emotions, aspirations, skills and qualities that each individual brings to any particular learning setting. Figure 16.1 illustrates the range of important factors relating to individuals and their learning context and which are crucial to the generation of energy for learning.

The term *learning power* has been used to capture 'that complex mix of human qualities that leads to positive personal and social growth, change

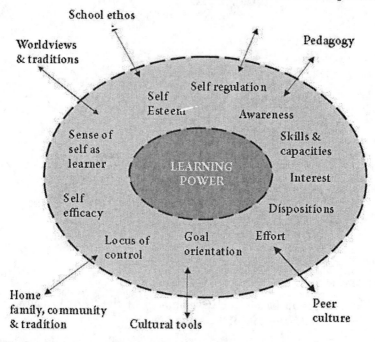

Curriculum & Assessment practices

School ethos

Worldviews & traditions

Pedagogy

Self regulation

Self Esteem

Awareness

Sense of self as learner

Skills & capacities

LEARNING POWER

Interest

Self efficacy

Dispositions

Locus of control

Goal orientation

Effort

Home family, community & tradition

Cultural tools

Peer culture

Figure 16.1 Factors influencing energy for learning.

and adaptation in relation to the social and natural world within a trajectory in time' (Deakin-Crick et al., 2004).

Figure 16.2 represents the integral relationship between the substance of education, typically the pursuit of knowledge, skills and understanding, and the engine that drives the acquisition of these things, namely the attitudes, values, feelings, dispositions, and motivations of each individual learner. As the analogy with the double helix of DNA suggests, the two are indivisible and mutually supportive. Sadly the language which we currently use in educational settings to articulate what might be called the 'affective dimension' of the double helix is severely limited, often confined to themes such as effort and interest. The truth is both much more complex and much more profound.

It was the need to gain a better understanding of this left-hand side of the double helix, namely the elements that contribute to an individual's 'learning power', which prompted the development of a new assessment instrument. *The Evaluating Lifelong Learning Inventory (ELLI)* project (Deakin-Crick et al., 2004), was designed to identify the components of learning power, and to provide a formative assessment tool which could be used by students and teachers to diagnose an individual's current profile and to use this as a tool for developing 'learning power' further, on an

Double Helix of Learning
(McGettrick 2002)

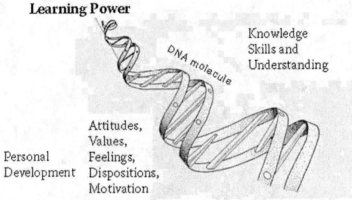

Figure 16.2 The double helix of learning.

individual or group basis. The development of the ELLI instrument has identified seven dimensions of 'learning power':

1. Growth orientation. The research suggests that effective learners know that learning itself is learnable, as opposed to less effective learners who believe that learning capacity is relatively fixed. In the latter case, difficulty in learning something tends to be experienced negatively rather than as a spur to greater effort.
2. Critical curiosity. Effective learners want to find things out and understand things, as well as enjoying asking questions. The opposite is passivity and an unwillingness to challenge or ask questions.
3. Meaning-making. Effective learners seek out the links between what they are learning and what they already know. They are interested in the big picture and how new learning fits within it. In contrast, less effective learners are more likely to approach learning piecemeal. They may be more interested in knowing the criteria for successful performance than in looking for joined-up meanings and associations.
4. Creativity. It would seem that effective learners are able to look at things in different ways, and to imagine new possibilities. They like playing with ideas and allowing them to bubble up in their minds. By contrast, less effective learners appear to be more rule-bound, preferring tried and tested ways of looking at things, which make them feel safer. Hence they feel uncomfortable in situations where greater creativity is required.
5. Resilience. Effective learners appear to thrive on challenges and accept that learning is sometimes hard for everyone. They have a higher level

of 'stickability' and can readily recover from frustration, in contrast to those who tend to go to pieces when they get stuck or make mistakes, and consequently are risk-averse.

6. Relationships. Effective learners appear to be good at managing the balance between being sociable and being private in their learning. Less effective learners are more likely to be either over-dependent on others or lack engagement with other people, tending towards isolation.

7. Strategic awareness. More effective learners appear to know more about themselves as learners and actively reflect on how well they are doing and why. They are good at managing themselves in terms of frustration and disappointment. Less effective learners appear to be less self-aware and less able, therefore, to explain the reasons for the way they choose to go about things.

These seven dimensions together constitute a 'language of learning'. They enable teachers to articulate to students the underlying factors that are likely to influence both the intellectual and emotional engagement of students with a given learning task. By the same token, they encourage both teachers and students to open up the 'black box' of learning so that both can think about and focus upon how to develop better learning orientations.

Using these dimensions, a detailed questionnaire has been devised which individuals complete to identify their profile in relation to the seven learning dimensions. Typically this is done online, so that an individual profile can be produced instantaneously, as well as one for a particular class or group. Figure 16.3 illustrates such a profile for an individual.

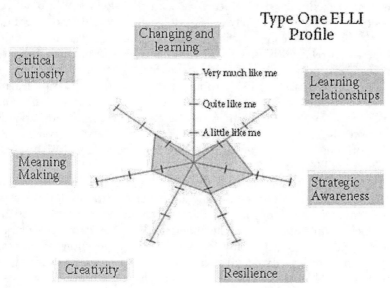

Figure 16.3 Example of an individual ELLI profile.

These individual profiles can be produced to explore a student's 'learning power profile' in a particular setting such as a specific subject, or more generically as the basis for a conversation between teacher and learner—or perhaps even between friends or within the family about the results and what strategies might be adopted to address areas of weakness. Equally, 'knowledge is power' for the teacher in planning teaching priorities and the Elli profile results can helpfully focus and guide teachers to address generic learning needs as well as specific subject weaknesses. Teachers will have a class profile which portrays the distribution of scores on the seven dimensions for the whole class.

Based on these profiles, teachers can design explicit learning interventions, such as fostering conversations about learning, encouraging self-assessment, agreeing explicit learning objectives, providing time for students to reflect, and so on. Development work in schools suggests that such activities are very fruitful in developing students' learning power (Deakin-Crick, 2006).

What should be clear from the above is that *ELLI* is an example of a new breed of formative assessment instruments that focus not on a particular body of curriculum content, but on the characteristics of the individual learner. As such, *ELLI* and any similar tool with such an alternative lexicon of assessment will help to develop a quite different centre of gravity in the classroom. It will encourage an emphasis on the development of *critical curiosity, creativity, collaboration* between students, the explicit *conceptualisation* of learning goals, *context* sensitivity, *confidence* building, and ultimately *commitment* on the part of the learner.

This kind of assessment language links what is widely known about how best to facilitate effective learning with actual classroom practice in terms of assessment. It is likely to lead to teachers who develop a commitment to learner-centred practices and who prioritize the creation of positive interpersonal relationships with their students as a foundation for future learning; relationships that are characterized by trust, affirmation, and challenge. This in turn is likely to lead to the creation of a safe learning environment where it is normal and expected that students will make mistakes and not know the right answer; where acceptance, rather than judgement prevails; and where the development of students' 'learning power' through the informed use of formative assessment is explicitly fostered as the primary objective.

It is also likely to mean that teachers will increasingly nurture the language of learning, encouraging students themselves to develop the capacity to articulate this language. Ultimately the development of assessment instruments which incorporate the understanding that learning is a holistic process, and hence do not only focus on cognitive learning outcomes, is likely to result in a fundamental change of focus for classroom activity. Students too would have to learn to focus on the learning process itself, rather than particular areas of subject content as at present. For them the challenge would be to develop the skills involved in monitoring themselves as learners and directing their energies in the most fruitful direction. Strategic awareness of strengths and weaknesses built up through regular self-assessment and reflection would encourage a sense of ownership and empowerment and, as a result, interest and motivation. If, in Perkin's (2006) words, there is no substitute for 'practising the hard parts', such efforts would be contextualized within a more general understanding of both 'the game' and 'the player'.

CONCLUSION

As our information-rich age makes the opportunities to build knowledge increasingly available, so it will become ever more important that learners are equipped with the skills to become autonomous, independent, self-motivated enquirers. This is a far cry from the treadmill of swotting for traditional summative tests and exams, the effects of which are described at the beginning of this chapter. If we have not yet found a cure for this disease, we are nevertheless beginning to make progress. But, as with all diseases, the first step is to recognize that there is a problem. As such recognition develops, so the search for a cure will become more urgent and widespread.

In this chapter, I have sought to add yet another voice to the many who for decades have been calling for the damaging effects of conventional forms of assessment to be addressed. I have suggested that the recent interest in the development of assessment for learning represents a positive and promising step forward in this respect. It is encouraging too that governments in many countries have shown great interest in such developments. However, the transition from 'teaching power' to 'learning power' will be a difficult one. The roots of contemporary systems of education lie in the perceived link between educational provision and national economic success and social solidarity—in 'gentling the masses'. These roots go very deep within modern societies and are embodied in a discourse of what it is to teach, to learn, and to assess, that is rarely questioned. Yet there is now a growing body of evidence to substantiate the need for change and the potential dividends of so doing. Such evidence presses the need to change the primary focus of educational and assessment discourse from *what is being* learned to *who is learning* as the basis for overcoming the very real inhibitions to effective learning that are currently present in formal educational settings. A truly 21st century approach to education is likely only to be possible with the advent of widespread assessment literacy and the development of a 'language of learning' that informs all that we do.

REFERENCES

Assessment Reform Group *Principles of assessment for learning* (http://arg.educ. cam.ac.uk/).

Assessment Reform Group (1999). *Assessment for learning.* Cambridge: University of Cambridge, School of Education.

Berliner, W. (2003) 'Testing, testing', *The Guardian*, 29 April, p. 2, Lexis-Nexis Professional [Online]. Available at: http://web.lexis-nexis.com/professional/.

Black, P. & Wiliam, D. (1998). Assessment and classroom learning. *Assessment in Education*, 5(1), 7–74.

Csikszentmihalyi, M., Rathunde, K., & Whalen, S. (1993). *Talented teenagers: The roots of success and failure.* Cambridge: Cambridge University Press.

Deakin-Crick, M., Broadfoot, P., & Claxton, G. (2004). Developing an effective lifelong learning inventory. *Assessment in Education*, 11(3), 248–272.

Deakin-Crick, R. (2006).*Learning power in practice.* London: Sage.

Deakin-Crick, R. et al. (2004). *ELLI 2 project report.* London: Lifelong Learning Foundation.

Gibbs, G. (2006). How assessment frames student learning. In C. Bryan & K. Clegg (Eds.), *Innovative assessment in higher education.* Abingdon: Routledge.

Harlen, W. & Deakin Crick, R. (2003). Testing and motivation for learning. *Assessment in Education*, 10(2), 169–207.

Hiscock, D. (2004) 'I'm sorry, I nodded off', *The Guardian*, 15 June, p. 17, Lexis-Nexis Professional [Online]. Available at: http://web.lexis-nexis. com/professional/.

Madaus, G. (1988). The influence of testing on the curriculum. In L. Tanner (Ed.), *Critical issues in curriculum*, 87th Yearbook of NSSE, Part 1. Chicago: University of Chicago Press.

Perkins, D. (2006, 20–22 April). Whole game learning. Keynote address at 'This Learning Life Conference', University of Bristol, UK.

Taylor, D. (2004). 'Parents: Testing times', *The Guardian*, 2 June, p. 16. Lexis-Nexis Professional [Online]. Available at: http://web.lexis-nexis.com/professional/.

Weeden, P., Winter, J., & Broadfoot, P. (2002). *Assessment: What's in it for schools?* London: Routledge/Falmer.

17 Academics' and academic developers' views of student self-assessment

Kelvin Tan

INTRODUCTION

Many writers have emphasized the importance of student self-assessment in higher education. It has been argued that self-assessment should be a continuing focus throughout undergraduate education (Burgess et al., 1999) and a main goal of higher education (Sluijmans et al., 1998). The development of self-assessment ability is also recognized as a distinct outcome of higher education (Boud, 1986; Dearing, 1997; Stefani, 1998) and a critical educational tool for learning beyond university education (Tamir, 1999; Taras, 2001). Consequently, many have noted that student self-assessment is a common feature in courses in higher education (Boud, 1995; Brown & Glasner, 1999; Dochy & Segers, 1999). Brew (1995) in particular observed self-assessment to be 'a normal and regular part of university teaching since the 1980's' (p. 52).

Whilst there is much emphasis on student self-assessment as a practice and as a goal in higher education, there is less attention paid to how it is understood and used by academics and academic developers. This study focused on the different ways that student self-assessment was experienced by 16 academics from a variety of disciplines and programs of study. The research findings describe a structure of progressive awareness of meanings and practices of student self-assessment. These results were compared with the views of academic developers on the benefits and dilemmas of student self-assessment practices. This chapter utilizes the views of academic developers concerning the institutional context for student self-assessment to suggest the contextual factors which influence academics' awareness of the meanings and practices of self-assessment. In turn, this raises issues as to how academic development practices may support academics' implementation of student self-assessment.

METHODOLOGY

The investigation utilized a phenomenographic approach to identify qualitatively different conceptions of student self-assessment. The word *phenomenography* first appeared in Marton (1981). Marton and Booth (1997) describe the basis of phenomenography as

> an interest in describing phenomena in the world as others see them, and in revealing and describing the variation therein, especially in an educational context. (p. 111)

The aim of phenomenography is to investigate the qualitatively different ways of experiencing a phenomenon rather than its quantitative dimensions. The focus here was on student self-assessment.

Sixteen academics from three metropolitan universities in New South Wales, Australia, were interviewed on their student self-assessment practices. The academics were selected on the basis that they had implemented a form of student self-assessment which fell within the scope of this study; that is, they provided distinct opportunities for their students to judge their own learning in a particular program of study. The range of self-assessment practices of the 16 academics reflects the general diversity of assessment practices in higher education. They include methods described in the literature such as group discussions and poster presentations (Butcher & Stefani, 1995), true and false self-testing assessment (Khan et al., 2001), and the use of self-assessment diaries (Fazey, 1993). The self-assessment practices of the respondents are consistent with descriptions of practices which indicate a significant degree of student involvement in judging their learning, such as collaborative assessment (Rainsbury & Hodges, 1998), co-assessment (Dochy & Segers, 1999), self-determined assessment (Baum & Baum, 1986), negotiated assessment (Gosling, 2000), and self-evaluation (Sullivan & Hall, 1997). Both summative and formative self-assessment practices were analyzed in this study. Unless otherwise stated, respondents in this study referred to both summative and formative student self-assessment.

Altogether, 12 different disciplines were represented. The diversity of disciplines and methods optimized the potential variation of meanings of student self-assessment amongst the academics. In turn, this enhanced the variation within and between academics' ways of experiencing student self-assessment in the sample.

ACADEMICS' VIEWS OF STUDENT SELF-ASSESSMENT

The aim of the interviews was to reveal the extent and complexity of each respondent's conceptions of self-assessment. In the phenomenographic approach, conceptions which have more critical aspects of the phenomenon discerned would imply greater awareness of the phenomenon. The extent of the awareness of the phenomenon lies in the configuration of the critical aspects in each conception of student self-assessment. A greater awareness of student self-assessment is denoted by a greater number of themes that are experienced. In this context, three conceptions of student self-assessment were identified. These represent progressively more complexity and greater levels of awareness of student self-assessment for academics. The three conceptions of student self-assessment are described as: teacher-driven self-assessment; program-driven self-assessment and future-driven self-assessment. Each of these is described in the next section with illustrative quotations from interviews.

Teacher-driven self-assessment

Teacher-driven self-assessment is experienced in terms of the teacher's control and regulation of the students' judgments of their learning. It is effective as a practice in itself for regulating and ensuring compliance in students' judgments of their learning. The teacher is the benchmark for the students' judgments of their learning. Student self-assessment is discerned in terms of the students' judgments complying with those of the teacher. The following quotes illustrate the academics' awareness of the teacher controlling and regulating the students' judgments of their learning in student self-assessment.

> Whatever I do, I give them all these assessment evaluation sheets so they will know where they are assessed and how we assess them. So they can prepare themselves in a way that they understand how they are preparing themselves towards the task and how, where, why we assess them below or above whoever.
>
> They'll usually come in and say 'Well, I'm interested in this', and I say, 'Well all right, if you are interested in that have you also looked at this theory and this theory which relates to this particular project. And then have a think about how these two are going to work; then think about evidence. How you're actually going to collect the evidence for that and then think about how you want me to judge how you've actually learnt it because I need to be able to determine how you've.'...

The focus of academics with a teacher-driven conception of self-assessment is only on the teacher's control and regulation of the students' judgments of their learning. The students' standards and proficiency within the program of study and the sustainability of the students' capacity for self-assessment beyond the program of study are not present in the academics' awareness. Self-assessment is relevant as an instrument of control in discrete activities. It is not seen as being relevant to the overall program of study.

Program-driven self-assessment

Program-driven self-assessment is experienced in terms of the program of study when providing students with opportunities to judge their own learning. Students' judgments of their own standards are used by the academic to educate them on the gap between their standards and the requisite standards of the program. Students' judgments of their learning revolve around how they may judge their relative proficiency in order to enhance their progress in the program of study. Academics are concerned with how students are enabled to understand the standards required in order to complete the program of study.

In program-driven self-assessment, the program of study is the benchmark for students' judgments of their learning. The program encapsulates the collective criteria for evaluating students' judgments of their learning. Students' judgments of their learning are deemed to be effective so long as they assist the students to advance in their course.

The following critical aspects of student self-assessment represent the constitutive awareness of academics with a program-driven conception of student self-assessment:

- Compliance/control of student behaviour;
- Contingent judgment of knowledge;
- Feedback on requisite standards;
- Development of requisite proficiency in self-assessment.

Within these four critical aspects, program-driven self-assessment fixes its focal awareness on the feedback and the development of the requisite standards and proficiency for the course. The sustainability of self-assessment is not within the academics' awareness of the phenomenon.

The following quotes illustrate the foregrounded aspects of student self-assessment. The focus is on the program of study acting as the composite set of standards and proficiency which benchmark and develop the students' judgments of their learning.

> I would expect that after they had done this task that they would bring all of those thoughtful learning results from that self-assessment; that when they come to their major work, they would be much more focused in what they've got to do. That they would be asking themselves those self-assessment questions. And that those questions would be uppermost in their mind. So it could end up playing a very important part in the worth of their final assignment.
>
> On the back, the student receives assessment grades as indicated for grades by university. So they all get this [academic grade descriptors] on the back.... So they can get an idea of where they're strong and where

they've got to improve. And then they look at that with the one they'd done and they identify areas where there is noticeable difference.

What would be the goal of self-assessment? Well to be able to judge your own performance better. To be able to reasonably accurately say what you're doing well in and badly. And I think probably I really like them to get even to the end of their first year with a world view that says you know, at any stage I'm monitoring how I'm going.

When academics focus on the program of study, the requisite standards and proficiency of the program is foregrounded and the control and regulation of students' behaviour and knowledge is in the background. However, self-assessment is effective only within the program of study for providing feedback and enhancing the students' proficiency. It is not discerned as being relevant to the students' future self-assessment ability beyond the program of study.

Future-driven self-assessment

Future-driven self-assessment is understood as the sustainability of student self-assessment beyond completing the program of study. The future need for students to be able to self-assess their own work in professional working contexts is the benchmark for students' judgments of their learning in the program of study.

The emphasis is on understanding and using student self-assessment to develop students' capacity for exercising their own judgments without depending on the academic. The program of study presents an opportunity for students to develop their self-appraisal skills in terms of constructing and refining assessment criteria. Through a developmental process, students may be able to construct their own assessment criteria and make judgments based on these criteria.

The following critical aspects of student self-assessment represent the constitutive awareness of academics with a future-driven conception of student self-assessment:

- Compliance/control of student behaviour;
- Contingent judgment of knowledge;
- Feedback on requisite standards;
- Development of requisite proficiency in self-assessment;
- Sustainability of self-assessment capability.

Within the five critical aspects, future-driven self-assessment fixes its focal awareness on sustaining students' judgments of their learning in the future beyond the program of study. By encapsulating all the critical aspects of self-assessment, future-driven self-assessment is the most comprehensive conception of self-assessment. It is arguably the most effective form of self-assessment in terms of displaying the greatest awareness of critical aspects of self-assessment. The following quotes illustrate the focus on sustaining students' capacity for self-assessment beyond the program of study:

> Because it is professionally imperative for nurses, for doctors, for teachers, for everybody, that you're able to realistically self-assess; that you can make a reasonable judgment about your work, of any piece of work that you do. And that then becomes the springboard if you like. That ability to self-assess is the springboard for your lifelong learning.
>
> And it's really important that if you are going to be able to provide consistent quality and be aware of your own deficiencies so that you will be able to improve them, you've got to be able to look at your own work objectively. And set yourself some criteria. And this is what I'm trying to encourage them to do, I suppose, extend it from not just an educational environment but through the professional life that they are going to be leading for the next 40 years. You know, see it as a professional skill as much as an educational tool.
>
> But I think there should be a form of self-assessment everywhere in tertiary education, in any tertiary education programme, because it is essential for lifelong learning. It is the pivot on which they know that they have a deficiency that they then have to address through lifelong learning. If they never learn to accurately self-assess, then they will never know when they have a deficiency that needs to be recovered and whether they've adequately recovered that deficiency once they've left the sort of structures of a university.

When the focus is on the student's future capacity to make sound and defensible judgments of their learning, the sustainability of self-assessment beyond the program of study is foregrounded. Self-assessment is effective within and beyond the program of study for sustaining students' capacity for self-appraisal. The academic discerns the importance of students developing their self-assessment capacity to complete the program of study and to prepare themselves for future learning contexts.

Academic developers' views of student self-assessment

Academic developers are professionals with expertise in teaching, learning and assessment practices, and with responsibilities for developing and supporting good practice amongst academic teachers. The aim of including this expert group in the study was to identify a wider range of perspectives on student self-assessment and also varying views on how good self-assessment practices might be developed. For example, academic development perspectives articulated issues on the institutional constraints impeding student self-assessment as well as the different forms of support available to academics intending to implement self-assessment for their students. Such perspectives illuminate the contextual factors influencing academics' awareness and implementation of student self-assessment.

Three academic developers were interviewed separately for their views on student self-assessment. They were selected on the basis of their familiarity with student self-assessment practice. In addition, the academic developers had many years of experience in teaching and assessment practice themselves and were well acquainted with institutional obstacles to implementing assessment innovation in a range of subjects and teaching contexts. One of the academic developers also held a managerial position and offered insights into the hierarchical perspective of assessment innovation and practice from a supervisory perspective. The collective views from these wide-ranging interviews identify several pertinent issues in relation to suitable academic development support for academics desirous of implementing student self-assessment. These views are described in terms of the benefits and dilemmas of supporting academics in their student self-assessment practices. These benefits and dilemmas are discussed in relation to the academics' conceptions of student self-assessment identified in this study.

Benefits of student self-assessment

A significant benefit of student self-assessment was identified as its potential for emancipating students from the teacher's dominance in the assessment process. The academic developers were in general agreement that self-assessment was unique amongst assessment methods because of its provision for students to make important decisions in their own assessment. Such a benefit extended to empowering students beyond formal assessment practices:

> Student self-assessment is just an assessment method but one that is very different from other methods. It has the power to emancipate that is absent in teacher-directed methods of assessment. Because it has emancipatory potential, it therefore has a potential for impact in wider aspects of the curriculum.

At the same time, it was perceived that self-assessment would entail a greater degree of transparency from teachers as compared to unilateral forms of assessment. This was based on the assumption that students play meaningful roles in negotiating the self-assessment criteria. One of the academic developers compares assessment transparency in self-assessment to other assessment methods:

> Student self-assessment implies that academics have to deal with transparency to a greater degree and details about how much control to yield. But it's a different sense of transparency compared to teacher

assessment because the student becomes the assessor and therefore the student must be able to assess properly. That means criteria and standards have to be transparent to the student and that students negotiate the extent to which their criteria and standards become transparent.

The potential for greater emancipation and transparency that was identified by academic developers may not be true of all student self-assessment practices. In particular, academics who practice teacher-driven self-assessment may not emphasize student emancipation since this would be at odds with privileging the teacher's judgments in students' self-assessments. Likewise, program-driven self-assessment accommodates student autonomy to the extent that students' judgments are consistent with the program's goals. Students' empowerment in their self-assessments is therefore limited to the confines of their program of study.

In contrast with the range of awareness of academics, academic developers in this study appear to confine their awareness of the benefits of student self-assessment to teacher-driven and program-driven self-assessment. For example, whilst suggesting the potential of self-assessment to emancipate students from teacher-directed methods, the academic developer was careful to limit its emancipatory potential to wider aspects of the curriculum. Likewise, the second quote by academic developers on the benefits of self-assessment emphasizes the issues of assessment transparency between teachers and students. The agenda for assessment transparency would appear to relate to ensuring that students 'must be able to assess *properly*', a reference consistent with appropriate self-assessment practices within the context of program-driven self-assessment, rather than developing students' ability to self-assess independently beyond the program of study in future driven self-assessment.

The limitation of the benefits of self-assessment to the program of study by academic developers may perhaps be explained by their organizational allegiance to the institution's goals. Since the academic developers in this study do not teach students directly, they may not closely identify with the future development and learning of students beyond the institution of learning. Such a tendency raises the possibility that higher education institutions may advocate the goals of program-driven self-assessment rather than extend the scope of self-assessment to future driven self-assessment. For academics, this may serve as a reminder that students' learning needs for future-driven self-assessment may not always be fully served nor supported by their institution. Hence, there may exist for academics the troubling question as to whether the institution's or the program's needs for student self-assessment are sufficiently broad to cater for future-driven self-assessment. Further dilemmas of implementing student self-assessment are identified by academic developers in the next section.

Dilemmas

Academic developers were forthcoming in identifying the dilemmas that beset the implementation of self-assessment practices. The major concern was that self-assessment practices would be perceived as a radical change in practice that would challenge the existing hierarchies. The academic developers in this study were highly sensitive to the institutional constraints and obstacles to any change in student assessment practices. Hence, the academic developers may have been more cognizant of their institution's reluctance to support changes to its student assessment practices rather than the widespread use of student self-assessment practices in other universities. As such, while academic developers felt that self-assessment had the potential for students to be empowered in their assessment, they were far more pessimistic that academics would be allowed to provide students with genuine self-assessment practices in the first place. One academic developer observed the institutional hierarchy to be the biggest obstacle:

> The biggest obstacle to student self-assessment is the hierarchy in organisations which means that student self-assessment must be accepted at every level of the hierarchy. Therefore it occurs only at individual instances and not at an institutional level.

A symbiotic relationship between institutional control and traditional assessment was observed to exist. One of the academic developers identified self-assessment as a radical practice that threatened the hierarchal levels of power in the institution:

> Not sure if students want to be involved in assessment. Student involvement may mean only responding to teachers' feedback. Traditional assessment cannot be displaced easily because of the top down approach in everything in the institution—learning, teaching, and assessment.

The reasoning was that teacher's traditional assessment of students was part of the overall hierarchy in the institution. Empowering students at the bottom of the hierarchy through self-assessment therefore threatened the upper tiers of power since it would correspondingly require more autonomy to be surrendered to teachers.

Academic developers on the whole were not optimistic that the institutional hierarchy would permit the necessary devolvement of power for self-assessment to occur. In particular, the notion of summative self-assessment was perceived as a practice that would be difficult to justify. Instead, only formative self-assessment or self-assessments that would not count towards the students' final grade were viable:

The main obstacle to student self-assessment is changing lecturers' and students' mindsets and the management's mindsets. Very difficult for summative self-assessment to occur—Can summative self-assessment actually be reliable? So I would say that only formative student self-assessment is viable.

Such a conclusion is at odds with the recent literature which argues for self-assessment to be used for formative purposes *in addition* to summative ones. In contrast, the academic developers in this study proposed that self-assessment could only be used for formative purposes *instead of* summative purposes. However, confining student self-assessment to formative purposes alone may not be viable. The risk is that students will not take self-assessment seriously unless their judgments count towards the final mark. Excluding summative assessment also limits the emancipatory potential of self-assessment. Taras (2001) argues that the real control of power is not challenged if students are excluded from summative graded assessment. However, student participation in grading their work may not necessarily mean that students are empowered. Race (1995) points out that if students know that tutors will intervene if they think that the marking process is unsatisfactory, then summative self-assessment cannot be claimed to be participative nor empowering.

CONCLUSION

This chapter maps academic developers' views of student self-assessment implementation in the institution against the variation of the different ways student self-assessment is experienced by academics. The first part of the investigation involved 16 academics from three universities. The aim was to differentiate between qualitatively different meanings and practices of self-assessment amongst academics who had practiced self-assessment in a range of different contexts. Secondly, academic developers from another institution of learning were interviewed for their views on the scope and purposes of student self-assessment as well as on the institutional context for student self-assessment.

The findings of the investigation describe a structure of academics' progressive awareness of meanings and practices of student self-assessment. Three conceptions were identified and discussed in terms of suggesting how student self-assessment may be evaluated in terms of their increasing scope. Each of the levels also has different consequences for the meanings and practices of power arising from experiencing student self-assessment in a particular way.

In teacher-driven self-assessment, the focus on the teacher emphasizes the teacher's retention and exercise of his or her commodity of sovereign power over students. In program-driven self-assessment, the focal awareness on the program of study emphasizes the academic as an agent holding epistemological power as well as being a subject of the same epistemological power situated within the program of study. The program of study represents a point at which epistemological power is applied on the students (through the academic) and on the academic.

In contrast, future-driven self-assessment moves beyond the meaning and practice of power as commodity. The greater awareness of more critical aspects of self-assessment is illuminated by dealing more reflexively with issues of power beyond the teacher's sovereign authority and the epistemological boundaries of the program of study. Academics are also aware of the disciplinary effects of self-assessment practices and attempt to minimize these effects by allowing students some discretion in the types of self-judgments they may elect to show the academic.

Much of the literature on power in student self-assessment focuses on relations of power between the teacher and the student. For example, Hinett and Weeden (2000) argue that the principal advantage of self-assessment is its capacity to elevate students to the status of a co-assessor with the teacher. Likewise, Butcher and Stefani (1995) and Stefani (1994) argue that self-assessment allows students to partner their teachers in the assessment process through being empowered to participate in their own assessment.

The dilemma for many teachers lies in vesting students with sufficient power to realize the benefits of self-assessment, and yet retain sufficient power for themselves to regulate the self-assessment outcomes of students. In contrast, the academic developers were more concerned with a different dilemma—with the forms of power and hierarchy that self-assessment challenges and whether institutions vest academics with sufficient power and autonomy for effective self-assessment practice. This has many implications for academic staff development in relation to articulating and promoting more effective uses of self-assessment and is beyond the scope of this chapter. Further research on issues of power between the institution and the teacher would advance our understanding of the contextual issues that surround academics' meanings and practices of power. In turn, such research would inform academic developers in supporting academics who wish to implement the 'radical practice' of student self-assessment.

REFERENCES

Baum, D. & Baum, C. (1986). Learner, know thyself: Self-assessment and self-determined assessment in education. *The New Era, 67*(3), 65–67.

Boud, D. (1986). *Implementing student self-assessment: HERDSA green guide no. 5.* Kensington, NSW: Higher Education Research & Development Society of Australia.

Boud, D. (1995). *Enhancing learning through self-assessment.* London: Kogan Page.

Brew, A. (1995). What is the scope of self-assessment? In D. Boud (Ed.), *Enhancing learning through self-assessment*, 48–62. London: Kogan Page.

Brown, S. & Glasner, A. (1999). Towards autonomous assessment. In S. Brown & A. Glasner (Eds.), *Assessment matters in higher education*. Buckingham: SRHE and Open University Press.

Burgess, H., Baldwin, M., Dalrymple, J., & Thomas, J. (1999). Developing self-assessment in social work education. *Social Work Education, 18*(2), 133–146.

Butcher, A. C. & Stefani, L. J. (1995). Analysis of peer, self- and staff-assessment in group project work. *Assessment in Education: Principles, Policy & Practice, 2*(2), 165–186.

Dearing, R. (1997). *Higher education in the learning society* (Summary Report). London: HMSO/The National Committee of Inquiry into Higher Education.

Dochy, F. & Segers, M. (1999). The use of self-, peer and co-assessment in higher education: A review. *Studies in Higher Education, 24*(3), 331–350.

Fazey, D. (1993). Self-assessment as a generic skill for enterprising students: The learning process. *Assessment and Evaluation in Higher Education, 18*(3), 235–250.

Gosling, D. (2000). Using Habermas to evaluate two approaches to negotiated assessment. *Assessment and Evaluation in Higher Education, 25*(3), 293–304.

Hinett, K. & Weeden, P. (2000). How am I doing? Developing critical self-evaluation in trainee teachers. *Quality in Higher Education, 6*(3), 245–257.

Khan, S. K., Davies, D. A., & Gupta, J. K. (2001). Formative self-assessment using multiple true-false questions on the internet: Feedback according to confidence about correct knowledge. *Medical Teacher, 23*(2), 158–163.

Marton, F. (1981). Phenomenography: Describing conceptions of the world around us. *Instructional Science, 10*, 177–200.

Marton, F. & Booth, S. (1997). *Learning and awareness*. Mahwah, NJ: Lawrence Erlbaum.

Race, P. (1995). What has assessment done for us—and to us? In P. Knight (Ed.), *Assessment for learning in higher education*, 61–74. London: Kogan Page.

Rainsbury, E. & Hodges, D. (1998). Academic, employer and student collaborative assessment in a work-based cooperative education course. *Assessment and Evaluation in Higher Education, 23*(3), 313–325.

Sluijmans, D., Dochy, F., & Moerkerke, G. (1998). *The use of self-, peer- and co-assessment in higher education: A review of the literature.* Open University of the Netherlands, Educational Technology Expertise Centre.

Stefani, L. (1994). Peer, self and tutor assessment: Relative reliabilities. *Studies in Higher Education, 19*(1), 69–75.

Stefani, L. (1998). Assessment in partnership with learners. *Assessment and Evaluation in Higher Education, 23*(4), 339–350.

Sullivan, K. & Hall, C. (1997). Introducing students to self-assessment. *Assessment and Evaluation in Higher Education, 22*(3), 289–305.

Tamir, P. (1999). Self-assessment: The use of self-report knowledge and opportunity to learn inventories. *International Journal of Science Education, 21*(4), 401–411.

Taras, M. (2001). The use of tutor feedback and student self-assessment in summative assessment tasks: Towards transparency for students and for tutors. *Assessment and Evaluation in Higher Education, 26*(6), 605–614.

18 Students' experiences of feedback on academic assignments in higher education
Implications for practice

Liz McDowell

INTRODUCTION

This chapter explores differences in higher education students' experiences of tutor feedback on assignments. In the UK, feedback on student work is effectively mandated through quality assurance systems such as the national Quality Assurance Agency's Code of Practice on assessment (http://www. qaa.ac.uk/public/cop/codesofpractice.htm). It features in the new National Student Survey (http://www.hefce.ac.uk/news/hefce/2006/nss.htm), which is used to evaluate the quality of education provided by universities. Nevertheless, the provision of feedback on students' academic work is also regarded as raising dilemmas in relation to feasibility and effectiveness. Feasibility is brought into question by the pressure on academic staff time and the difficulties of providing individual feedback to students who are taught in large groups (Knight & Yorke, 2003, p.43). Modular curriculum structures are also said to give rise to problems of getting feedback to students in a timely manner (Weaver, 2006). Questions of effectiveness frequently centre on debates about whether students actually use feedback (Higgins et al., 2002), whether they understand it (Chanock, 2000; Higgins et al., 2001; Weaver, 2006), and whether the feedback is appropriately constructed (Ivanic et al., 2000). The positioning of feedback systems as part of auditable procedures is considered to damage the dialogic functions of feedback (Crook et al., 2006).

One very important message from research in formative assessment is that, if feedback is to have any effect on learning, the learner must respond to it (Black & Wiliam, 1998). We therefore need to understand how students respond to assignments and to feedback. Higgins et al. (2001, p. 272) suggest that students are likely to 'conceptualise feedback in qualitatively different ways'. However, most of the research to date treats higher education students as a group, either students 'in general' or all of the students on a particular course or at a specific level, such as first year undergraduates. This chapter explicitly addresses *differences* in the ways that students experience feedback and suggests that we can identify a small number of significantly different experiences which can sensitize us to new dimensions and considerations in feedback practice.

RESEARCH METHOD

The research study illuminates some of the different ways in which university students experience academic assignments and associated feedback. The study adopted a learner-centred, phenomenographic approach (Marton & Booth, 1997).

This methodology is the basis of what has been, arguably, the most influential body of student learning research in higher education in recent decades. According to Richardson (1999, p. 72), phenomenography has 'revolutionized the way in which both researchers and teachers think about the process and outcomes of learning in higher education'. Phenomenography is an interpretive methodological approach focussing on 'the ways of experiencing different phenomena, ways of seeing them, knowing about them, having skills related to them' (Marton & Booth, 1997, p. 117).

An aspect of methodology which is specific to phenomenography is the representation of experience in terms of a limited number of mutually exclusive categories. These represent the critical differences in the collective experience of some phenomenon and these are generally few in number; for example, five conceptions of university teaching experienced by academics (Prosser & Trigwell, 1999). It is experiences rather than individuals that are placed in categories. The same students may experience assignments and feedback differently at different times depending on the context, the particular features of the assignment and so on.

In this research study data was gathered from undergraduate students in two different universities in the north of England: biology students in their second year of study and social science students in their third (final) year of study.[1] The main data source was in-depth interviews with a total of 15 students concerning their experiences of study and specifically their experiences of doing assignments. In addition, contextual data on the study context, including class observation and lecturer interviews, were also collected. Written assignments in both programs were intended to serve both summative and formative assessment purposes, as is often the case in higher education. Assignments counted towards module grades but were also being used as a tool for learning. Students practised their skills by undertaking a number of coursework assignments and were given advice and feedback, before and after assignment submission. However, lecturers and students placed considerable emphasis on written feedback comments returned to students alongside their assignment marks. A number of categories termed assignment *pathways* were developed in the research. The four pathways represent variations in the student experience that are distinct but do not represent a hierarchy or developmental continuum.

Table 18.1 Variation in the experience of feedback across the four pathways

Pathway	Primary focus	Meaning	Affective impacts
Gathering: Feedback as judgement	Subject matter	Judgement of capability	Lack of confidence Feel threatened
Connecting: Feedback as learning	Subject matter	Integral to good learning	Affirmation Sense of involvement
Minimalist: Feedback as checkpoint	Marks	Check and regulate effort	Relief Detachment and distancing
Performing: Feedback as guidance	Generic assignment requirements	Guidance for subsequent performances	Builds confidence Sense of achievement and purpose

RESULTS

Aspects of the research findings relating to students' responses to feedback and written assignments are presented here. Two of the pathways, termed *gathering* and *connecting*, share a common feature in relation to feedback. In both cases feedback in relation to the content or subject matter dealt with in the assignment is of primary importance. In the case of the other two categories, *minimalist* and *performing*, it is the generic aspects of feedback concerning the expectations and standards for academic work that are a primary focus for the student. Although the categories are illustrated by quotations from students it should be stressed again that they represent distinctive experiences rather than being labels attributed to individuals. Table 18.1 illustrates the main features of the model.

THE GATHERING PATHWAY

At the core of this pathway is the student's aim to find out about or understand the topic in order to complete the assignment.

Overview

The student following the gathering pathway believes that he or she needs to gain a good understanding of the topic in order to produce a good assignment, and works conscientiously to *gather* information and read widely or in depth. Although students attempt to reorganize the ideas and information and present them in their own way, they tend to build up the assignment in sections from the information and materials that seem relevant to each part, which may result in a lack of coherence in the written piece. At the end of the assignment, the student likes to feel a sense of satisfaction in relation to having completed the task and understood some new material, but is concerned about the marks and uncertain about how well they have done.

Feedback

In the gathering pathway, students regard feedback as indicating how well they have understood the topic and presented their assignment. They are likely to view feedback in negative terms as indicating 'where you have gone wrong'. Students find it difficult to make use of feedback for subsequent assignments. They attribute the problem of using feedback at least partially to the vagaries of individual lecturers who, it seems to the student, want different things. Students may see the comments they receive as rather arbitrary or specific to a single task, with little underlying consistency that might indicate generic requirements for academic work. Students tend not to actively seek feedback on their work, simply accepting whatever is presented to them. In most situations, they prefer not to actually discuss their work with a lecturer as they find this too threatening.

What is attended to?

It is important to students to feel that they have understood, and to them this means 'the right understanding' as judged by the expert lecturer. The mark gained is the primary indicator of this but students also pay attention to specific comments about the content of their assignment. Feedback which might be regarded as more generic and focuses on how they have, for example, structured their assignment or developed an argument, is viewed as less helpful.

What does it mean to the student?

Feedback is seen as a judgement on the assignment and, importantly, of the students' personal ability. This is because the students equate a good assignment with a good understanding of a topic, and developing a good understanding as a test of their own capabilities. A good mark and positive feedback are reassuring but negative feedback is difficult to cope with especially as students find it difficult to see how to use any feedback to improve subsequent performances. Selena,[2] a social science student, said that she was aware of all of the general requirements but still found it difficult in relation to each specific assignment: 'you know all [the lecturers'] comments by now, but you don't really know what's going to apply'.

How do students feel about it?

Students enjoy learning and may become very involved in the process of investigating a topic and producing an assignment. It is important to them to feel that they are learning something and to be a 'good student'. Although they may feel they have gained a good understanding when they submit the assignment, they do not have confidence in this until they receive validation from a lecturer. They find feedback threatening and are reassured if it is good and upset if it is bad. They may rationalize negative feedback by saying that it is actually about the presentation of their assignment and how they wrote it rather than 'really' meaning that they did not understand the topic. Sadiyya, reflecting on an essay said: 'I daren't say I didn't really understand it because…I'd done the reading'. Even consistently good feedback over a number of modules did not seem to help students to build confidence in their own capabilities or enable them to judge for themselves how well they have done. Even as a final year student, Shahira said about an assignment: 'I don't know what she is after, or what any lecturer is after'.

CONNECTING

In this pathway students try to develop their understanding and knowledge about the topic in ways that make sense to them and have some relevance to their own interests and ideas.

Overview

The starting point is learning by building on previous knowledge and exploring or developing it further. Students undertake reading as a process of connecting, following trails of ideas and links from one source to another, and will look quite broadly for relevant materials. They tend to integrate their work on the assignment so that they are finding materials, reading, and writing all at the same time. The end point of the process is a personal sense of understanding within the subject. Students gain satisfaction from this achievement and through the responses of other people to their ideas.

Feedback

Feedback is viewed as a dialogue rather than as merely receiving feedback from a lecturer. Students following this pathway regard discussion prior to submitting an assignment as valuable. They actively seek opportunities to discuss the topic and their ideas about it with fellow students and friends and, in some cases, with lecturers. Feedback is a way of testing out and developing their own ideas through sharing with others and a way of receiving an acknowledgement of their ideas and contribution. Whilst feedback about generic matters, such as assignment structure, is also recognized and acknowledged, students like to write assignments 'in their own way' and do not necessarily follow a standard approach.

What is attended to?

In relation to feedback received with a marked assignment, students look for comments which indicate a response to the content of their assignment and their own ideas. They hope that the lecturer will indicate some appreciation or interest in what they have written and, ideally, continue the dialogue by, for example, suggesting ways in which the work could be developed. The mark gained is relevant but of secondary importance. However, since students are sometimes concerned that their approach to writing an assignment, being somewhat unconventional, might be marked down by certain lecturers, the mark is a confirmation that, as Sophie said, she had 'got away with it'.

What does it mean to students?

In this case feedback is about developing understanding through dialogue and discussion and is seen as an important, perhaps vital, part of learning. Students expect to give as well as receive feedback, not necessarily in the sense of giving marks or formal comment, but as part of discussing their subject with other interested people, so that they contribute to the development of their own and other people's understanding.

How do students feel about it?

Students have a strong sense of personal ownership of learning. Feedback, in the broad sense, is viewed very positively as an opportunity for learning rather than as a threat or judgement. Feedback which is purely generic would tend to be disregarded and students would be dissatisfied if feedback did not contain within it a genuine discussion of ideas about the topic. Written feedback on assignments can be 'nice to have' but students regard other forms of feedback as more relevant.

In contrast to the strong subject or content focus above, in the minimalist and performing pathways there is a focus on generic feedback giving indications of the requirements for academic work.

MINIMALIST

This pathway stems from a concern to complete the academic task as quickly and easily as possible, without necessarily learning very much but demonstrating to the assessor that the task has been done. It is a 'classic' example of a surface approach to study (Martonet al., 1997).

Overview

The pathway is task-centred and students minimize their own time and effort by, for example, basing their assignment on lecture notes or a few resources that they find quickly and easily. As they write the assignment there is a flavour of 'cut-and-paste' in terms of selecting and rearranging the information obtained, with very limited, if any, personal transformation. The main outcome for students is the mark obtained, although they would prefer to feel *some* sense of satisfaction by having, in their own terms, done a reasonable job.

Feedback

Feedback is viewed as a way for the student to check that they have 'done OK'. They may use feedback to regulate their study approaches, especially to gauge the amount of effort and time that they need to put in.

What is attended to?

Students pay most attention to the marks received and may not even read comments. What is most important is that they know they have 'got through'. When they do pay attention to comments they may focus particularly on 'surface' features such as grammar, spelling, general structure, word length, and referencing, using them as guidelines to follow for the next assignment.

What does it mean to students?

The purpose of receiving marks is that students are guided in their future efforts in deciding how much they have to do. If they have done badly they may decide to 'put more work in'. If the mark is what they hoped for, the comments are unlikely to be used. If they have done less well than they hoped they may look at the comments for guidance on what they need to do in future. They may also use the comments to work out what lecturers want so that they can try to show that they have done what is wanted in future, but with little intention of engaging with the more complex aspects of assignment writing such as development of an argument.

How does student feel about it?

From some of the data it appears that students using a minimalist pathway are rather detached and dismissive of the academic context. They make an implicit 'bargain' to do the minimum needed to obtain a reasonable mark. This might be considered as a strategic approach to academic study where students have other priorities. Feedback and the marks they receive allow students to check whether they are making sufficient effort. It would therefore appear that they have no personal concerns about negative feedback. However, other data suggests that this apparent detachment may be a distancing strategy for some students who find that they cannot cope in their studies. Some comments suggest a sense that there is no point in trying to do better: 'Even if I spent hours and hours doing an essay, I could not get something that someone else in my class could, because they're just a better writer' (Salim).

PERFORMING

This pathway is based on students using a process of producing an assignment and meeting academic requirements that they have tried and tested but continue to refine.

Overview

The primary starting point is task-centred. Although students are very likely to develop some understanding of the subject matter involved, this is a secondary concern, almost a by-product. The students aim to find relevant and high quality materials quickly and efficiently. In writing the assignment they keep in mind what is going to satisfy the assessor. In this study, students talked about, and showed some evidence of using, skills in critical thinking, use of evidence, academic writing and so on, in order to produce an assignment which had an argument, theme or viewpoint, giving it some coherence supported by evidence. At the end of the assignment, students feel a sense of satisfaction in having clearly demonstrated that they have done what is required to a high standard and expect a good grade.

Feedback

Students actively seek feedback, which helps them understand and meet course requirements. For example, in biology, the second year students undertaking an extended essay on a self-selected topic were allocated a lecturer as an essay supervisor to help them with this unfamiliar task. However, the module leader reported that, in his experience over many years, very few made more than one brief contact with a supervisor, and it was exceptional for students to give their supervisor a draft essay for comment. Brian, a student identified as taking a performing approach to this assignment, saw his supervisor on a number of occasions, and submitted a draft essay for comment.

What is attended to?

In this pathway students receiving feedback on an academic assignment are looking for guidance on the lecturers' expectations and on the criteria used for judging their work. They pay attention to general guidance, rather than comments specific to the topic of the particular assignment, and try to transfer and adapt this guidance to future assignments. The mark obtained for the assignment is very important, but they would be dissatisfied if they did not also receive feedback in the form of comments to help them in future work.

What does it mean to the student?

Feedback has very positive connotations for the students. It provides guidance enabling them to improve or maintain their academic performance, to ensure that they are 'on track'. They are seeking to discern and then to adopt and refine a model or template for their assignments, so they take and use comments which can be 'generalized' to future assignments.

How do students feel about it?

Students are confident in their current performance or in their capabilities to learn how to do well, with sufficient resilience to learn from feedback even if they have received a low grade. Stuart, as a final year student, felt that he generally knew for himself when he had produced a good assignment because, over time, he had built up an understanding of what was required. Nevertheless he liked to have confirmation through feedback. Sometimes the lecturer's view was in conflict with the student's own view. The student might be unconvinced or even angry but, pragmatically, accepted that it was the lecturers who defined what was needed and worked out how to adjust to requirements.

DISCUSSION: SUPPORTING DIFFERENT PATHWAYS THROUGH FEEDBACK

This research shows some of the variation in students' approaches to feedback and its purposes and use. When we view this within the context of students' overall approaches to academic assignments, it can illuminate some reasons why feedback may be used in particular ways, not used appropriately, or not used at all. Although students can do well in terms of course grades using the different pathways, in each case there are some problems associated with using feedback, which may limit the quality of the student's experience of learning and their academic achievements, alongside some positive responses to feedback. If students' experiences and achievements are to be enhanced they may need different kinds of feedback or be given help to see feedback in a different way.

Students who use a gathering pathway take feedback very personally as a judgement on their own capability. They are in a dependent and vulnerable position where they rely on external judgement which appears to them as threatening and somewhat arbitrary, even when they receive good grades. Their identity remains one of the 'good student'. As suggested by Black and Wiliam (1998), non-specific, comments such as 'A good essay' or 'Excellent structure and conclusion' are not helpful. Drawing on the work of Dweck (2000) we can suggest that these students hold a fixed view of intelligence and they seek confirmation of their capability from each 'test'. Feedback needs to direct them to consider successful strategies and approaches that they have used and encourage them to take on challenges and develop their approaches still further. Students seem to have problems in recognising generic principles or criteria which they can transfer from assignment to assignment, perhaps because they focus on getting the subject matter 'right'. They tend to keep their own ideas out of their academic writing, because as Bridget said: '[lecturers] know more than I do and I think I might look a bit stupid if I wrote the wrong thing'. Perhaps because of this, students may 'play safe' and concentrate on reproducing knowledge, albeit often in a skilled and sophisticated way.

The connecting pathway suggests committed and personally engaged students but those who make high demands on the study context in terms of feedback and engagement. Again they focus on the subject matter of assignments, and may be willing to take a risk in order to produce the kind of assignment that satisfies them personally. Such students will be dissatisfied if they do not have opportunities within their studies to discuss their ideas. In order to be valued, feedback on an assignment needs to focus on what the students have to say and, ideally, be dialogic in nature (Ivanic et al., 2000). Students are able to accept, and even welcome, feedback which not only acknowledges and endorses their work but is also critical and challenging. However, generic feedback may not be attended to, and students need to be encouraged to engage with the requirements for academic writing in their subject, in order to further develop their academic performance and progress. One way of approaching this is to include, in feedback, not only what needs to be done but also why, in order to help students to fully understand the basis of academic practices. There is a danger that otherwise they will view such requirements as restrictive, arbitrary, and irrelevant conventions. For example, Sean explained how he would get to a point in doing an essay where he was satisfied and knew what he wanted to say, then he would take what he had written and completely re-organize it in order to provide what he perceived that lecturers wanted, and he saw this as creating 'two opposed sets of knowledge...one academic and one personal'.

The performing pathway is likely to be followed by some highly successful students. There appears to be no problem in giving feedback to such students. They welcome it and use it effectively, picking up on comments and suggestions, applying them to other assignments, and developing a set of generic principles for themselves. In stark contrast to the gathering pathway, these students are extremely 'cue-conscious' (Miller & Parlett, 1974). Guidance and feedback may help students to overcome two specific limitations of their approach. Firstly they can become too fixed and 'formulaic' in their approach to assignments. Stuart did not do as well as he hoped in his dissertation and this was perhaps because he 'treated it just like a long essay' rather than realising that the expectations were somewhat different. Feedback may be needed to help students to see that specific types of assignment or topic may require variations in approach. Secondly, feedback which addresses what the assignment says rather than how it is said may encourage students to engage more fully with the academic content, avoiding the danger that they see assignments only as hurdles to be overcome rather than also as opportunities for learning and developing their understanding. Brian performed very well in his assignments but was bemused when a lecturer tried to engage him in some discussion about one of the topics covered; he said, in tones of amazement 'The lecturer seems to think I'm interested!'

The minimalist pathway, at least in this research study, did not lead to academic success. It may have been personally successful for some students who did not wish to engage in their studies but to use their time and energies in other ways. However, there was also the suggestion that students were using their energies elsewhere because they were struggling academically. For students who use this pathway most or all of the time, something more than enhanced feedback is likely to be needed to make any significant change. In this case it is perhaps the form of the feedback which could make the most difference. Discussions with a lecturer rather than written comments might succeed in engaging the student with feedback which they would otherwise ignore. However, if this is not an academic requirement, such students are unlikely to actively seek discussion with their lecturers. Assignments which include a component of peer feedback may also make a difference since the views and responses of fellow students might carry more weight than those of academics. There is the danger that these students will remain only marginally engaged in their studies.

CONCLUSIONS

The different experiences of assignments and feedback presented here may give lecturers a deeper insight into students' responses and what they signify. They also suggest some general principles for feedback that may help a range of students. Importantly, feedback given by lecturers needs to engage with *both* the subject-related, content aspects of student work and the generic features of structure, presentation, use of evidence, and so on. This suggestion runs counter to those in some other research (Higgins et al., 2002; Weaver, 2006) where it is suggested that feedback focussed on the subject matter of an assignment may be irrelevant for the student who has moved on to other assignments or modules. Feedback should include clear pointers to ways forward, but I argue that these should address both the general approaches that students have taken and the ways in which they have dealt with specific subject content. This may help students such as those taking a gathering pathway to absorb the generic principles through their illustration in specific examples tied to the content of assignments. The focus on subject content may help students experiencing a performing approach to realize that *what* they say is relevant alongside *how* they say it, and it will also help to foster the commitment of those adopting connecting pathways.

There were examples in the research study, beyond the confines of tutor feedback on assignments, which illustrate how students may start to view feedback differently. For example, biology students were required to give a presentation to fellow students on a topic they had researched. This was an important experience for some who began to think differently about presenting a topic, realising that they had to *communicate* with their peers. Some were much more active in seeking feedback on their ideas and their presentational approach in this oral presentation assignment than they had been in relation to written work. In social science, all students in the study were taking an area studies module where the lecturer encouraged students to draw on firsthand experience and 'non-academic' knowledge. For some students, it was the first time they had ever felt that they had anything of their own to say in a university classroom, and they began to get more of an insight into the 'feedback' value of exchange of ideas and opinions. In conclusion, coming to view academic work as communication and dialogue, supported by feedback, may be a key to successful and satisfying learning.

NOTES

1. The universities and the degree courses are not identified in order to maintain confidentiality as agreed in the research protocol.
2. Social science students have been given pseudonyms beginning with S, biology students with B.

REFERENCES

Black, P. & Wiliam, D. (1998). Assessment and classroom learning. *Assessment in Education*, 5(1), 7–74.

Chanock, K. (2000). Comments on essays: Do students understand what tutors write? *Teaching in Higher Education, 5*(1), 95–105.

Crook, C., Gross, H., & Dymott, R. (2006). Assessment relationships in higher education: The tension of process and practice. *British Educational Research Journal, 32*(1), 95–114.

Dweck, C. S. (2000). *Self- theories: Their role in motivation, personality and development.* Philadelphia: Taylor & Francis.

Higgins, R., Hartley, P., & Skelton, A. (2001). Getting the message across: The problem of communicating assessment feedback. *Teaching in Higher Education, 6*(2), 269–274.

Higgins, R., Hartley, P., & Skelton, A. (2002). The conscientious consumer: Reconsidering the role of assessment feedback in student learning. *Studies in Higher Education, 27*(1), 53–64.

Ivanic, R., Clark, R., & Rimmershaw, R. (2000). What am I supposed to make of this? The messages conveyed to students by tutors' written comments. In M. R. Lea & B.Stierer (Eds.), *Student writing in higher education: New contexts,* 47–65. Buckingham: SRHE & Open University Press.

Knight, P. T. & Yorke, M. (2003). *Assessment, learning and employability.* Maidenhead: Open University Press.

Marton, F. & Booth, S. (1997). *Learning and awareness.* Marwah, NJ: Lawrence Erlbaum.

Marton, F., Hounsell, D., & Entwistle, N. (1997). (Eds.) *The experience of learning* (2nd ed.). Edinburgh: Scottish Academic Press.

Miller, C. & Parlett, M. (1974). *Up to the mark: A study of the examination game.* London, SRHE.

Prosser, M. & Trigwell, K. (1999). *Understanding learning and teaching: The experience in higher education.* Buckingham: SRHE & Open University Press.

Richardson, J. T. E. (1999). The concepts and methods of phenomenographic research. *Review of Educational Research, 69*(1), 53–82.

Weaver, M. R. (2006). Do students value feedback? Student perceptions of tutors' written responses. *Assessment and Evaluation in Higher Education, 31*(3), 379–394.

19 Assessment beyond belief
The cognitive process of grading

Janice Orrell

INTRODUCTION

A central dimension of assessment is the interpretation of the learning attainment and grading, or marking, of students' learning products. This is a significant and time-consuming task at all levels of education. Often there is much at stake for students' futures in this aspect of assessment, since grades may affect progression in a course, scholarships, admission to higher levels of study, and sometimes selection for employment. Grading can have a profound psychological impact on students. Students are often defined by the grades attributed to their learning outputs and, in turn, they so define their own personal worth.

Cox (1985) indicated that the two most pressing problems of assessment were firstly, to arrive at a reliable grade and, secondly, to do so through a process that supports desirable learning goals. Ideally, the interpretation and grading of students' learning products should be guided by predetermined learning outcomes that encourage deep learning. These should include student mastery, analysis, application, creativity, ethical reasoning and critical evaluation of concepts, and a body of knowledge generally identified as desirable qualities of university education (Biggs, 1991, 1992). Furthermore, it has been found that assessment is pivotal in shaping students' learning outcomes (Biggs, 1991) and determining whether students adopt a reproductive or transformative approach to learning. Assessment is at its best, therefore, when it is integral to the teaching learning process and promotes desired learning outcomes.

RESEARCH STUDIES ON GRADING

The findings of experimental studies over many decades provide considerable evidence that interpreting and grading is highly context dependent (Geisinger, 1982) and significantly influenced by factors that have little bearing on students' learning achievements. Some influences that were found pertain solely to the assessors themselves. Branthwaite et al. (1981)

identified the point that assessors' personalities and dispositions significantly influenced their attribution of a grade, such as their desire either to be liked by their students or to be regarded as tough markers. Other assessor-related factors include assessors' beliefs about, and past experience of, grading (Orrell, 1997) and assessors' prior knowledge and expectations of students (Branthwaite et al., 1981; Terwilliger, 1977). The individual assessor's pedagogical objectives and content knowledge (Noizet & Caverni, 1978) are also relevant. Further studies have also been conducted on another set of factors, namely the potential risk of assessor bias due to student or assessor gender and ethnicity. However, findings from these studies are largely contradictory and inconclusive (Heywood, 2000).

A second set of factors influencing grading includes those relating to the immediate context. These include the quality of the preceding papers just assessed (Daly & Dickson-Markman, 1982), recent classroom events and conditions, and prior assessment events (Noizet & Caverni, 1978).

A third set of factors found to be influential in grading is the presentational or surface features of students' texts; that is, performance attributes not directly related to stated learning outcomes. These include the graphic quality of students' texts (Marshall & Powers, 1969; Hughes et al., 1983) and students' accurate use of expected writing grammars and citation conventions. For example, in the case of an essay, there is an expectation that it will include an introduction, body, conclusion, and references. There are other grammars for specific forms of assessment such as case studies or field reports. If one of the components is missing or is incomplete, the grade may be profoundly affected despite the quality of the work submitted and its relevance to the publicly stated learning outcomes (Orrell, 1997). On the other hand there are factors relevant to students' attainment of learning outcomes which also influence grading. These include general readability of the text (Chase, 1979, 1983) and the quality of the introductory paragraph (Townsend et al., 1983).

It is clear from this brief summary of several decades of research that the task of grading students' texts is influenced by a wide range of surface factors, many of which do not always relate to students' achievements of stated learning outcomes. It might be expected that assessors could exercise some control and mitigate the effects of these surface influences if they were apprised of the potential limitations and biases in their judgements of students' learning products. However, many assessors are not aware of the tacit extraneous influences on their grading. Highly technical knowledge is required to construct valid assessment tasks and devise reliable grading procedures. In universities, assessors are rarely trained for the task of interpreting and grading their students' learning products. Universities usually adopt a *natural* approach to assessment (Berieter & Scardamalia, 1988). That is, assessors' knowledge of, and expertise in regard to the subject matter, as well as their experience in grading, seem to be the only required qualifications for the task. Furthermore, it has been demonstrated that even where assessors *were* trained to ignore particular surface factors such as handwriting when grading written tests, the influence of these surface factors on the resultant grade was not reduced (Marshall & Powers, 1969; Sweedler-Brown, 1992).

Prior research into grading has been limited and its utility has been criticized. Tittle, (1989, 1994) argues that because studies of grading are largely the domain of assessment theorists rather than practitioners, they provide little insight into the complex human factors that influence the grading decision. Much of the research is experimental and is not located in the context of teaching and learning. It largely uses grade outcomes as data, is atomistic, often focusing on a single factor (e.g. the influence of handwriting). Alternative qualitative studies are largely interview-based. This data may merely reveal assessors' ideals and rationalisations and are subject to 'social lies'. These studies offer assessors little insight.

RESEARCH STUDY: GRADING IN HIGHER EDUCATION

This study set out to investigate assessors' thinking in the context of everyday practice and from this generate a framework that might aid assessors' critical scrutiny of their own grading practice. Two previous studies (Noizet & Caverni, 1978; Rapaille, 1986) were highly influential in the design and analysis of the study. Although neither was conducted in higher education, they were the only studies found that examined the thinking of assessors as they graded student work. Noizet and Caverni undertook a large scale, experimental study that examined the thinking of a large number of assessors as they graded a standardized, simple dictation task. From this, they produced a very plausible model of cognitive processing during the interpreting and grading phase of assessment, which also identified the possible foci of assessors' attention. The subsequent study by Rapaille identified that authentic data regarding thinking and decision making while grading could be generated if *natural conditions* were maintained. Natural conditions required that assessors grade their own students for real grades that attracted all the normal consequences.

In the current study, 16 academics, with between 4 and 20 years experience in teaching and assessment in higher education, volunteered and were then trained in executing concurrent 'think aloud' protocols; that is, *thinking out loud while performing a task*, in contrast to describing one's thinking (Ericcson & Simon, 1993). The participants were then tape-recorded as they thought out loud while they assessed their own students' text-based learning products that were for real grades. The research was conducted under *natural conditions* building on the work of Rapaille (1986).

The protocols generated were analysed using a taxonomy derived from the data. It included seven basic cognitive processing codes (Table 19.1), with their definitions grounded in cognitive processing theory, and five

Table 19.1 Taxonomy of cognitive processing during grading

Cognitive process codes	
Recognition	Perception of an attribute or component of the student's product
Reactions	A positive, negative, neutral value assigned to a perceived attribute.
Recall	Something expected, previously known or believed is remembered. (Sub-codes Beliefs, Expectation, Knowledge)
Monitor	Assessors' self-management and meta-awareness of assessment processes (Sub-codes: Self-Management, Perception, Comprehension, Pose Problem, Predicting, Planning, Establishing the Context)
Judgements	An opinion is stated relating to local components or global product features (Sub-codes local, global)
Reasoning	A number of propositions are processed together with the idea that they are logically linked, to infer beyond what is immediately perceivable, or to justify an opinion or inference that has just been formed (Sub-codes, Inferring, Justifying)
Actions	Reports of assessors' actions including writing on student's text / checking backwards and forwards in the text/ making notes for assessors' future use (Sub-codes: Teaching, Editing, Feedback, Checking, Noting, Assigning grades)

basic foci of attention codes (Table 19.2). All thinking in the protocols was segmented in to a single unit of meaning and each unit assigned to the relevant codes and the codes' frequencies were calculated. The total number of elements coded was 2095.

Table 19.2 Taxonomy of attention during grading

Focus of attention codes	
Content	Statements that relate to the substance or content of the essay
Approach	Statements that relate to :(a) the way in which students managed the assessment task; (b) students' level of understanding; (c) students use of learning strategies implied in the student product.
Presentation	Statements that relate to writing conventions and graphic quality of the text
Student	Statements that relate to the particular *student* who produced the paper, or that relate to *students* in general
Assessors' concerns	Statements that relate to the task of assessing itself pertaining to either the grading scheme and the assessment process
Unclassifiable	Non-task related statements and general indefinable statements

Raw frequencies, mean percentage frequencies and standard deviations of both the process codes and focus of attention codes were calculated. Consistency in the use of the taxonomy in the analysis was verified using co-coder and main coder reliability tests using Cohen's Kappa (Bakeman & Gottman, 1986). The between-coder Kappa value was 0.77. Fliess (1981, cited in Bakeman & Gottman, 1986) considered Kappa values estimated at 0.60 to 0.75 as good agreements and values estimated over 0.75 as excellent. The results of this level of analysis were further investigated using a matrix of both sets of data to produce more finely specified assessment behaviours.

IDENTIFYING ASSESSMENT BEHAVIOURS

The *cognitive processing* and *focus of attention* code matrix produced 182 specific assessment behaviours. For example, three subsets of cognitive process code Recall were Beliefs, Expectations, and Knowledge. In the matrix these three sub-codes produced 15 categories of potential behaviour. However, only 71 different categories of actual behaviour out of the 2095 coded occurrences were identified in the data. The most frequent behaviour was Recognition of Content (15.94 %, n=334). The matrix also indicates some potential behaviour that did not occur at all, such as Judging the student and other behaviours that occurred very seldom, such as Recalling a belief about the student (0.14 %). If a particular behaviour occurred only once, it would have a score of 0.05 %. The Process/Attention frequency matrix is shown in Table 19.3.

FEATURES OF COMMON ASSESSMENT PRACTICE

The following propositions regarding common assessment behaviour have been derived from the analysis of think-aloud data illustrated in Table 19.3. The frequency analysis indicated that assessors predominantly engaged in simple cognitive processing (40.39 %), which comprises the total processing of the first three categories of cues; namely, *recognition, reaction,* and *recall*. These were all simple, brief, unelaborated cognitive processes. Elaborated cognitive processing was far less frequent (28.69 %). Elaborated thinking included judgements and reasoning. That is, less of the total thinking, but more sustained thought was involved in making *Judgements* (local and global), as well as *Reasoning*. Assessors' reasoning involved making inferences about student learning behaviour and attainment that largely went beyond the immediately available information. Reasoning also involved assessors justifying the judgements they had just made. In addition, assessors monitored their own management of the assessment task (15.51 %). Surprisingly, little processing indicated any deliberate recall of

Table 19.3 Process/attention code matrix of think aloud protocols

Process/focus N=2095	Con[a]	Appr[b]	Pres[c]	Stud[d]	Asses[e]	Non-task	Total Proc
Recognition	15.94	3.20	1.72	0.00	0.00	0.00	20.86
Reaction	12.41	3.96	3.15	0.00	0.00	0.00	19.53
Recall	6.11	2.83	1.44	1.81	1.14	0.14	13.46
Knowledge	4.06	0.19	0.10	1.48	0.95	0.14	6.92
Expectation	1.67	2.53	1.34	0.19	0.00	0.00	5.73
Belief	0.38	0.10	0.00	0.14	0.19	0.00	0.81
Monitoring	2.06	3.03	0.91	0.48	8.74	0.34	15.51
Self-management	0.53	0.72	0.43	0.00	6.73	0.24	8.69
Perception	0.57	1.34	0.19	0.19	0.91	0.10	2.39
Comprehension	0.53	0.10	0.05	0.24	0.00	0.00	1.73
Problem posing	0.43	0.77	0.19	0.05	0.24	0.00	1.68
Review & planning	0.00	0.10	0.00	0.00	0.86	0.00	0.96
Judgements	4.01	6.11	1.15	0.19	0.00	1.71	13.18
Local	3.10	4.29	0.81	0.05	0.00	0.00	8.26
Global	0.91	1.82	0.34	0.14	0.00	1.71	4.92
Reasoning	1.81	4.29	0.10	0.00	0.48	0.00	6.68
Inferential	1.48	2.67	0.10	0.00	0.00	0.00	4.25
Justificatory	0.33	1.62	0.00	0.00	0.48	0.00	2.43
Actions	5.43	2.53	2.83	0.00	0.00	0.00	10.79
Response	4.00	2.05	2.44	0.00	0.00	0.00	8.49
Teach	*2.91*	*1.29*	*0.29*	*0.00*	*0.00*	*0.00*	*4.49*
Edit	*0.14*	*0.00*	*2.15*	*0.00*	*0.00*	*0.00*	*2.29*
Feedback	*0.95*	*0.76*	*0.19*	*0.00*	*0.00*	*0.00*	*1.91*
Checking	1.43	0.48	0.19	0.00	0.00	0.00	2.10
Total focus	47.78	25.92	11.26	2.48	10.69	2.19	100.0

[a]Content/[b]Approach/[c]Presentation/[d]Student/[e]Assessor

beliefs, expectations, or knowledge (13.46 %), and only 10 % of the thinking was involved with reporting of writing actions such as giving students feedback, teaching new information, editing, or checking.

The protocols indicated that during assessment and grading, academics executed routines, such as brief teaching, editing, and providing reactive feedback. These routines were largely triggered by cues situated within the students' texts rather than by a predetermined marking guide. Academics engaged in self-regulatory behaviour and monitored their own comprehension of students' intentions as writers. Self-regulation was predominantly in the form of strategic management of personal assessment behaviour, with little focus on pedagogical concerns or problems. Overall, academics' thinking while they assessed student work focused on gathering information to generate a mental representation of exactly what the student had written. To a lesser extent, assessors looked for evidence of students' effort and management of the assessment task; namely, whether students had done what they were asked to do.

STAGES IN THE ASSESSMENT AND GRADING PROCESS

Further analysis was conducted to address the question of whether the assessors' thinking behaviour changed over time. A quartile analysis indicated that there were changes over time in both the cognitive processing and the focus of assessors' thinking. The first and the last quartiles have some quite specific features suggesting that there are three observable phases, each with a distinctive purpose:

Phase 1. Initial task elaboration
Phase 2. Cue acquisition and construction of a mental model
Phase 3. Grading and Summing up

The first phase was pre-reading thinking and was conceptualized as an *Initial Task Elaboration Phase*, a behaviour described in most cognitive models of problem solving. The function of this phase was to establish the context of the 'interpreting and grading problem', and this was accomplished by recalling the demands of the task and the assessor's knowledge about the student who had produced the text. Simple processing, elaborated reasoning, and self-monitoring were also included in this phase. The initial, simple cognitive processing, involved assessors' recognition of surface presentation attributes and their expression of brief reactions to them. Initial elaborated reasoning generated inferences about how students had approached the assessment tasks. Initial self-monitoring focused on assessors' management of their own assessment behaviour. Attributes relating to the student who had produced the text were brought into consciousness early in this initial phase of the assessment process. This created conditions for a primacy effect, whereby this initial perception predetermined the nature of future perceptions and opinion-formation regarding the text.

The second phase involved *cue acquisition* in which assessors read and noted cues in the learning product. The cognitive processes in this phase enabled assessors to make local judgements about: the accuracy of the content; the appropriateness of the students' approaches to their task; and the suitability of the presentation features. The process/focus analysis of the data suggests that the processing during in this phase was non-problematized with the focus of assessors' thinking prompted by cues in the students' texts rather than being engaged in a complex analysis of students' levels of learning achievement or the ideas that students had generated. The cognitive analysis in this phase was dominated by assessors' recognition of content cues so they might construct a mental representation of their students' texts in order to judge their quality intuitively against a tacit, norm product (Noizet & Caverni, 1978). Judgements made during this phase focused mostly on students' understanding of content, their approach to their assessment tasks, and their compliance with academic writing conventions. Academics written responses to students were brief and executed largely to teach new content and to edit spelling, sentence structure, and compositional grammar. By contrast, there was little feedback written on students texts that might guide students' future learning and that might indicate students' level of mastery of the content and the quality of the ideas they had generated.

The third phase has been conceptualized as a *Grading and Summing up Phase*. The major significance of the final phase was that this was when the grade was most likely to be assigned. This last stage was characterized by more global judgements, more written responses to students, and more self-monitoring by assessors' regarding their own behaviour. The notations on students' texts were largely justifications of the grade with little feedback that would provide the students with a guide to improving their learning product in the future. Reasoning emphasized making inferences about how students' had approached their tasks and justifying assessors' judgements. Assessors' thinking when deciding on a grade was exceptionally brief and it was characterized by considerable uncertainty in every case.

This time analysis is important because it illustrates how assessors' attention to writing discourse conventions and recalling the students who have produced the texts is greatest in the first phase. Furthermore, the focus on presentation attributes or on the students who had produced the texts also occurred at the critical final phase, influencing global judgements about students' products and the grade. The cognitive concepts of anchoring and primacy effects (Cowan, 1988) suggest that prior subjective knowledge about students has considerable potential to influence grading of texts. After the initial task elaboration phase, however, attention to these factors was minimal until critical moments, in the last phase, when assessors were forming global judgements and justifying grading decisions. It is at this point that presentation attributes and student attributes, heeded in the early phases, were more like to be recalled.

THE RELATIONSHIP OF ASSESSMENT
TO TEACHING AND LEARNING

The analysis of assessor behaviour raises questions about the validity and reliability of grading. It also challenges idealized conceptions about the relationships between assessment, grading, teaching, and learning.

Validity and standards

The thinking-in-assessment analysis identified that, when assigning grades, assessors paid significant attention to graphic and other surface presentation cues. Presentation cues are surface features of a text and, as such, should not be the major determinant of a grade. Ideally, we should expect to see more focus on evidence of students' attainment of higher learning goals. At the moment of grading, assessors did engage in some general-ized observations about students' thinking, but generally there was very little evidence that these experienced assessors were seeking cues to identify the extent to which students had interpreted and transformed ideas. There was little attempt to view the assessment process in terms of learning and pedagogy.

Assessment is considered a vehicle for the maintenance of academic standards in higher education. While assessors did focus on simple aspects of cognitive mastery, such as correct understanding of concepts, they did this in atomistic and non-specific terms, so that their appreciation of the levels of cognitive attainment they were assessing or expecting was not observable. In other words, the 'think aloud' data did not reveal explicit grade-related standards of learning performance, such as that described in Biggs's (1992) SOLO taxonomy. Neither did assessors make judgements about the student's learning product by comparison with publicly agreed standards. The lack of explicitly articulated standards and expectations has immediate impacts, in terms of validity and, indeed, reliability, but also has long-term consequences (Sadler, 2003).

In contrast with a standards-based approach, assessors were observed to undertake a comparison of the text in terms of its quality relative to other students' performances. Other students' performances exercised a tacit influence over the grading decision. The qualities of other students' performances, however, do not provide a stable basis for maintaining standards because as a basis for grade decisions they are unpredictable and highly variable.

Bias and reliability

The study raises questions about the reliability of grades due to potential bias, because grades were clearly influenced by assessors' knowledge of the students who had produced the text. An interesting finding was the preva-lence of assessors' abstracted concepts of students as members of norma-tive categories. When they made mention of an individual student, assessors were inclined to then assign that particular student to a tacit 'category' of students that attracted other qualities such as 'effort' or 'ability'. Asses-sors then relied on this tacit knowledge to make inferences, predictions and judgements about a student's capabilities, and ways they had generated their learning product, that went beyond the immediate tangible evidence in the text. These inferences were not subjected to self-critique by academics.

Feedback

There was an observable failure to provide students with sufficient feed-back about the evidence of their attainment or shortcomings regarding higher level thinking and about how their learning achievements could be enhanced in this respect. This brings into question the validity of assessment procedures if they do not focus students' attention on higher learning attributes and attempt to encourage deep approaches to learning. Sadler (1989) and Moore and Smith (1989) argue that teachers' failures to be explicit about transformative learning and critical thinking limit students' capacities to critique and improve their own written products in the future and to function as transformational learners.

The use of classroom-based knowledge was rarely observed in the protocols, with few links between the assessment and the classroom mentioned. Similarly, there was little evidence of explicit plans to use feedback from the specific assessment under consideration to shape future teaching or assessment practice. Assessment thinking, therefore, seemed to have a largely postscript relationship with classroom activities. This is a tension for students and assessors.

Lack of problematisation of grading

Assessors consciously manage the assessment process, but this management is largely practical, responding to cues in the texts rather than being part of a deliberate interpretation and grading strategy. There is little evidence in the protocols to suggest that assessors adopt a *problematized* approach; that is, one in which assessors engage with the pedagogical problem of diagnosing students' cognitive competence or achievement. This would also include active use of predetermined attainment standards. It would also require assessors to demonstrate standards of assessment literacy that enabled them to critically self-regulate their own potential fallibility or bias. Instead it seemed that they adopted what Berieter and Scardamalia (1988) call a *natural* (or easy) approach in which knowledge of the learning domain is all that was required to make judgements about students' levels or standards of learning attainment.

The low frequency of problem posing behaviour, the largely non-pedagogical nature of the problems that were posed, the low frequency of checking backwards or forwards in the text, and assessors' failures to make review notes to use in planning future teaching, all suggest that a relatively non-problematic and surface approach was taken to the assessment task. This does not imply that the assessors *never* give deeper pedagogical consideration to the overall implications of their teaching and the levels of student learning. They may perhaps do this in reviewing the assessment exercise as a whole. It does indicate, however, that even when assessment thinking was known to be the object of observation by a researcher, it was largely driven by the content of the students' text, and by a need to produce and justify a grade, not by pedagogical problem posing or a qualitative profile of expected cognitive attainment.

CONCLUSION

The everyday, common practice of interpreting and grading revealed in this study illustrates that assessment may be a mere *postscript* to the learning and teaching process in order to generate a grade to represent students' learning attainment in response to students' compliance by engaging in assessment performances. Collectively, these factors represent surface, subjective, and normative frames of reference in grading; frames of references that do not fully represent the desirable attributes of graduates. Furthermore they do not represent the hallmarks of a university education, which could be expected to include the acquisition of a body of knowledge and a capacity to interpret, use, and transform it in novel contexts.

There is considerable defensiveness surrounding interpreting and grading which will make changes to practice difficult to implement. Academics often consider their execution of the task of judging and grading student work as a measure of their status and worth as academics. Competence in one's disciplinary or professional domain is regarded as synonymous with competence to assess. Experience in assessing becomes the justification and guide for future assessment behaviour. The considerable amount of scholarship and theory in the field of assessment research is neglected or unrecognized. This study has shown that common assessment practice is largely subjective, normative, tacit 'wisdom of practice' (Shulman, 1987) that has not been subjected to personal or public critical scrutiny. Improvement in practice may be possible if institutions and systems pay far better attention to the quality of grading practice and ensure that not only academics, but also other stakeholders, have a far greater literacy about its conduct.

The key implication from this study for better practice is that assessment design and grading need to be less private and the subject of far greater public scrutiny, so that individuals and institutions are able to more clearly articulate what students have achieved. This is important to internal and external stakeholders who expect good quality assurance to lead to students leaving university with valid and trustworthy credentials (Yorke et al., 2000). Good practice in assessment and grading can also lead to better learning outcomes and not merely more trustworthy certification of outcomes. When students are clearer about what they have to achieve in their learning as a result of specific feedback on their performance, they are more likely to improve their learning efforts and achievements in an effective manner. Assessors who are more critical of their own practice, aware of ways of improving it and of ways to integrate assessment with teaching and learning, will also contribute to improvements. Assessment and grading can be vehicles for learning for both students and teachers.

REFERENCES

Bakeman, R. & Gottman. J, (1986). *Observing interaction: An introduction to sequential analysis.* Cambridge: Cambridge University Press.

Bartlett, F. (1932). *Remembering: A study in experimental and social psychology.* Cambridge: Cambridge University Press.

Berieter, C. & Scardamalia, M. (1987). *The psychology of written composition.* Hillsdale, NJ: Laurence Erlbaum.

Biggs, J. B. (1991). Teaching: Design for earning. In B. Ross (Ed.) , *Teaching for effective learning: Research and development in higher education,* vol. 13. Sydney, Australia: HERDSA.

Biggs, J. B. (1992). A qualitative approach to grading students. *HERDSA News, 14*(3), 3–6.

Branthwaite, A., Trueman, M., & Berrsiford, T. (1981). Unreliability of marking: Further evidence and a possible explanation. *Education Review 33*(1), 41–46.

Chase, C. (1979). Impact of handwriting quality on scoring essay tests. *Journal of Educational Measurement 16,* 39–42.

Chase, C. (1983). Essay test scores and reading difficulty. *Journal of Educational Measurement, 20*(3), 293–297.

Cowan, W. (1988). Evolving conceptions of memory storage, selective attention and mutual constraint with the human information processing system. *Psychological Bulletin, 104,* 163–191.

Cox, R. (1985). Higher education: Assessment of students. In T. Husen & T. N. Postlewaite (Eds.), *The international encyclopedia of education research and studies,* vol. 2. Oxford: Pergamon Press.

Daly, J. & Dickson-Markman, F. (1982). Contrast effects in evaluating essays. *Journal of Educational Measurement, 19*(4), 309–316.

Ericcson, K. & Simon, H. (1993). *Protocol analysis: Verbal reports as data* (rev. ed.) Cambridge, MA: MIT Press.

Geisinger, K. F. (1982). Marking systems. *Encyclopedia of educational research, 3,* 1139–1149.

Heywood, J. (2000). *Assessment in higher education: Student learning, teaching, programmes and institutions.* London: Jessica Kingsley.

Hughes, D. C., Keeling, B., & Tuck, B. (1983). Effects of achievement expectation and handwriting quality on scoring essays. *Journal of Educational Measurement, 20*(1), 65–70.

Marshall, J. C. & Powers, J. M. (1969). Writing neatness, composition errors, and essay grades *Journal of Educational Measurement, 6*(2), 97–101.

Moore, B. S. & Smith, R. (1989). *Curriculum leadership and assessment and reporting.* Adelaide: South Australian College of Advanced Education.

Noizet, G. & Caverni, J. (1978). *Psychologie de l'evaluation scolaire.* Paris: P.U.F.

Orrell, J. (1997, September). *Assessment in higher education: Academics' personal practical theories.* Paper presented at ISATT '97, Teachers' Work and Professional Development, 8th Biennial Conference of the International Study Association on Teacher Thinking, Kiel, Germany.

Rapaille, J. P. (1986). Research on assessment process in 'natural' conditions. In M. Ben-Peretz, R., Bromme, & R. Halkes (Eds.), *Advances of research on teacher thinking.* Lisse, Netherlands: ISATT/Swets & Zeitlinger, 122–132.

Sadler, D. R. (1989). Formative assessment and the design of instructional systems. *Instructional Science 18,* 119–144.

Sadler, D. R. (2003, 6–7 November). *How criteria–based grading misses the point*. Presentation at Effective Teaching and Learning Conference, Griffith University.

Schon, D. (1983). *The reflective practitioner: How professionals think in action*. New York: Basic Books.

Shulman, L. (1987). Knowledge and teaching: Foundations of the new reform. *Harvard Educational Review, 57*(1), 1–22.

Sweedler-Brown, C. O. (1992). The effect of training on the appearance bias of holistic essay graders. *Journal of Research and Development in Education, 26*(1), 24–29.

Terwilliger, J. S. (1977). Assigning grades-philosophical issues and practical recommendations. *Journal of Research and Development in Education, 10*(3), 21–39.

Tittle, K. C. (1989). Validity: Whose construction is it in the teaching and learning context? *Educational Measurement, 8*(1), 5–34.

Tittle, K. C. (1994). Toward and educational psychology of assessment for teaching and learning: Theories, contexts, and validation arguments. *Educational Psychologist, 29*(3),. 149–162.

Townsend, M., Hicks, L., Thompson, J., Wilton, K., Tuck, B., & Moore, D. (1983). Effects of introductions and conclusions in assessment of student essays. *Journal of Educational Psychology, 85*(4), 670–677.

Yorke, M., Bridges, P., & Woolf, H. (2000). Mark distributions and marking practices in UK higher education. *Active Learning in Higher Education, 6*(1), 7–27.

Part V
Epilogue

20 Balancing dilemmas

Traditional theories and new applications

Dylan Wiliam

INTRODUCTION

In his 'Prosepoem towards a definition of itself' Brian Patten (1967) suggested that poetry 'should guide all those who are safe into the middle of busy roads and leave them there'. This seems to me a good analogy for the kinds of critiques of traditional assessments that are contained in this volume. To all those who are comfortable with the existing state of affairs regarding assessment in higher education, the chapters in this book will have been unsettling. They may well, and indeed, should, feel that they have been guided from their complacency to the middle of a busy road and left there.

Elsewhere in the poem Patten specifies another function for poetry: 'On sighting mathematicians it should unhook the algebra from their minds and replace it with poetry; on sighting poets it should unhook poetry from their minds and replace it with algebra'. This reciprocal challenge is my guiding theme for this chapter. While the chapters in this book have challenged the status quo, I want to ensure that the authors in this book, in turn, have no easy resting place—I want to problematize the problematizers. In particular, I want to suggest that while the authors of the chapters in this book are innovative in their visions of what assessment can and should do, the existing theoretical foundations of assessment are quite adequate to encapsulate these. Indeed I will argue that the use of validity theory, and especially the work of Samuel Messick, provides a powerful framework within which the balancing of dilemmas can be more rigorously debated.

WHY DO WE ASSESS?

Hanson (1993) defined a *test* or an *assessment* (I shall use the two terms interchangeably in this chapter) as 'a representational technique, applied by an agency to an individual with the intent of gathering information' (p. 19). The crucial feature of this definition is that a test is *representational*; we are not interested in the results of the test itself, but in our ability to make inferences about some wider range of things once we know the results of the test. Even if we give a class of students a list of 20 words to memorize, and test them the following day, we are interested not in the specific performance on the test, but on that specific performance as an index of performance on other occasions (e.g., that they will be able to do as well at some point in the future).

The fundamental problem of assessment is therefore one of generalizability. How do we move from a series of observations of student performance on a particular occasion to making inferences about other occasions, or to things that were not specifically assessed? How do we know that skills that nurses demonstrate in the classroom will be generalized to the hospital wards? How do we know that the skills that the apprentice demonstrated in her 'apprenticeship piece' will be generalized to her subsequent productions? How do we know from the work presented in a portfolio that a student teacher will be able to create effective learning environments for his students? As the chapter by Havnes makes clear, what we describe, sometimes carelessly, as 'transfer' is an extremely complex process which involves negotiating multiplicities of meaning across different contexts.

THE VALIDITY OF ASSESSMENTS

The process of establishing what kinds of inferences are warranted on the basis of assessment outcomes, and what kinds of inferences are not, is called validation. The validity of an assessment is therefore not a property of a test, but rather of the inferences that can be made. As Lee Cronbach (1971) noted, 'One validates, not a test, but an *interpretation of data arising from a specified procedure*'(p. 447, emphasis in original).

This is an important point, because even in modern texts, it is common to find validity defined as a property of an assessment, and in particular, that an assessment is valid to the extent that it assesses what it purports to assess—a definition that first appeared over 70 years ago (see Garrett, 1937), and was comprehensively discredited over 50 years ago (Cronbach & Meehl, 1955).

The problem with defining validity as a property of an assessment is that an assessment may be valid for some students but not for others. For example, a traditional timed written examination in history requires a student to write legibly at high speed for an extended period of time. For students who can do this, then the scores they get may be an accurate representation of their capabilities with regard to history, but for students who cannot write legibly at speed, their scores are likely to be as much a reflection of their writing ability (or lack of it) as their knowledge of history. High scores are relatively easy to interpret, but low scores may be due to lack of historical knowledge, lack of writing skill, or a combination of both. The important point here is that if all the students taking the examination are skilled and fluent writers, then differences in scores are likely to represent differences in the ability to think historically—the construct we are interested in. But if our students differ in their writing skill, then differences in scores are harder to interpret. Some of the variation (or, in statistical terms, *variance*) in scores will be due to differences in historical thinking, but some will due to factors that are irrelevant, such as writing skill. The scores will suffer from what is called 'construct-irrelevant variance' (Messick, 1989)–in other words, some of the variation in scores is attributable to factors that are irrelevant to the construct in which we are interested.

Put simply, construct-irrelevant variance occurs where the assessment assesses something it shouldn't so that the assessment is in some sense 'too big'. On the other hand, it is just as serious a threat to validity (in other words to the inferences that we can make) if the assessment fails to assess something it should, and is therefore 'too small'. The technical term for this is *construct under-representation* because the assessment outcomes under-represent the construct of interest.

These themes of construct under-representation and construct-irrelevant variance play out throughout most of the chapters in this book. For Broadfoot, and Falchikov and Boud, current assessment methods under-represent the constructs that will be important in the coming century, and in particular, that of preparation for future learning (Bransford & Schwartz, 1999). For Gioka, the kinds of things that can be assessed through timed, written examinations under-represent the construct of science. On a finer-grained level, the chapter by Orrell deals with the interplay of construct-irrelevant variance and construct under-representation. Where some markers take the quality of presentation into account, this will be regarded as construct-irrelevant variance by some, because differences in the quality of presentation, which are deemed not relevant to the construct of interest (in this case, writing) lead to differences in scores. In contrast, for others, presentation is part of the construct of interest, and so these individuals will regard a failure to take into account the quality of presentation as construct under-representation.

In the chapter by Dysthe et al., the explicitness of the assessment criteria is the central theme. Where assessment criteria are vague, then some of the variation in the scores achieved by students will be attributable not to the capability of the students, but to whether they knew what the person who graded the portfolio was looking for. Some observers will regard this as construct-irrelevant variance. Others, however, will regard knowing what the assessor was looking for as highly relevant to the construct of interest, since they regard internalizing the criteria for success as signalling the student's inauguration into a community of practice (Sadler, 1989; Wiliam, 1998). On the other hand, when the assessment criteria are specific and clear, the opportunity for students to be rewarded for novel approaches to the task is reduced. Where observers value creativity highly, the failure to reward it would be regarded as construct under-representation. The same sorts of considerations arise in Smith and Tillema's discussion over the relative merits of structured and unstructured portfolios.

The debate about the relative merits of process and product, particularly in fields such as performing arts, visual arts, design and technology raises similar issues. In Japanese calligraphy, the order in which the strokes that make up a character are made is important. So, amongst experts in calligraphy, it is acceptable to deduct marks where the strokes were made in a non-standard order, even where it is impossible to determine the stroke order in the final product. Lindström's chapter, on craft and design, discusses the relative importance attached by different assessors to process and product. For one of the artisans interviewed, speed was an important aspect of competence, so to assess without time-limits would be seen as under-representing the construct of interest. For other artisans, to place time-restrictions on students would introduce a degree of construct-irrelevant variance.

The debate about the merits of student self-assessment within summative assessment in the chapter by Tan can also be examined within the competing concerns of construct-irrelevant variance and construct under-representation. Where students' self-assessments contribute to the final score, there is a danger that variation in students' scores will be in part due to differences in self-confidence, which many, if not most, observers would regard as construct-irrelevant variance (as well as being strongly linked to gender). For others, not to use the students' own knowledge of their strengths and weaknesses in arriving at a final grade or score ignores relevant information, resulting in construct under-representation.

While these debates may be seen as more or less academic in some settings, they can become matters of life and death in others. The chapter by Smits et al. deals with assessment in the education of nurses, and here, failure to attend to concerns of construct under-representation can be dire. In a study of the mathematical competence of nursing students, Pirie (1987) found that in many nursing schools, students who had achieved a pass in the national school leaving examination in mathematics in England were exempt from further study of mathematics, while the remainder had to attend special classes on the kinds of mathematical calculations needed in nursing (typically ratio calculations, where drug dosages needed to be scaled to take account of the mass of the patient). The inference being made was that those students who had achieved a pass in the mathematics school leaving examination could perform such calculations accurately. However, when Pirie examined the mathematical competence of the nurses, it turned out that the students who had been exempted from further study on the basis of their scores on the mathematics school leaving examination could not, in fact, accurately complete ratio calculations. The irony of this situation was that only those nurses who had failed the mathematics school leaving examinations were safe to administer non-standard drug dosages!

The central feature of all the tensions and dilemmas identified above is that the debate is not about the technical quality of the assessment, but about the construct to be assessed. In short, *these dilemmas are not about assessment at all*. Rather they are debates about what should be assessed. Many of the debates are therefore conducted at cross-purposes, since the argument is conducted as if it were about assessment, but in fact is about the construct of interest. Such debates are impossible to resolve, because the arguments fly past each other, with neither side accepting the premises of the other.

Quite apart from the futility of such arguments, there is another danger that arises from the lack of construct definition. When we embark on assessment without being clear about the construct to be assessed, we end up allowing the assessment to dictate what gets assessed. Especially in high-stakes settings, we slip from wanting to make the important assessable to making the assessable important. This is why many experts in the field of assessment, and validity theory in particular, have stressed the need for construct definition prior to assessment development (see for example, Braun et al., 2001).

Perhaps the main benefit of clarity about the construct of interest is that the validation process becomes much less subjective. Different observers will disagree about whether presentation should be assessed as part of writing. However, once we agree that it is (or is not) to be included, then the debates focus on the much narrower issue of the extent to which a particular student response meets the requirements of the construct.

This conceptualization of validity as a property of inferences made on the basis of assessment outcomes subsumes the traditional notions of content validity, construct validity, and criterion-related validity. Where the construct of interest can be defined in terms of a content domain, then validation will be concerned with the extent to which inferences are warranted about elements in the content domain that were not specifically assessed. Where the assessment is concerned with the student's likely performance on some criterion, then obviously the correlation between the assessment and the performance on the criterion will be paramount. Where there is no clear domain definition, nor a focal criterion, then the evidence that the assessment really does assess the construct of interest (convergent evidence) and evidence that it does not assess related, but distinct constructs (discriminant evidence) will be paramount (Messick, 1989). It is important to note, however, that while content considerations may be paramount for some inferences, criterion-related inferences for others, and construct-related inferences for yet others, all are relevant for any assessment. The 'trinitarian' doctrine of validity (Guion, 1980) does not allow one to pick and choose which aspect of validity one will focus on. Validity is an overall evaluative judgment that integrates content, construct, and criterion-related concerns (Messick, 1989). It is also important to note that in this view, reliability is a part of validity, since if random factors affect assessment outcomes, then any inferences made on their basis are likely to be unwarranted (Wiliam, 2001, in press).

MEANINGS AND CONSEQUENCES OF ASSESSMENT

For many authors, this completes the picture. However, in a groundbreaking paper published in 1980, Samuel Messick argued that, with educational assessments in particular, the social context in which the assessments were used could not be ignored (Messick, 1980). He argued that the relationships between assessment outcomes and the inferences made from them were not static, and therefore inferences that might be valid at one point in time might not be valid at some subsequent point in time. To embrace this broader perspective, while at the same time retaining the central idea of validity as a unified concept, he distinguished 'two interconnected facets of the unitary validity concept. One facet is the source of the justification of the testing, being based on either evidence or consequence. The other facet is the function or outcome of the testing, being either interpretation or use'. (Messick, 1989, p. 20). Crossing the facet for the source of the justification (evidential basis or consequential basis) with the function or outcome of the testing (result interpretation or result use) yields the four-fold classification shown in Table 20.1.

The top left cell represents the evidential basis of result interpretation. This includes traditional content considerations, and much of what was called construct validity in the 'trinitarian' approaches to validity. The top right cell represents the evidential basis for result use. This includes criterion-related concerns, such as whether an assessment can be used to predict important outcomes, but also evidence about the relevance and utility of the assessment in its proposed use.

The bottom row of Messick's model deals with the consequential basis of assessments. The bottom left cell represents the consequential basis of result interpretation. The central idea here is that when particular aspects of a domain are included in an assessment, and others are not, whatever the impact on traditional notions of ability validity (i.e., content, construct, and criterion-related concerns), the assessment carries value implications. So

Table 20.1 Facets of validity argument, after Messick (1980)

		Function	
		Result interpretation	*Result use*
Justification	Evidential basis	Construct validity	Construct validity + Relevance/utility
	Consequential basis	Value implications	Social consequences

for example, it is common to find that scores on tests that consist entirely of multiple choice items give substantially the same outcomes as performance assessments, which are much more expensive to administer, and indeed, are often much less reliable (Linn, 1994). In terms of traditional conceptualizations of validity, and especially when we take utility into account, the argument in favour of multiple-choice tests seems unanswerable. However, when we take value implications into account, we can see that adopting a multiple-choice test, whatever its advantages in traditional validity terms, sends the message that only the aspects of the domain that can be assessed via multiple-choice tests are important. The concerns of face validity identified in the chapter by Smits et al. would be an example of the value implications of assessment. Conceptually, face validity is completely irrelevant to construct validity—what people think something is assessing is irrelevant to what something is actually assessing—but can have significant value implications.

These value implications in turn have social consequences, for the collection of evidence, for its interpretation, and for its use, as reflected in the bottom right cell in Messick's model—the consequential basis of result use. For example, the chapter by Gulikers et al. notes the importance of the meaningfulness of a task. If students perceive the task as meaningful, then it is likely that their responses are reasonably accurate indications of what they can do. If, on the other hand, students see a task as meaningless, then we cannot conclude that the outcomes are indications of their capability. In such situations, inferences made on the basis of assessment outcomes are likely to be of questionable validity.

When results are used, particularly in high-stakes contexts, the consequences include changes in, for example, what is taught. Where assessments use only multiple-choice items, the value implications include the idea that the only kind of knowledge that is important is that which can be tested in a multiple-choice test, and the consequence is often that teachers then change what they are teaching to focus on those aspects of the domain. In drawing attention to the social consequences of result use, Messick was not primarily interested in the negative effects of testing highlighted by Broadfoot in this volume. Rather he was pointing out that the social consequences of test use can change the inferences that are warranted on the basis of an assessment outcome–in other words, social consequences of test use can change the *meaning* of assessment outcomes. For example, as noted above, it is frequently observed that the results of multiple-choice assessments accord to a high degree of accuracy with those derived from authentic assessments. Proponents of multiple-choice tests therefore argue that we can use results from multiple-choice tests as proxies for the results of authentic assessments. However, if the concordance between multiple-choice tests and more authentic forms of assessment was established when teachers were teaching all aspects of the curriculum, we cannot assume that the concordance will hold forever. In particular, when the stakes are high, the social consequence is likely to be that teachers teach only to the aspect of the domain that is assessed. This change in practice changes the relationship between the multiple-choice test and the authentic assessment. Whereas previously the multiple-choice test might have been a good proxy for other, more authentic forms of assessment, the concordance will weaken where teachers teach only those aspects of the domain assessed by the multiple-choice tests. In arguing for the importance of the consequential basis of result interpretation and use, Messick was not proposing that this should include all the social consequences of the use of assessments:

> As has been stressed several times already, it is not that adverse social consequences of test use render the use invalid, but, rather, that adverse social consequences should not be attributable to any source of test invalidity such as construct-irrelevant variance. If the adverse social consequences are empirically traceable to sources of test invalidity, then the validity of the test use is jeopardized. If the social consequences cannot be so traced—or if the validation process can discount sources of test invalidity as the likely determinants, or at least render them less plausible—then the validity of the test use is not overturned. Adverse social consequences associated with valid test interpretation and use may implicate the attributes validly assessed, to be sure, as they function under the existing social conditions of the applied setting, but they are not in themselves indicative of invalidity. (Messick, 1989, pp. 88–89)

It is also worth noting that Messick expressly rejected the idea that there were different kinds of validity. For him validity remained an integrated concept, albeit with different aspects, each of which needed attention: 'Validity is an integrative evaluative judgment of the degree to which empirical evidence and theoretical rationales support the adequacy and appropriateness of inferences and actions based on test scores or other modes of assessment' (Messick, 1989 p. 13). Because of his careful delineation of the limits of the social consequences in his model, and his insistence that validity should be an integrated evaluative judgment, Messick would be horrified to learn that he is now widely associated with the idea of 'consequential validity'. We need to be concerned about the broader social consequences of assessments, but we should not try to squeeze these concerns into the concept of validity—a position that was neatly summarized by James Popham in the title of a paper: 'Consequential Validity: Right Concern, Wrong Concept' (Popham, 1996).

Perhaps the most obvious way in which valid assessments have adverse social consequences is in their impact on the learners themselves. While the arguments of Messick and Popham lead us to consider these issues separately from validity, there is a vast and growing literature on the harmful effects assessments can have on learning, as noted in the chapter by Broad-foot (see also Black et al., 2002).

Partly in an attempt to ameliorate some of the more egregious effects of assessment, there has been an interest in recent years in providing students with more than just the results achieved on assessments. For a variety of reasons, some comprehensible and others less so, in most institutions the result has been that students receive both evaluative and formative feedback on their work, despite the evidence that the presence of the former means the latter is ignored; see, for example, studies reviewed in Black and Wiliam (1998).

At the same time, it is becoming clearer from both qualitative studies such as that reported in the chapter by McDowell, and from a range of quantitative studies, that feedback that just tells students how they did, even when combined with information about what they should have done, is the least effective form of feedback.

In reviewing 185 research studies on the effects of feedback in higher education, Nyquist (2003) developed the following typology of different kinds of formative assessment:

Weaker feedback only: students are given only the knowledge of their own score or grade, often described as 'knowledge of results'.

Feedback only: students are given their own score or grade, together with either clear goals to work towards or feedback on the correct answers to the questions they attempt, often described as 'knowledge of correct results'.

Weak formative assessment: students are given information about the correct results, together with some explanation.

Moderate formative assessment: students are given information about the correct results, some explanation, and some specific suggestions for improvement.

Strong formative assessment: students are given information about the correct results, some explanation, and specific activities to undertake in order to improve.

Table 20.2 Standardised effect sizes for different kinds of feedback interventions

	N	Effect
Weaker feedback only	31	0.16
Feedback only	48	0.23
Weaker formative assessment	49	0.30
Moderate formative assessment	41	0.33
Strong formative assessment	16	0.51
Total	185	

He then calculated the average standardized effect size for the studies for each type of intervention, and the results are given in Table 20.2 below.

Unless feedback engages students in mindful activity, little or no learning will result, no matter how much time and care is spent by assessors in crafting that feedback. Furthermore, even where feedback is helpful in boosting achievement in the short term, if the effect is to persuade the learner that he has reached some kind of threshold, and that further progress is unlikely, then the overall effect will be negative. As the chapter by Falchikov and Boud makes clear, we cannot ignore the effects of assessment on the extent to which individuals become lifelong learners, although for the reasons discussed above, I think it is a mistake to try to shoehorn these adverse impacts into the concept of validity. But as Kvale makes clear in his chapter, if we can incorporate some of the features of assessment in apprenticeship, then the impact of assessment on learning can be positive.

In the remainder of this chapter, I want to discuss two specific issues that I think are particularly important in developing more appropriate forms of assessment for contemporary education: the relationship between continuous and one-off assessment, and the issue of norm- versus criterion-referencing.

CONTINUOUS VS. ONE-OFF ASSESSMENT

The relative merits of summative assessment that is distributed throughout the program and assessment that takes place just at the end of the program have been debated for years. The traditional argument against one-off assessments has been that they reward those students with good memories, those who work well under pressure, and those who like leaving things to the last minute. In the technical language introduced above, scores on such one-off assessments display construct-irrelevant variance, in that some part of the variation in scores is attributable to differences that are not relevant to the subject being assessed. Others disagree, however, and argue that such variation is not construct-irrelevant. Some people want to use examination results to get information about the ability of students to work under pressure, so for them, the pressure produced by examinations is essential (and therefore construct-relevant).

Assessment distributed throughout the program tends to incorporate a greater range of sources of evidence, and generally also involves a greater volume of evidence. All other things being equal, therefore, such assessments tend to be superior in validity and reliability to end of course assessments. However, all other things are rarely equal. The scoring of distributed assessments tends to be less standardized than the scoring of end-of-course assessments, so there is a greater possibility of inter-rater variability. Also, the conditions under which the assessments are actually undertaken are less easily controlled, leading to problems of authentication (i.e., how do we know who has completed the work?). However, there are two more serious problems with distributed assessment that are rarely acknowledged, let alone discussed, both of which are related to the issue of evidence accumulation (Almond et al., 2003). When the assessment is distributed across a course or program, we are forced to aggregate evidence about student achievement from early on in the program with that obtained later on, which raises issues of *value* and *generalizability*. The issue of value is this: How are we to value achievement in the first part of the course relative to achievement in the later part of the course? One student may get the lowest possible passing grades for the first half of the course, and the highest possible grades for the second half of the course. Do we rate this student as higher than, equal to, or lower than the student who gets the highest possible passing grades for the first half of the course, and the lowest possible grades for the second half of the course? In many US universities, it is common to weight all grades from non-introductory courses equally, while universities in the UK tend to attach a higher weight to later performance. The important point is that any such decision is arbitrary, and normalizing. Whatever rule we adopt will advantage some students, and disadvantage others.

The second issue related to evidence accumulation is that of generalizability. Quite apart from the value we attach to performances at different parts of the course is what we can conclude from them. If we assess students on some material in the beginning of the course, can we assume that they still know it some months later? This may be an issue that people are content to ignore in liberal arts degree programs, but it is crucial in areas where degrees confer licenses to practice, such as medicine, dentistry, nursing, law, and teaching.

This is an important issue because it interacts so strongly with pedagogy. For example, many degree programs operate with what might be termed a 'banking' model of assessment. A student takes a course, is assessed on the course, and then receives a score or grade, which is then 'banked'. In other words, even if the student forgets everything she or he has ever known about that material, no-one can take the grade away. This supports an approach to pedagogy that emphasizes 'coverage' of the curriculum at a shallow level, where students are required to remember what they have learned only for a short period of time, until the grade is 'banked'. In contrast, where the assessment involves a significant 'synoptic' component, so that at the end of the program the student is assessed on everything they have learned in the program, both teachers and students are forced to take a longer-term perspective on learning. While loading all of the assessment into final examinations is certainly counter-productive in terms of student learning, abolishing all terminal assessment in favour of assessments distributed throughout the program will almost certainly be worse. The challenge for contemporary education is to develop models of assessment that are both *distributed* and *synoptic*.

INTERPRETING ASSESSMENT OUTCOMES

For much of last century, the standard way of interpreting an assessment outcome was to compare the outcome with the performance of some group. In the original applications of the Scholastic Aptitude Test in the United States between 1926 and 1940, any individual student's score would be interpreted with respect to the other students who took the test that year—in other words the interpretation of the meaning of the test score was *cohort-referenced*. The important point about a cohort-referenced interpretation of an assessment outcome is that it is competitive; one's ranking is dependent on the performance of one's peers. From 1942 onwards, however, each student's score was compared to a group of students who took the test in 1941. The test was no longer cohort-referenced, but *norm-referenced*, with the score of each student being interpreted relative to the norm group. Such an assessment is not competitive, in that one's own ranking does not depend on the performance of one's peers.

The problem with norm-referenced interpretations of assessment outcomes is that all such interpretations require is that we are able to put students in rank order, and we can put students in rank order without having any idea what we are putting them in rank order *of*. In other words, we can rank students without any clear construct definition. Knowing that someone is above average, below average, at the 92nd percentile or whatever may be acceptable for a whole range of applications, but is practically useless for supporting learning. This was the driving force, in the 1960s, behind the development of assessments that could provide evidence not only about where a student ranked, but what they knew and what they did not (Glaser, 1963), although Glaser himself acknowledged that the key distinction—between absolute and relative standards of quality—had been made much earlier by Flanagan (1951). The crucial need, Glaser argued, was for assessments that could support *criterion-referenced* interpretations. The important point here is that, properly speaking, there is no such thing as a criterion-referenced assessment. We have assessments that may or may not support criterion-referenced interpretations, norm-referenced interpretations, or indeed both.

While criterion-referenced interpretations were intended to be absolute, rather than relative, the criteria themselves were not completely independent of norms. All criteria derive their value from their utility with respect to a population. 'Can high-jump 1 metre' is not an interesting criterion for healthy adults, since it is too easy, while 'Can high-jump 3 metres' is not interesting because it is too hard. But 'Can high jump 2 metres' is an interesting criterion, at least for adult athletes, because it discriminates amongst them, and tells us something we did not know before. However, the same criterion is useless for different populations, such as children below the age of 8, where the first criterion might be more relevant. This is the point Angoff (1974) was making when he said:

> And although it would be foolish of us to deny the fact that criterion-referenced evaluations are similarly valid and useful, we should be aware that lurking behind the criterion-referenced evaluation, perhaps even responsible for it, is the norm-referenced evaluation. (p. 4)

What happened subsequently was a series of disastrous attempts at what Popham has called 'criterion-referenced hyperspecification' whose effects were shown to be 'stultifying' (Popham, 1994), although the ripples are being felt in the competency movement today, as noted in the chapter by Orr. While some clarity about what is to be assessed is essential if we are to move away from norm-referenced interpretations of assessment outcomes, there are many ways of doing this.

In higher education in particular, it is important to note that most of the interpretations being made are neither norm-referenced nor criterion-referenced. They are not norm-referenced in that in most institutions, proportions gaining the highest classifications are allowed to change over time, sometimes quite rapidly. Nor, on the other hand, are they criterion-referenced, since there are rarely explicit criteria for the awards of different scores or grades. Instead, most assessments in contemporary education would be better described as *construct-referenced* (Wiliam, 1994). The student's work is interpreted with respect to a set of constructs of quality that are more or less widely shared by the community of assessors. Effective summative assessment requires shared meanings of these constructs across the community of assessors, while, as noted above, effective formative assessment requires the students also to become members of the same community (Sadler, 1989; Wiliam, 1998). As noted by Dysthe et al., criteria have a role to play in enculturating learners into the community, but it is a mistake to regard the criteria as definitions of quality—they are encapsulations of pre-existing insights about quality, but by themselves cannot establish that understanding of quality (Polanyi, 1958).

CONCLUSION

To paraphrase Mark Twain, I believe that reports of the death of traditional validity theory have been greatly exaggerated. While the chapters in this book have raised important issues about the nature and effects of the kinds of assessment used in contemporary education, I have tried in this concluding chapter to show how debate about the important trade-offs and dilemmas can be made more rigorous within the theoretical frameworks that exist, rather than by re-inventing new ones. This does not make balancing the dilemmas any easier, but it does, I believe, mean that the arguments that we have will be more productive, the resolutions that we reach are more transparent, and, as a result, assessment is increasingly used to advance the learning of students, rather than just measure it.

REFERENCES

Almond, R. G., Steinberg, L. S., & Mislevy, R. J. (2003). *A four-process architecture for assessment delivery, with connections to assessment design* (CRESST report number 616). Los Angeles: University of California Los Angeles Center for Research on Evaluations, Standards and Student Testing (CRESST).

Angoff, W. H. (1974). Criterion-referencing, norm-referencing and the SAT. *College Board Review*, 92 (Summer), 2–5, 21.

Black, P., Broadfoot, P. M., Daugherty, R., Gardner, J., Harlen, W., James, M., Stobart, G., & Wiliam, D. (2002). *Testing, motivation and learning*. Cambridge: University of Cambridge School of Education.

Black, P. J. & Wiliam, D. (1998). Assessment and classroom learning. *Assessment in Education: Principles Policy and Practice*, 5(1), 7–73.

Bransford, J. D. & Schwartz, D. L. (1999). Rethinking transfer: A simple proposal with multiple implications. In A. Iran-Nejad & P. D. Pearson (Eds.), *Review of research in education*, 24, 61–100. Washington, D.C.: American Educational Research Association.

Braun, H., Jackson, D. N., & Wiley, D. E. (Eds.). (2001). *The role of constructs in psychological and educational measurement*. Mahwah, NJ: Lawrence Erlbaum.

Cronbach, L. J. (1971). Test validation. In R. L. Thorndike (Ed.), *Educational measurement* (2nd ed.), 443–507. Washington D.C.: American Council on Education.

Cronbach, L. J. & Meehl, P. E. (1995). Construct validity in psychological tests. *Psychological Bulletin*, 52, 281–302.

Flanagan, J. C. (1951). Units, scores, and norms. In E. F. Lindquist (Ed.), *Educational measurement* (2nd ed.), 695–763. Washington, D.C.: American Council on Education.

Garrett, H. E. (1937). *Statistics in psychology and education*. New York: Longmans, Green.

Glaser, R. (1963). Instructional technology and the measurement of learning outcomes: Some questions. *American Psychologist*, 18, 519–521.

Guion, R. M. (1980). On trinitarian doctrines of validity. *Professional Psychology*, 11, 385–398.

Hanson, F. A. (1993). *Testing testing: Social consequences of the examined life*. Berkeley: University of California Press.

Linn, R. L. (1994). *Assessment-based reform: Challenges to educational measurement*. Paper presented at the Angoff Memorial Lecture. Princeton, NJ: Educational Testing Service.

Messick, S. (1980). Test validity and the ethics of assessment. *American Psychologist*, 35(11), 1012–1027.

Messick, S. (1989). Validity. In R. L. Linn (Ed.), *Educational measurement* (3rd ed.), 13–103. Washington, D.C.: American Council on Education/Macmillan.

Nyquist, J. B. (2003). *The benefits of reconstruing feedback as a larger system of formative assessment: A meta-analysis.* Unpublished master of science thesis, Vanderbilt University.

Patten, B. (1967). Prosepoem towards a definition of itself. In A. Henri, R. McGough, & B. Patten (Eds.), *The Mersey sound* (Penguin Modern Poets, vol. 10). Harmondsworth, UK: Penguin.

Pirie, S. E. B. (1987). *Nurses and mathematics: Deficiencies in basic mathematical skills among nurses—Development and evaluation of methods of detection and treatment.* London: Royal College of Nursing/Scutari Press.

Polanyi, M. (1958). *Personal knowledge.* London: Routledge & Kegan Paul.

Popham, W. J. (1994). *The stultifying effects of criterion-referenced hyperspecification: A postcursive quality control remedy.* Paper presented at the Symposium on Criterion-Referenced Clarity at the annual meeting of the American Educational Research Association, New Orleans, LA.

Popham, W. J. (1996). *Consequential validity: Right concern–wrong concept.* Paper presented at the annual meeting of the American Educational Research Association, New York.

Sadler, D. R. (1989). Formative assessment and the design of instructional systems. *Instructional Science, 18,* 119–144.

Wiliam, D. (1994). Assessing authentic tasks: Alternatives to mark-schemes. *Nordic Studies in Mathematics Education, 2*(1), 48–68.

Wiliam, D. (1998). *Enculturating learners into communities of practice: Raising achievement through formative assessment.* Paper presented at the European Conference on Educational Research (Annual Conference of the European Educational Research Association), Ljubljana, Slovenia.

Wiliam, D. (2001). Reliability, validity and all that jazz. *Education, 3–13, 29*(3), 17–21.

Wiliam, D. (in press). Quality in assessment. In S. Swaffield (Ed.), *Unlocking assessment.* London: David Fulton.

Contributors

Theo J. Bastiaens is professor at the Ruud de Moor Centre, Open University of the Netherlands and at the Institute for Educational Science and Media Research, Fernuniversität, Hagen. His research interests are e-learning, learning in organizations, electronic learning environments, instructional design methods and systems, and open and distance education.

David Boud is professor of adult education, at the University of Technology, Sydney. He is been president of the Higher Education Research and Development Society of Australasia and has written extensively on teaching, learning and assessment in higher and professional education and more recently on workplace learning. He has particularly focused on self-assessment and building assessment skills for long-term learning. His work can be accessed from www.davidboud.com

Patricia Broadfoot is vice chancellor, the University of Gloucestershire, UK. She was formerly pro vice chancellor and professor of education, University of Bristol. She has written extensively on assessment development and reform and has worked with both policy-makers and practitioners in many countries to help achieve this. She was the founding editor of the journal *Assessment in Education,* and was for many years a member of the Assessment Reform Group.

Olga Dysthe is professor, Department of Education and Health Promotion, University of Bergen, Norway. Her main research interests are teaching and learning in higher education, with special focus on writing, supervision, and assessment. She has published several books and articles based on socio-cultural and interactive perspectives on learning.

Knut Steinar Engelsen is associate professor, ICT in learning, Department of Teacher Education, Stord/Haugesund University College, Norway. Engelsen has worked with ICT in learning since 1986. He has been a partner in several studies about ICT and assessment, and has published books and articles about this topic.

Nancy Falchikov completed her postgraduate research at the University of Edinburgh, where she is now a research fellow in the Department of Higher and Community Education. She is also a visiting academic at the University of Technology, Sydney. Current research activities include work on aspects of student involvement in assessment. She has published two books and many papers on this topic.

Olga Gioka holds a BSc in Physics and a MA and a PhD in Science Education. She has taught physics and general sciences in secondary schools in Greece and the UK. She is currently teaching science education at the Department of Education, University of Crete. Her research interests centre on assessment for learning in science education and science teachers' professional development.

Judith T. M. Gulikers has been a PhD student at the Educational Technology Expertise Centre, Open University of the Netherlands. She is now at The Education and Competence Study Groups, Wageningen University, The Netherlands. Her research interests are competence-based education, competence development, and authentic assessment.

Anton Havnes is associate professor, Centre for Educational Research and Development, Oslo University College. His research interests are student learning and assessment in higher education, workplace learning, developmental research, and boundary crossing between professional education and professional practice.

Frøydis Hertzberg is professor of Norwegian Language at the Department of Teacher Education and School Development, University of Oslo. Her main academic interests lie in the theory and practice of writing, academic rhetoric, the training of oral skills, assessment of writing, and the teaching of grammar. Her present research interests relate to argumentative writing across the curriculum.

Wim M. G. Jochems has been professor and general director of the Educational Technology Expertise Center at the Open University of the Netherlands. He is now founding Dean of the Eindhoven School of Education at Eindhoven University of Technology, The Netherlands, and full professor in educational innovation. His research focuses on innovation of professional and science education.

Paul A. Kirschner is professor at the Educational Technology Expertise Centre of the Open University of the Netherlands. His research interests are in educational technology and design of learning environments, the use of media and ICT in education, practices in higher science education, learning materials and curriculum development, development of teacher extensive and distance education, and computer supported collaborative learning.

Steinar Kvale is professor of educational psychology, and director of the Center of Qualitative Research, University of Aarhus, Denmark. He has a PhD from the University of Oslo, his dissertation being *Prüfung und Herrschaft* (1972). He has edited *Psychology and Postmodernism* (1992) and written *InterViews —An Introduction to Qualitative Research Interviewing* (1996). He has, with Klaus Nielsen, edited *Mesterlære*[Apprenticeship] (1999) and *Praktikens læringslandskab* [The learning landscape of practice] (2003).

Per Lauvås has been professor of education, Oslo University, and is now on the faculty of Ostfold University College. He has broad experience in staff development in higher education. He is the author/co-author of a number of publications on supervision, consultancy, mentoring and coaching, both in pre- and in-service training of (university) teachers and in other professions. Assessment issues have become a major devotion during recent years.

Lars Lindström is professor of Education and Arts Education, Stockholm Institute of Education, Sweden. In a previous project, he used portfolios to assess Swedish students' creative skills in the visual arts, from ages 5 to 19. The results are summarized in *The International Journal of Art and Design Education* 1/2006 under the heading "Creativity: What Is It? Can You Assess It? Can It Be Taught?" (pp. 53–66).

Tjalve Gj. Madsen is assistant professor in Pedagogical Science, Department of Teacher Education, Bergen University College, Norway. His main interests are developmental work within the field of practice and research in both secondary school and teacher education. The main focus is on assessment and supervision.

Liz McDowell is director of the national Centre for Excellence in Assessment for Learning and professor of Academic Practice, Northumbria University, UK. She has been active in research and development in assessment since 1994 and has published widely with a particular focus on the student experience. Liz was the founder of the Northumbria/EARLI Assessment Conference series.

Sandra Murphy is professor, School of Education, University of California, Davis and teaches graduate-level courses on research on writing, reading, and assessment. She has written several articles on the teaching and learning of writing and reading and has co-authored several books on writing assessment. Areas of special interest in her research and scholarship include writing assessment and its impact on teachers and curriculum, reading comprehension, and critical perspectives on literacy.

Susan Orr is deputy dean of the faculty of Arts, York St. John University College. Her doctoral research is on assessment as a social practice in art and design. She has presented papers at a number of conferences in the UK, Europe, and the United States and has authored and co-authored (with Dr. Margo Blythman) a range of articles, papers, and chapters.

Janice Orrell is a director, Carrick Institute for Learning and Teaching in Higher Education, Australia. Her portfolio is Discipline-Based Initiatives, Resource Identification Networks, and Special Projects. The current special project is a critical analysis of assessment policies in Australian universities. Her research fields are assessment in higher education, in particular interpreting and grading, work-integrated learning, clinical education and assessment, and the induction of academics to their roles of teaching and supervision.

Dominique M.A. Sluijsmans is assistant professor, Educational Technology Expertise Center (OTEC), the Open University of the Netherlands. Her main interests are student involvement in assessment, teacher education, and instructional design.

Kari Smith is professor at the Department for Education and Health Promotion at the University of Bergen, Norway, and is also Head of International Affairs at Oranim Academic College of Education, Israel. Her main research interest is evaluation and assessment for and of learning, teacher education, and professional development. She is the co-author with Harm Tillema of the book *Portfolios in Professional Development—A Research Journey.*

Marieke H.S.B. Smits is a PhD student at the Educational Technology Expertise Center (OTEC), the Open University of the Netherlands. Her project is focused on feedback in performance assessment.

Kelvin Tan is assistant professor, Policy and Leadership Studies Academic Group, National Institute of Education. His current teaching, research, and consultancy interests focus on alternative assessment, formative assessment, student self-assessment, and power. Kelvin is also a trained lawyer and conducts courses on legal issues in educational and school contexts.

Harm Tillema is senior lecturer, Leiden University, The Netherlands. His main field of interest is professional learning and development, especially in teaching and teacher education. A special field of interest is assessment as a tool of professional learning. In his research, he has studied the impact of beliefs and dispositions in student teacher learning as beginning professionals, as well as assessment intervention techniques such as portfolio and development centres.

Dylan Wiliam is deputy director, Institute of Education, University of London. He was former director of the Learning and Teaching Research Center, Princeton University. His principal research focus is the professional development of teachers through the use of evidence about student learning to adapting teaching to better meet student needs. His current interests focus on how school-based teacher learning communities can be used to create effective systems of teacher professional development at scale.

Line Wittek is a research fellow, Centre of Educational Research and Development, Oslo University College. Her main research interest is the role of new educational tools in student learning, with a special focus on the implementation of portfolio assessment in higher education. She has conducted several studies and published books and articles about the topic.

Index